P9-DIG-780

Bee Cave Public Library
4000 Galleria Parkway
Bee Cave, Texas 78738

Praise for

GRIEF IS A JOURNEY

"Securely grounded in contemporary bereavement studies and seasoned with decades of clinical experience, *Grief Is a Journey* clearly delivers. In chapters on life's many losses and the challenges they entail for those who suffer them, Dr. Doka offers both practical principles and compassionate counsel for the griever in straightforward, readable prose. Whether the reader is seeking to understand the everyday complexity of mourning in all of its emotional, cognitive, social, and spiritual aspects or trying to discern the 'red flags' that call for professional consultation, this compact volume does much to close the gap between science and practice, and to offer the wisdom of the field to bereaved readers who greatly need it. I, for one, will buy several copies to distribute to my clients."

—ROBERT A. NEIMEYER, PH.D.

"This guide through the long valley of grief is written by one of the foremost therapists and researchers in the field of bereavement studies. Yet it is a straightforward instruction manual covering most of the problems that cause bereaved people to seek help from outside their network of friends and family. Dr. Doka writes with great clarity and good sense, giving advice that is appropriate, respectful of his reader's unique experience, and encouraging to all those who are on a journey through grief."

—COLIN MURRAY PARKES OBE, MD, FRCPSYCH, DL

GRIEF IS A JOURNEY

Finding Your Path through Loss

DR. KENNETH J. DOKA

ATRIA BOOKS

NEW YORK LONDON TORONTO SYDNEY NEW DELHI

Note to Readers: Some names and identifying details have been changed, and some people portrayed are composites.

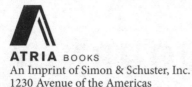

ATRIA BOOKS
An Imprint of Simon & Schuster, Inc.
1230 Avenue of the Americas
New York, NY 10020

This publication contains the opinions and ideas of its author. It is intended to provide helpful and informative material on the subjects addressed in the publication. It is sold with the understanding that the author and publisher are not engaged in rendering medical, health, or any other kind of personal professional services in the book. The reader should consult his or her medical, health, or other competent professional before adopting any of the suggestions in this book or drawing inferences from it.

First Atria Books hardcover edition April 2016

ATRIA BOOKS and colophon are trademarks of Simon & Schuster, Inc.

For information about special discounts for bulk purchases, please contact Simon & Schuster Special Sales at 1-866-506-1949 or business@simonandschuster.com.

The Simon & Schuster Speakers Bureau can bring authors to your live event. For more information or to book an event, contact the Simon & Schuster Speakers Bureau at 1-866-248-3049 or visit our website at www.simonspeakers.com.

Interior design by Kyoko Watanabe

Manufactured in the United States of America

10 9 8 7 6 5 4 3 2 1

Library of Congress Cataloging-in-Publication Data

Doka, Kenneth J.
Grief is a journey : finding your path through loss / Dr. Kenneth J. Doka.
pages cm
Includes bibliographical references and index.
1. Grief. 2. Death. 3. Loss (Psychology) I. Title.
BF575.G7D638 2016
155.9'37—dc23
2015014071

ISBN 978-1-4767-7148-9
ISBN 978-1-4767-7153-3 (ebook)

To my son, Michael, and my daughter-in-law Angelina
and my grandchildren, Kenneth (Kenny) and Luzelenia (Lucy)
for the joy, support, and unconditional love
they freely give—daily

CONTENTS

Part 1

The Journey of Grief

Part 2

The Many Losses in Life

Part 3

The Unacknowledged Losses of Life: Disenfranchised Grief

Part 4

Helping Yourself—and Others

PART 1

The Journey of Grief

Whatever you love—whether a person, a pet, or even an object—you may one day lose, for loss is a universal occurrence. And when you lose what you love, whether by separation or death, you grieve that loss; so grief, too, is a universal experience.

Yet, while the experience of loss is universal, the reactions to that loss are as distinct and individual as you are. Everyone grieves each individual loss in a unique way.

That fact is paradoxically both troubling and comforting. Troubling, since you want certainty: *What can I expect in grief? When will these feelings and reactions end? What is normal?* But comforting, too, because it accounts for the wide range of reactions you may be experiencing, and it reminds you that, just as each relationship is unique, so is each loss. Your own reactions have no less worth or validity than those of others around you.

Yet you still wish for a guide, and *Grief Is a Journey* offers that guide. Its opening chapters explore the many myths that trouble you as you grieve, and other chapters explore the varied reactions you may experience, as well as the factors that influence the particular manner of your grief.

This book affirms that as you go forward, you are going to retain a part of the one you have loved. It affirms that grief *is* truly a journey—as lifelong as your love—and it shows that you need not journey alone, or without hope.

CHAPTER 1

The Myths and Realities of Grief

It has been eight months since Vicky's husband died, and Vicky is very confused by her own grief. In the first two months she seemed to be coping so well, but in the past six months she feels worse—not better. She cries often and is short-tempered at work and at home. She is angry—angry at her husband for not taking care of himself; at friends who are not attentive; and even at her children, who are pressuring her, as she says, "to suddenly get better."

Brian is grieving the loss of his son. He thinks of Shay often and lovingly plans an annual carnival in his young son's memory. But his wife, Marla, worries that Brian has not dealt with his grief because he has never cried or talked about his feelings.

Steve is mourning the death of his lover. He misses him terribly. They spoke daily—sharing events and offering advice. Though it has been over a month, Steve still picks up the phone and begins to dial Henry and expects to hear Henry's voice when the phone rings. He wonders if he is going crazy.

> So does Carla, who is mourning her brother. She and her brother both were married and had kids, and they often socialized together, even vacationing as families. It seems so unfair that her brother died so young, only in his forties. But Carla resents everyone who asks how John's wife and children are doing. "What about my grief?" she says.

Though their losses and reactions are different, all of these people share a common experience—an experience that each one of us will encounter during our lifetime. They are grieving. Grief is the price we pay for love.

Loss is universal, but our reactions to it are not. Our responses are individual. Psychologists and clinicians have known this for years, but when people are suffering—the elderly woman left in an empty home without her husband, the adolescent son of a newly divorced couple, or the mother of a child struck with a debilitating illness—grief feels like an uncontrollable burden they must bear alone. Psychologists have learned so much useful information about grief, and how it unfolds, that can help people with their pain. But this information hasn't been given out widely to the public, or even made known to other therapists and clergy. At the same time, there are several myths about grieving that persist and that are damaging people's health and well-being.

Misconceptions about grief lead more than one million people each year to seek out chemical solutions to their pain, either through alcohol, recreational drugs, or prescription medication. Almost all report that they feel abandoned by family and friends who think that they have failed to "get over it" in time. Millions experience their grief alone, and they ask themselves, *Am I going crazy?*

This is why I felt compelled to write this book. I want to help people better understand their grief and to cope with it. I also want to help other counselors who may not know about recent important discoveries about how grief works.

Although grief is a universal, critical life experience, we often journey through it privately, isolated, afraid to share our feelings—

worried that our responses may be misunderstood or dismissed. And there is limited public understanding or conversation about the ways we cope with loss. For years, as I have lectured publicly about grief, I am inevitably asked variations of the question raised above. *Am I going crazy? What's wrong with me that I am crying all the time?* Or, *What's wrong with me that I am* not *crying all the time? What's wrong with me that my grief ebbs and flows? Why do I seem to be getting worse, sadder, rather than better?*

I want to reassure you that whatever your response is to grief, it is natural and normal for you. You may cry or not cry; you may feel much sadder at some times than others. For some people, grieving takes a long time; for others it takes less time. But it takes you the time that it takes. There are no rules that make one person's response normal and another's abnormal.

The journey through loss and grief does not have an effective road map that helps us to understand our experiences and pain, although I hope that in this book I will help you create your own route through your grief.

When we are grieving, we have a variety of perfectly normal, natural reactions that we may feel are "wrong" for one reason or another—they're strong or inconvenient or unexpected or condemned by our culture or family. We become fearful of sharing these reactions with others, who may not know how to offer support. They may even compound our problem by suggesting, when our reactions are truly natural and normal, that we need professional help. We may lose confidence in our ability to cope at a critical time when we need to adapt in order to survive. Our fears can become reality.

So I want to try to reassure you that you can cope. You may need some guidance in dealing with your pain, but you can create your own map for navigating your grief. First of all, your feelings are your feelings. You feel what you feel. You may feel sad, angry, or anxious; or a number of other emotions; or a jumble of emotions all at once.

In my teaching and lecturing, my counseling, and the hundreds of letters I receive as editor of *Journeys: A Newsletter to Help in Bereavement,* I have learned that most people have two models of how grief works. The first model is that *each day, it will get a little easier*. That model usually fails because many people get surges of pain that arise from time to time, especially around holidays, birthdays, or anniversaries. Another model of grief is that it proceeds in *stages,* which is based on Elisabeth Kübler-Ross's five stages.[1] These bereaved persons expect, or are expected by others, to go through phases of denial, anger, bargaining, and depression—before they reach acceptance. But the fact is that Kübler-Ross originally saw these stages as reflecting how people cope with illness and dying, not as reflections of how people grieve. Actual experiences of grief are far more individual, often chaotic, and much less predictable.

Grief is not a single process that everyone experiences the same way. This is critical for you to try to remember. Since we do not experience grief in a predictable set of stages, there is no "one size fits all" way to cope with loss.

There is also no closure to grief. Grief is not about letting go of past relationships or closing yourself off from them. Even in bereavement, you continue your bond—albeit in a different way.

Grief is not an illness you get over. It is a journey.

Here are some major principles to keep in mind about this new understanding of grief:

- You have personal, individual pathways in grieving
- Grief is not only an emotion. It includes physical, behavioral, cognitive, social, and spiritual reactions. Your own responses are influenced by your religion or sense of spirituality, culture, class, gender, and life experiences.
- Grief is not at all a relinquishing of ties to the deceased. It is understanding the complex ways that you retain a continuing bond to the person you loved.
- You experience many related losses as a consequence of a single loss or death. These secondary losses will also influence your life, and you will want to name and grieve them, too.

- You do not simply cope with your loss. There are possibilities for growth inherent in your grief, even though you may not see them for some time.

People feel grief for many kinds of losses. We grieve the deaths of family members, friends, lovers, and coworkers; sometimes even people we once loved, such as ex-spouses. We mourn the end of a valued friendship whether through death, relocation, or conflict. We grieve transitions and changes in our life. We become attached to dreams, to ideals, to our pets, to possessions, and to people we admire, whether politicians or celebrities, and grieve these losses, as well.

Twenty-six years ago, Donna angrily divorced her husband Nolan after she became aware of his multiple infidelities. She is stunned by her own grief reactions to hearing of his death. After all, she reasoned, it had been so long and the divorce had been so bitter. Married again now for near twenty years, she finds it difficult to sort out her feelings. Her friends do not understand why she would grieve "the creep." She feels awkward to share it with Austin, her present husband. She thinks he would just not understand—in fact, it took years for her to trust Austin after her past experience. How can he be expected to understand her grief?

We grieve other types of losses, too, as we journey through the different stages of life. A mother will feel pain after her preadolescent son objects to a public hug for the first time. Elderly people grieve their loss of independence when they have to give up their driver's license.

Losses like this are often disenfranchised—they are unrecognized and unsupported by other members of society. Sometimes we even discount or dismiss our own pain.[2] We feel *disenfranchised grief* over losses that are not openly acknowledged, socially sanctioned, or publicly shared. We experience these losses, but we come to believe we do not have the right to grieve them. Frequently, other people in society prohibit our right to grieve losses like these. As a result, we often suffer in silence, not knowing the true cause of our reactions, having no context in which to understand this, and receiving little support and recognition. While the concept of disenfranchised grief has been recognized by researchers and professionals for the past twenty years, this concept has rarely moved beyond specialists in the field.

Grief Is a Journey starts with this groundbreaking yet basic idea from the latest findings on grief: *We each have to find our own personal pathway as we deal with loss.* Grief is as individual as fingerprints or snowflakes. After all, each of us has our own set of experiences and distinct ways of coping. Every loss is different. Its consequences emerge from our unique relationships and arise from our own singular circumstances. Once you truly accept that basic but liberating concept—and once you identify your personal pathway—you are empowered to cope. You will find the right way to deal with your pain and memories, you will identify sources of meaningful support, and you will find the right resources to help you cope with your grief.

Once you identify the ways that grief manifests itself in your own life—and in the lives of those you care about and love—you can better help yourself, and you will see more clearly how to reach out effectively to support your family and friends who are grieving. This new understanding of grief allows you to answer three critical questions: *How can I understand my own pathway? How can I use this knowledge to help me deal with my grief? How can I support those I care about in their grief?*

I'd like to dispel some prevalent myths about how we grieve before we move forward. These myths have been perpetuated for years by laypeople as well as psychologists and counselors, but they have caused pain to millions of people who would otherwise experience their grief in a more natural, healthful way. These myths are pervasive but unsupported by scientific research. Identifying them can keep you from creating unrealistic expectations and allow you to explore a more individualistic and personalized truth—your own truth about your loss and your grief.

OFFERING CONDOLENCES

- Nothing you say can ease the pain of the loss. You can show support and empathy by your presence.
- Culturally appropriate actions such as bringing food, sending flowers, or making memorial donations are ways that show caring and support
- Do not invalidate or minimize the loss. Comments like *You are young, You can get married again, Think of the children you still have, She had a very long life,* and *At least he did not suffer* may attempt to comfort, but they do not acknowledge the loss and grief the person is experiencing.
- Do not offer platitudes such as *He is in a better place* or *God must have wanted her*. Grieving individuals may eventually find comfort from their beliefs, but right now they want the person with them—alive.
- Do simply say you are sorry for the loss
- Do share any special memories of the deceased, as well as the lessons you learned from the deceased or the impact they had on your life. While you may share them at the funeral, send them as well in a letter or card. They will be cherished.
- If you wish to help, be specific in what you can do. "Can I help get people to and from the airport?" or "Would you like me to pick up Cody after practice?" are far better than "Let me know if I can help."

Myth #1: Grief Is a Predictable Process

It would be easier if grief were predictable. If only we knew what we would experience, when we would experience it, and just how long it would last. Some of the earliest medical doctors and therapists looked at grief as an illness and believed that, like many illnesses, grief would simply run its course. They believed that counseling, much like medicine, might alleviate the symptoms and even shorten the experience, and that, given sufficient time and without complications, the grieving person eventually would be fine.

This notion that grief is predicable is one reason for the popularity of the "stage theories" of grief,[3] even though research has never supported the existence of stages.[4] But the idea that we can progress through stages promises resolution. It follows a story line in which a protagonist faces a challenge and, after various trials, emerges stronger and wiser. You may indeed grow stronger and wiser in dealing with your loss, but the journey you take can be just as unpredictable as the loss that brought about your grief.

Reality: Grief Is Individual

We are individuals, each with distinct beliefs. We come from different cultures. We live our own individual lives. We have our own relationships with those we love—our own histories. Every loss we experience is unique. The death of a parent is unlike that of a child or spouse—not necessarily easier or harder—just different. Each death occurs in a distinctive way. Some follow a long, lingering illness, while others are sudden and traumatic. Given all these differences, we will not all respond to grief in the same way.[5] Your grief is as unique as you are.

While there are some patterns to how grief unfolds, each of us responds to a different loss in a different way. We wish that we could establish with certainty what to expect. We hope that one day we may come to live with what now seems so wrong, so unacceptable. Yet reality is more complicated than the stages present in their inaccurate road map. Because the stages create false expectations of what grief is supposed to be like, when reality does not follow the stages and meet our expectations, we become confused and begin to doubt ourselves, our own feelings and thoughts. Grief may begin to feel like a tidal wave that hurls us along without our having any control. We feel as if grief just happens, and that we can do little about our emotions.

At my lectures, I am asked questions such as, *How long will my mother be in the depression stage? How long will my son remain angry?* But we rarely experience one dominant emotion at a time. We can feel depression, anger, disbelief all at once. We are a hive of emotions. If you have a history of depression or anger, your depression or anger at your loss may be consistent with your response to other life crises. Nonetheless, depression can be treated, and you can resolve your anger.

As we will explore in later chapters, grief can affect every part of your being, physically, emotionally, spiritually, socially, and mentally. You can feel ill, experiencing aches and pains. The stress of a significant loss can actually threaten your health. You may experience all sorts of emotions—guilt, relief, sadness, even at times a sense of liberation. For instance, Jim felt that sense of liberation, among other feelings, when his father died. Even though Jim was in his forties, married, and independent, he had struggled with his father's obsessive, controlling expectations of him.

Grief also can influence your thinking and challenge your beliefs. You may feel alienated from your beliefs. You may find it hard to concentrate. Thoughts about the person who died and images of the death may constantly intrude. To try to fit your reactions to your loss into five stages disenfranchises your reactions, creating confusion and more pain.

Grief simply does not follow a predictable set of stages.

Myth #2: There Is a Timetable to Grief

Belief in a timetable is another attempt to make the unpredictable predictable. After all, illnesses follow a certain course: We get a cold and it lasts a week or two. So how long does grief last? Common allowances of time off from work after a close family death seem to imply that in a few days or weeks, everything should be back to normal. It is a common myth that given a certain amount of time, perhaps at most a year, we should "get over it."

Reality: There Simply Is No Timetable to Grief

Grief is not an illness that runs its course. Rather, grief will wind its way through your life. There is no way to predict its course or time or when and where it will change for you. We are all different.

I often describe grief as a roller coaster. Each roller coaster is a different ride, even though all the tracks have ups and downs. In most roller coasters, the very beginning of the ride—that slow climb up the first peak—is more about anxiety than action. Grief is like that, too. Often the very beginning of the journey is not the roughest part. We may still be in shock. Even with prolonged illness, we often experience the actual death as somewhat sudden and unexpected. It was that way with my dad. He was in hospice care, dying of cancer. He knew it. We knew it. We all lived with the reality for months. We saw the steady decline. Yet the very slowness of the decline lulled us. He made it through Thanksgiving. We thought he might make it to Christmas. He died in his sleep, on November 30. Even that death was unexpected.

While we are shocked by the finality of a death, other factors cushion us in this early period. We have a lot to do. Funerals have to be planned. Cards and flowers have to be acknowledged. Forms need to be filed. Various documents and papers require review. In the period immediately following a death, our very busyness protects us from the rawness of our grief. For many of us, friends and family offer a blanket of care that covers and comforts us during this early time.

Later, perhaps a month or two after the death, many people experience a deep plunge. The shock has receded. The tasks related to death have eased. Support has faded as those around us have moved on. One of my clients remarked about the first day she returned home from work and there were no sympathy cards in the mail, no supportive messages in her voice mail. "Then," she stated, "I realized I was alone—really alone with my grief."

On the roller coaster of grief, you experience ups and downs. You will have good days and bad days, days that you feel the brunt of your loss, and days where you focus on a now different, perhaps previously unimagined future.

Some low points are predictable. The holidays tend to be difficult, as do special days such as birthdays or anniversaries. The anniversary of the death may be a difficult time as well. Seasonal cues remind you of your loss. If you experienced a death in the late summer, the seasonal back-to-school sales may prompt reminders of your loss. Certain days take on significance. *This was the day we brought him to the hospital for the last time. This is the last day we spoke before she lapsed into a coma.* Because of the persistent myth that grief lasts a year, you might even believe that you are feeling worse when you should be getting better. Please remember that there is no "should" in grieving.

Depending on the nature of your relationship, who you are, and the type of loss you suffered, the course of your journey may differ. From day to day some routes may be relatively easy, while others shock us with their intensity. The intensity will take some time to diminish, for most of us—and perhaps can be helped as we work to understand our grief. The bad days will come less often, will become less intense, and will not last as long. But in grief we never really get off the ride.

That is why there really is no predictable timetable. The intensity of grief may be over quickly—or barely experienced at all. It may be a year, but it may even be two years, which is common. And you may find that you need counseling, or other assistance and support, if the intensity does not cease. There may be times—even decades after your loss—when you feel surges of grief. For me, at the happy birth of my grandson, I so much missed not sharing that moment with my dad and not sharing the delight that he was named after me.

While there is no timetable, I will try to give you some guidelines to help you along your journey and to help you do some things for yourself that will help you cope.

Myth #3: Grief Is About Letting Go

I cannot think of a more destructive myth than this one. It may date back to when Sigmund Freud first began to write about grief. He suggested that the mourning process involved slowly disengaging from the emotional energy once invested in the person who died, and then slowly reinvesting it in other people and relationships.[6] Grief, in other words, was about letting go. The mourning process was about reviewing and releasing emotions we had invested in a relationship. This outdated view of grief is simply not the way to look at your loss.

When Martin Luther King Jr. died, for instance, Coretta Scott King made a conscious decision to live to carry on King's legacy and life's work. As part of that decision, she decided that she would never remarry, as it would dilute the moral authority she carried as King's widow. In this role, Coretta King continued to advance the struggle for human rights. No one can say that maintaining her connection in her way of mourning was wrong.

Letting go just does not work for us. In my practice, I have found that many clients are fearful that the easing of their pain would be at the cost of the fading of their memories. They would rather retain the pain than forget. I want to reassure you, as I always reassure them, that as your pain ebbs, you will have a greater ability to gain access to your memories. One of the first signs that you are doing better is when you can laugh about a story of the person you so deeply miss—a story too painful to recall in the early days after the death.

When I first began teaching, I lived in my home community of Astoria, in the northwestern corner of Queens, one of the five boroughs of New York City. Astoria is a multiethnic neighborhood characterized by semi-detached homes with small backyards. New York has a unique form of torture for car owners called "alternate side of the street parking," which means that, on certain days, parking is allowed on only one side of the street to permit street cleaning. So most homeowners paved over their back lots to provide for a small garage or off-street parking. But not my older Italian neighbors, Rosa and Joe. Their backyard was a tomato garden, as Rosa insisted that her "gravy"—tomato sauce—should be made of only the freshest ingredients. Growing tomatoes in the midst of New York City, in the shadow of the Manhattan skyline, is a challenge. The weather is variable, the pests (including neighborhood kids) burdensome, and the soil needs constant fertilization.

Joe would constantly bicker with Rosa about her tomato garden. Fresh tomatoes are readily available at many vegetable stands, he constantly reiterated. Why not change the backyard to a carport? Rosa was unmoved and would say, "If I die first, do whatever you want." Joe would joke that the hearse would be followed by a cement truck.

Rosa died first and, until the end of his life, Joe lovingly tended Rosa's garden. And as he shared his bounty with his neighbors, he would welcome a glass of wine and recount warm memories of his wife.

Would we say that Joe is stuck in his grief?

Reality: We Retain a Continuing Bond with Those We Love

In recent years, we have moved 180 degrees from the idea that grief is about detachment.[7] Rather than cutting bonds with the deceased, we can and generally do maintain a continuing bond with anyone we love. This bond is expressed in many ways. Certainly we retain memories of that individual—memories that continue to inform, advise, and guide us. Memories also nurture and warm our very being. People we love become part of our own biographies. We cannot really separate ourselves from them. They have left an indelible mark on who we are, how we see ourselves. Being my sister and brother's kid brother, as well as my mother and father's son, helps define the person I have become.

Our families leave their legacies, and perhaps even some liabilities, with us. The most obvious might be physical—the turn of a smile we share, or the color of our eyes and hair. The deeper ones are the lessons we learned and the insights we gained from those relationships. Some may be small—almost idiosyncratic. For example, I begin each day by drawing up a list of things I need to do—something I observed my dad do. My son does it as well.

Some people experience extraordinary moments of connection, such as a dream or an indefinable moment where we feel a sense of presence. These times may be difficult to describe, but we never forget them. We feel other bonds in our spiritual beliefs. We may believe that the person we grieve is in heaven, awaiting an eventual reunion. We may believe that one day, in some future life, our spirits will somehow reconnect.

What we do want to be careful of, however, is when continuing bonds can become restricting. Do not feel compelled to keep promises you made that no longer make sense or that are not good for you. One of my college students, for example, felt compelled by a promise to his dying father to go into the ministry—something that he no longer wished to do. Another client, a widow, was troubled by a promise to her dying husband that she would never remarry. You will want to reexamine any bonds that may impair your growth.

You never fully lose your connection with someone you loved. They remain with you. In fact, one task of mourning is deciding how to carry those memories and feelings with you in ways that still allow you to reengage fully in life. We'll discuss that in a later chapter.

Myth #4: After a Loss, We Need Closure

You may be told that there is some action or event that can bring you some sort of closure—or release—from your grief. A widespread belief is that the funeral provides closure, that once we see the deceased lying serenely in the casket, we may feel that his or her suffering is over, that he or she is at peace. We may look to an autopsy report to offer closure, as if once we really learn the cause of the death we can seal that chapter of our life. We may be told that closure lies in a private ritual or memorial, in getting a memorial tattoo, or in writing a letter to the person who died.[8] These actions all can be very helpful and healing, but they will not bring your emotions to a close.

The concept of closure is built on two discredited myths—that grief has a timetable, and that we can somehow move beyond our grief by letting go or detaching from the person we loved. The concept of closure simply added that this finality could be achieved by some ritual or activity.

The concept of closure, misguided though it is, has a history. It was first used almost a century ago by Gestalt psychologists, and was later adopted by the crime victims' rights movements. Victims asked to be able to attend the trial, make a victim impact statement, be present for sentencing, or witness an execution as means to achieve closure. Yet even in those dramatic cases, closure never really occurred.

Reality: There Can Never Be "Closure"

Closure is simply not useful in coping with loss. Most bereaved people find that over time their pain lessens and they can function as well—sometimes even better—than they did before the loss. Yet even over time, we may experience short surges of grief, moments where we deeply feel our loss. Grief is not an illness from which we recover, or an event on the way to a destination. Rather, grief involves a lifelong journey, and no single act, or even a combination of actions, changes that.

Of course, there are significant moments in our journey. Funerals are important. A meaningful funeral can have great therapeutic value. In the same vein, an autopsy report might offer information that answers troubling questions. It did so for Georgia. When her twenty-year-old son died of a particularly virulent bacterial meningitis, Georgia was deeply troubled that perhaps she had missed an early symptom or a treatment possibility. Painful as the report was to read, it reassured her that she did all she could. A competent diagnosis and autopsy report can be extremely important in cases like Georgia's, or in similar situations such as sudden infant death syndrome (SIDS) deaths where our grief can be deeply complicated by fears that something we did or omitted to do caused a death. For Manuel, the autopsy report of a SIDS death eased his fears and those of his wife. While these events might offer a sense of relief or an answer to troubling questions, however, they certainly do not "close" our grief. We need to bring closure to the use of the term *closure*.

Rituals and memorials can help you as you deal with loss. Writing a letter to the deceased and reading it at graveside is an excellent way to convey a feeling that you need to express, or even apologize for something you did or failed to do. But these meaningful steps on your journey do not end your passage. When Georgia was questioned by her friends about whether the report brought her closure, her response said it well: "The report answered many questions. It reassured me—and that was important. But grief is about learning to live with loss."

Myth #5: We Need to Process the Loss in Order to Reach Resolution

This myth also arises from Freud's conceptions of grief a century ago. He believed that when we experience a loss, we also expect to experience some form of great distress. He thought that not showing distress is a sign that something is seriously awry with our grief, that we are denying our loss or repressing our grief. Freud believed that people need to *feel* their grief—to cry, to yearn, to show some evident sign of pain—and that only by experiencing and processing that pain could they ever hope to recover from their grief and resolve their loss.

Much self-help literature also assumes that people who openly express emotions in grief, and publicly show their grief, are healthier than those who do not. Because of this mistaken assumption, people who are really dealing well with their grief may be influenced to think that something is wrong with them.

The danger of this myth, like the myth of the five-stage model, is that it sets up one way to grieve—a single road map—and implies that if we are not following this road map, something is wrong with us. It may make us believe that we are repressing or denying our grief—or, even worse, that perhaps we did not love or care about the person who died as much as we had believed we did. Other people may wrongly assume that our lack of visible emotion means a lack of love for the person we lost. I once knew a couple whose young daughter died of leukemia. Her mother constantly cried whenever something reminded her of the loss. Her father began a scholarship fund to perpetuate his daughter's memory. His wife struggled with his lack of tears, wondering if he ever really loved their daughter. He was perplexed that his mate could not see the love and devotion inherent in keeping alive her legacy.

This expectation of showing our emotions may have come out of what might be called an *affective bias* in counseling. Often the question we most associate with counseling is "How did you feel about that?" This affective bias finds its boldest expression in literature about men and grief. Many clinicians see men at a disadvantage in grieving when compared to women, who are seen as more ready to accept help and express emotion, both of which are viewed as essential to the process of grieving. Since men are perceived as less likely to show emotion or accept help, they are seen as having more difficulty in responding to loss. Recently at a lecture, one counselor suggested that when grieving men use the word "fine" in answer to how they are doing, it should be viewed as an acronym for "feelings inside, never expressed." The underlying assumption is that there are limited ways that we can effectively cope with loss.[9] Yet there is little research underlying the premise that we need to emotionally process our grief.[10] We must make a distinction between emotionally processing our grief and processing grief at all.

Reality: We Each Process Loss in Our Own Way

Perhaps a better way of looking at this is that while we all need to process our losses, we do that in our own ways. For some of us it is a long, arduous, and emotionally challenging task. Others may deal with grief more quickly and with less inner turmoil.

We can also differ in the ways we process our grief and experience, express and adapt to loss. Certainly, coping by openly expressing our grief is one way, but other styles are equally effective.[11] The emotional style of grieving is an *intuitive* pattern—individuals cope with grief by expressing and exploring their emotions. For Alicia, processing her grief involved joining a support group where she could cry among a circle of supportive parents who understood her loss. She could process her difficult emotions—her anger at God for her loss, her guilt, and her relief when death finally came, ending her daughter's tortured last days—in a compassionate setting where, she said, "People got it."

In an *instrumental* pattern, grief is experienced physically, such as in restlessness or bodily pain. Here we *think* or *do* our grief. That is how Bob handled his loss. When his son, a pilot, disappeared over the ocean on a training mission, Bob's wife availed herself of all the counseling the airline provided. All Bob wanted to do was to study the tidal patterns. Every afternoon he would take up his own plane to search for signs of wreckage.

Many people exhibit more *blended* patterns that are both intuitive and instrumental reactions and responses.

While you do need to process your loss, there is neither a timetable nor a single way to do so. The way you grieve, how you show your loss, whether you cry, break down, or respond in a stoic manner, is not a measure of how much you loved the person you lost.

Myth #6: Human Beings Are Naturally Resilient to Loss

Many people do adapt well to loss.[12] Their grief reactions are relatively minimal and they continue to cope well with all the demands of work, home, or school. And many people cope with loss without additional assistance.[13] Not everyone needs counseling, but some do, particularly those dealing with complicated loss and those who do not have strong support systems.

Reality: Many Individuals Are Resilient in Experiencing Loss, Yet Many May Find Grief Difficult—Even Disabling

Grief is not necessarily a crippling experience. I always begin our support group asking if anyone has anything they would wish to discuss. One woman, Sylvia, began almost apologetically. "I think," she stated tentatively, "that I am doing better than I should be doing." She seemed worried that there was something that she was missing—that the pain of grief would come crashing down upon her.

The truth is that her response was as natural and as normal as the responses of others in the group. In fact, a recent study showed that just fewer than half the people surveyed indicated relatively few manifestations of grief and an ability to function well even after a loss.[14] Researchers labeled these people *resilient*.

Resilient grievers often share certain characteristics. For example, resilient grievers reported fewer losses in their lives—deaths were not frequent; one loss did not follow another. Resilient grievers were psychologically healthy before the loss. They reported few earlier psychological problems or stressors, and had good social support. They had a strong intrinsic spirituality that offered comfort and support.

In addition, resilient grievers generally had not experienced the sudden deaths of people they were close to. Nor were the deaths perceived to be "preventable"—that is, they saw little that they could have done to prevent the loss. Most said that they found great comfort in being able to say good-bye to the person who died. Often in more sudden deaths, such as a car crash or even a stroke or heart attack, grieving people are haunted by guilt from asking what-ifs.

Even though, generally, the circumstances of death are barely within our control, we can learn from these resilient grievers. Resilient grievers tend to have an optimistic mind-set, and they believe that even out of the most tragic situations can eventually come opportunities for learning and personal growth. Sylvia strongly believed that. The loss of her spouse was exceedingly painful, but Sylvia looked at the changes that followed his death as a challenge. She viewed each new accomplishment or a task she took on—even mundane ones such as doing the household bills—as a personal triumph.

This leads to another characteristic of resilient grievers—they believe that something good can come out of even the worst events. Alan's son died in a tragic accident on a hike when he slipped and tumbled off a cliff. While Alan continues to grieve deeply for his son, he takes comfort in the fact that a new guardrail he helped to install will keep others from a similar fate. We all have the capacity to grow even in the midst of trauma.

Resilient grievers also consciously try to engender positive memories of the person who died. Over time, they report that these comforting memories spontaneously emerge. Sylvia, for example, would return to a beach her husband loved. "I would replay events in my mind—very consciously at first. Then, soon, whenever I was at a beach—even if I saw a photo of a beach—I would be flooded by these warm thoughts."

You need not worry if you are doing better than you think you should be doing. You can be comforted by it. You can also learn from those who are doing "better than they should"—even in the midst of your own grief.

However, if you are having trouble coping with loss, you will find help in the coming chapters in finding your own path.

Myth #7: It Is Easier to Accept a Death after a Prolonged Illness

There are many variations of this myth—for example, "Long illnesses are harder on the deceased person, but make grief easier for survivors; while sudden deaths are easier for the deceased person, but more difficult for survivors." Underlying this myth is a misunderstanding of the concept of *anticipatory grief*—the sense that we would grieve a loss in anticipation of the death. That is, if we were already grieving the death before the person died, we will have less of a shock and we will already have completed some of the grief. This almost seems to assume that we have just so many tears or so much grief that anything expended earlier would mean less would be needed or available after a death.

Reality: All Deaths Are Difficult

One of my mentors, Rabbi Earl Grollman, used to stress that the worst loss is the one we are dealing with now. Each loss is difficult in its own way. Prolonged and sudden losses create different issues for survivors. In sudden loss, there may be a sense of trauma—a loss of a sense of a safe and predictable world, as well as a profound sense of shock over the loss, and a legacy of unfinished business. In a prolonged loss, we may experience a sense of ambivalence—waiting for the inevitable death and yet seeking to avoid the finality of death. Anticipatory grief or anticipatory mourning is a misnomer. What we grieve throughout the illness are often all the losses associated with the illness—the fact that someone we love often daily loses different capabilities and aspects of self. When the person does die—we now grieve their loss.[15]

Two Other Myths

While I implicitly mentioned these two myths at the beginning of this chapter, I want to briefly explain them further here:

Myth: Grief Is Solely a Reaction to a Death.
Reality: Grief Is a Response to any Loss

Here Freud got it right. Freud often began his pieces with case studies or illustrative anecdotes. In his essay "Mourning and Melancholia,"

Freud began with a case anecdote about a bride abandoned at the altar—a woman jilted by her fiancé.

We sometimes overlook that it is loss—not death—that arouses grief. We grieve the deaths of people we loved, but we also grieve other losses as well. Any break in our relationship to something or some person to whom we are attached generates grief. We can grieve divorces and separations. We can grieve the loss of things such as a home, job, or car that was important to us. We may grieve things of symbolic importance such as the loss of reputation or social status. We can grieve the losses of people we never met—witness, for example, the reactions to the deaths of varied celebrities or public figures such as Nelson Mandela, Princess Diana, or Elvis Presley. We can grieve the loss of animals. Many times we may be surprised by the grief generated by relationships we thought were long over—such as the loss of an ex-spouse. We grieve our own illness—or the illnesses of people we care about. Here, too, we face a series of losses as health ebbs and we need to give up treasured activities, or face decreased abilities to engage in even normal activity. The point is that as humans we emotionally invest or attach to many different people and things. Whenever these attachments are severed we grieve.

Myth: Some Types of Losses Are More Difficult Than Others. Reality: All Loss Can Hurt

It is easy to think that our loss is more difficult than any other loss. But we cannot calibrate the pain that comes from the death of a child, nor compare it to the loss of a beloved partner. As we will see in the forthcoming chapters, every type of loss creates its own issues. Each hurts in its own unique way.

In the remainder of this book, we explore the most current understanding of how we grieve. I'll present individual strategies that you can adopt to help you cope most effectively with your grief. In this first part, I will show you the common ways we process grief and learn to live with loss, and the different patterns and styles of dealing with loss that you may be experiencing.

In part 2 we explore the unique nature of the challenges of different losses that we commonly experience in adulthood—the losses of spouses, children, parents, and siblings. You may have to deal not only with your own grief but also the grief of others—your parents, your in-laws, your children and grandchildren. You may struggle to be supportive of relatives, friends, and colleagues in their grief. Whatever situation you find yourself in, I offer concrete suggestions for understanding and coming to terms with grief in order to begin rebuilding your life.

CHAPTER 2

The Experience of Grief

Dictionaries define grief as a great sorrow or sadness associated with loss. Grief is that—or certainly can be that for many people. However, grief is also more than that. Grief is a highly individual reaction. Some people have profoundly debilitating reactions to a loss, while others have more muted or resilient reactions. Some reactions, such as sadness and tears, we may clearly identify as part of grieving. Yet other reactions, such as irritability, an inability to concentrate, or even physical pain, may be less identifiable as stemming from grief, and so cause concern and confusion.

The truth is that loss can affect every dimension of our being, so grief can express itself in our emotions, behavior, and thought processes. Grief can also manifest itself physically and spiritually. In this chapter, you will discover some of the surprising and unexpected ways we can experience grief. We will also take note of "yellow flags" and "red flags," warning signs that tell you when grief is not typical.

Grief Can Hurt—Physically!

> Ever since Jay lost his job, he has felt physically sick, experiencing tremendous pain around his back and shoulders. A battery of tests failed to isolate his problem. In his last visit to a neurologist, the doctor could not find a biological foundation for Jay's complaints but suggested that Jay listen to his own words. Jay noticed that as he discussed his plight, he would often state, "Everything is on my back now—it's all on my shoulders."

Could reactions to a loss really be this physical? The answer is definitely! Physical manifestations of grief are common. Such physical reactions can include (but are not limited to) headaches, muscular aches, menstrual irregularities, fatigue, chest pains, tightness in the throat or chest, abdominal pains, shortness of breath, weakness, and oversensitivity to stimuli. Some people experience physical symptoms that are similar to those suffered by the person who died. Sometimes the reactions have a strong symbolic connection to the loss, such as heartache. In the 1970s, Jane Nichols spoke about the "empty arms syndrome" in women who had miscarriages and stillbirths. At a time when grief for such losses was generally not validated, these women complained of pain in their upper arms—in the same muscles they would use to lift or hold a child.

Physical manifestations are particularly common in grieving children. In my classes on Children, Adolescents, Grief, and Loss, I ask my students, "Who sees the homesick kids first at sleepaway camp?" The answer is the camp nurse. Children struggling with separation often seek help for physical ailments that are a symptom of their distress. When their emotions remain unidentified and unspoken, they may be converted to physical reactions. Children learn early that being sick elicits care.

Sometimes, as we effectively deal with grief, our physical symptoms abate. That happened with Pat. She came into my office raging that her physician thought her problem was related to her grief. She had severe tremors in her hands, which were visibly shaking when she entered my office. She asked if I thought this was only in her head. I simply asked her if she had ever had those symptoms earlier. She noted that her parents told her that when she was a young girl she would often shake in the middle of her temper tantrums. I asked her if she was angry now. She nodded and whispered, "Furious." An Irish Catholic, Pat often buried her emotions. Both she and her husband worked and, typically, Pat would return first and get the dinner ready. After her husband retired, she would return home—to a mess left by her husband. Angry and resentful, she never confronted her husband or suggested that he at least clean up after himself and begin dinner. Instead she simply seethed. He had been home all day alone and now wanted Pat's attention. He would call out to her as she worked in the kitchen, perhaps to comment on some trivial event or have her see something on the TV. If she would be late in responding, he would simply give a dismissive "never mind." On the evening before Pat's husband died in his sleep from a massive stroke, he had done this a number of times. Pat felt guilty that perhaps he would have shared some symptom if she had only paid attention. She was also angry over the persistent game, as well as now having to confront a life alone. As she expressed her anger, the shaking ceased.

While physical reactions are common in grief, you should never ignore them. Any persistent physical symptom—any ache or pain—should be checked out by a physician—but go to a physician who understands that experiencing a loss has physical manifestations. The reason for this is simple—*grief is dangerous to your health!*

Studies have shown that there is a higher mortality among grieving persons, especially older widows and widowers, in the first year following loss. As early as 1969, researchers noted what they called the "broken heart syndrome" in describing the increased mortality among widowers.[1] Later, scientists found increased rates of cardiovascular disease and an impaired immune system in bereaved persons that can play a role in the onset of many diseases including some forms of cancer. They also found increased rates of depression and anxiety (which have negative effects on physical health).[2] Yet a strong sense of spirituality, good social networks, and a sense of purpose and meaning can mitigate these negative effects.

There are a number of reasons for this increased mortality and morbidity in older widowers and widows. Many older individuals die of chronic diseases, and these diseases often are related to lifestyle factors such as diet or other habits—often shared within a marriage. For example, if one spouse smoked, the other spouse lived—at the very least—with secondhand smoke.

Grief is stressful. Stress negatively affects health, especially among aging individuals. Finally, when a spouse dies, lifestyle practices such as diet, sleep, exercise, or adherence to a medical regimen may also change for the worse. The wife who once made three nutritional meals for her husband may eat erratically out of cans after his death. My dad was very time conscious—especially about my mother's medications for her minor chronic illnesses. When my father died, we wondered if my mother would be able to adhere to her regimen, as she was often casual about following such directions. She did and lived a decade after his death. In her case, keeping careful time about her medications was one of the bonds she retained with her husband—*it was something Frank would have wanted.*

Understanding these dangers allows you to assess how grief may be affecting your own health. It may help your loved ones to recognize these signs and symptoms. It also reminds you of the importance of self-care as you struggle with your losses. Are you experiencing any persistent physical symptoms or changes in your health?

You can be proactive about your health by asking yourself questions about what you are doing to maintain your health in this stressful time. Are you eating regular nutritious meals? Have your sleep patterns significantly changed? Are you exercising regularly? Are you adhering to any medical regimens, such as taking medications as directed?

It is equally important to acknowledge the stress you may be experiencing following your loss. Is that stress affecting your health? For example, if the stress is regularly interrupting your sleep, you may want to develop strategies to sleep more soundly. You may want to establish a quiet and regular routine around bedtime, or make sure you are taking prescribed medications correctly. Look for other ways to deal with your stress. Perhaps you want to carefully assess which obligations to address and which can be delayed or delegated. If you like massage therapy, aromatherapy, meditation, or even a walk on the beach or in a park, you may want to use them. The point is that while grief affects our health, we can take some action to minimize those negative effects and ease our physical manifestations of grief.

The Emotions of Grief

Sadness, Yearning, and Loneliness

Sadness, yearning, and loneliness are often part of grieving. We may also experience guilt or anger, relief, or even fear of further loss. The emotions themselves can be challenging and complex—creating a sense of shame and isolation that complicates mourning.

It is natural to feel sadness. We yearn for the person we loved to come back to us or for things to return to the sense of normality that we once felt. We may feel lonely because someone who shared part of our life is no longer there. One of my mentors, Dr. Robert Kastenbaum, a pioneer in the field of grief and the founding editor of the first journal on grief, *Omega: Journal of Death and Dying,* lost his daughter years before in an accident after she had visited him on Father's Day. When I offered my condolences, Bob's response was to wonder whether he would ever get over the "profound absence of her presence."

That is the heart of grief—the absence of a presence we once felt dear. Nonetheless, we can do things to help ourselves as we encounter loneliness and sadness. I once suggested to a support group of surviving spouses that they identify the times they experienced loneliness and sadness most. For one surviving spouse, Friday nights were toughest. She and her husband had busy independent lives, but Friday night was *their* night. They would always meet at a local pizzeria, enjoying dinner and a glass of wine while reviewing their day. Another surviving spouse indicated that Friday nights were difficult for her as well, and so these two widows decided to go out for dinner together. In the beginning, they were simply lonely together, but over time, they both began to look forward to this night out, this time with each other.

The point is that while you have little say in how you feel and how you will experience grief, you do have choices about how to deal with those feelings. Even in grief, you are not without resources or devoid of any power. In acknowledging your grief and in recognizing that your emotions are normal and natural responses to loss, you can begin to cope with your feelings.

Navigating Guilt

Guilt is one of the most common—and crippling—unexpected emotions. In a recent study, four prominent grief researchers found excessive guilt to be corrosive—affecting both physical and psychological health.[3] Guilt eats us up from the inside, creating pain, and troubling memories. Research into mothers grieving the death of a child identified six different types of guilt.

Causation guilt means that we believe we contributed to the death by something we did or failed to do. For example, we may be fixated that if only we had taken the person to a doctor or recognized a symptom, death could have been avoided. A wife may feel guilt because she could never get her husband to stop smoking even as he was being treated for lung cancer. These thoughts do not have to be rational to be real. We can even feel guilty over things that we recognize we could not really control.

Role guilt comes from feeling we could have been a better father, mother, brother, sister, son, or daughter. When my dad was ill, we had a moment of conflict. Dad was bed-bound and he asked me to raise the shade. I raised it about six inches but it was too high, so he asked could I lower it. I did this for about twenty minutes—raising or lowering it less than an inch each time. Finally, in frustration, I said I would do it just once more. Later I realized this was not about the shade at all. It was about his lack of control. I began to torture myself—I, of all people, studying dying for decades, should have been more sensitive. Yet hindsight is easy. In the end, I reacted as a son—not a counselor. I needed to forgive myself—and my dad. Such guilt often can arise within the tense and difficult days as one struggles with the disease or the demands of caregiving.

Guilt may result from earlier events in the relationship. Candy, for example, felt guilty over the years she had not spoken to her brother following an argument after their mother's death. Even though they eventually reconciled, she regretted all those missed years.

With *moral guilt,* we see our loss as a cosmic punishment for something we have done. When I worked at Sloan Kettering with children dying of cancer, parents frequently repeated the verse "the sins of the fathers will be visited on their children." They confessed all sorts of sins—infidelity, misdemeanors and felonies of their youth, even poor attendance at their place of worship—which they thought, however unfounded, might be responsible for their child's illness.

With *survivor guilt,* we wonder why we are alive when someone else died. This is a very common reaction of siblings when a brother or sister dies. Parents and other adults may idealize the child who died as having been a perfect child. The surviving siblings then can easily believe that they—the "less than perfect" children—should have died. Older persons feel this guilt when someone younger dies and they believe that they should have died instead.

Grief guilt means we feel guilty or ashamed at how poorly we seem to cope with our loss. However, in *recovery guilt* we think we are doing too well. We can experience both of those emotions. Grace, for example, felt so ashamed after her husband died that she was finding it difficult to enter into the Christmas spirit for her younger children's sake. Yet at times when she did find enjoyment, such as her son's Christmas pageant and her daughter's holiday concert, she felt guilty that she was enjoying herself so soon after her husband's death.

Once you identify your guilt, you can examine it. What is its source? Is it realistic? So often we hold unrealistic expectations of what we can control or accomplish. In fact, there are many things we cannot control. In Grace's case, I challenged her to close her eyes and envision what she could have done to make her husband stop smoking. After she did so, she said, "I did everything I could think of to hide his cigarettes. Once I even shot his lighted cigarette with a water pistol!"

Ask yourself: *Given the circumstances, what could I have done differently? How can I learn—even grow—from the experience?* Sometimes we can gain perspective on our guilt by simply reflecting on the question, *Would others find me guilty?* If you feel guilty over something, you may want to write a letter to the person and perhaps read it at his or her grave site, or even talk to a chair while pretending the person is sitting in it. One of the exercises I do with clients who address unfinished business in that way is to then have them sit in the other person's chair and respond as they believe the other person might.

As you work to resolve your feelings, rituals of affirmation and reconciliation can be very useful. Rituals of reconciliation allow you to finish business that was interrupted by death. They can allow you to say good-bye and to give or accept forgiveness. For instance, you might write a note and burn it to symbolically release the words into the sky. Rituals of affirmation celebrate the life of the person who died and recognize his or her legacy or accomplishments. When a popular grade-school teacher died, her students wrote notes about the most important lesson the teacher had taught them, which were sent to the family.

Your faith system may have rituals or beliefs that help you cope with guilt. One of my clients, Herb, felt guilty that in the last year of his wife's life, he became interested in another woman. His wife, Rebecca, had dementia for many years. In the past two years, he reluctantly placed her in a nursing home when her needs far exceeded his abilities to care for her. Yet he remained a dedicated husband—visiting daily to the end of her life. However, in the last year before Rebecca died, Herb became friendly with a neighboring widow.

They would share meals, walks, and watch television together. Both sets of adult children appreciated their new relationship, as it eased their parents' isolation and loneliness. When Rebecca died, Herb felt guilty that he had been adulterous—in love with another woman even as his wife was alive. Counseling seemed unproductive in easing Herb's guilt until I asked him how, if he felt guilt, he found forgiveness in his faith. He decided that, since he was "unfaithful" for a year, he would volunteer in a dementia day program one day a week for a year before he began traveling with his new partner. He called a few months later to say he was now volunteering three days a week so they could begin traveling in April.

How Dare You Die! Anger in Grief

Anger, too, is a common, sometimes confusing or surprising reaction. The root of the word *bereaved* means to have something yanked out or taken away from you—forcibly. It would probably be best translated by a seventies expression, *ripped off*. Anger and rage are familiar responses to having someone we love and care about ripped away from us.

Sometimes that anger is directed at an individual we hold responsible for the pain. For example, the anger may focus on a nurse or physician, perhaps a clergyperson or friend, who we feel was not as attentive, sensitive, or supportive as we had expected. We may even be angry with the person who died—blaming that individual for not taking proper care, for dying, for leaving us alone in our grief. At other times, the anger is cosmic. We become angry with God, a higher power, or the world. We may find that our anger does not have a specific target. We are filled with a sense of rage and simply lash out at anyone in our way. Often those individuals to whom we are closest feel the sting of our anger. They become safe and convenient targets of our wrath.

Anger is natural and understandable, but it can isolate you at a time when you most need support. It can drive away the very people you need most.

So how should you deal with the anger? The first thing to do is to explore your anger. When do you get angry? What seems to trigger it? Is your anger proportional to the cause? How do you express it? What does it do to others?

If you find that you do have legitimate cause for your anger, you can consider how to channel that emotion in constructive ways. For example, mothers angry at lax laws and ineffective enforcement that allowed convicted drunk drivers to repeat offenses with little more than a slap on the wrist formed Mothers Against Drunk Driving (MADD). Over the years, MADD changed not only our laws but also our society's perspective on driving while intoxicated.

Many times, however, anger is not really focused on any responsible person or legal inequity or injustice. You may realize that most times you are not angry at an individual. You are angry at your own grief, loss, and isolation. Here, too, you have to consider how to channel that anger. Sometimes physical exercise can help you cope. You may find it useful to write a letter (and not send it), talk about your feelings, punch a pillow, or scream on an empty beach. Even fantasies can be an effective way to cope with anger. Grace, for example, would imagine what she would tell her husband when she met him in a future afterlife. "He will first have to hear what his death did to me. How I wished he had watched his own health better."

Other Emotional Responses

You may feel anxiety and fear after a loss. After traumatic, unexpected, or sudden deaths, survivors may see the world as dangerous and unsafe. Even a death from a long illness can make survivors frightened to face the world alone. Fear can be debilitating. It can keep you from participating fully in life. You may be afraid to go out alone or engage in activities you once enjoyed. Even more dangerous is when your fears affect others. For Maryanne, the drowning death of her son Bobby created tremendous anxieties about her younger son, Billy. Though she lived in a community near a beach, she forbade Billy to swim on the beach and built a backyard pool where she could keep an eye on him and his friends. As Billy reached adolescence, the lure of the beach—the local hangout for youth—proved irresistible to him. Maryanne realized that in a community where ocean swimming was the primary activity, Billy was not as strong a swimmer as his friends. In fact, Maryanne's anxieties kept him from developing his skill. As Maryanne worked on her anxieties, she found a swimming program for adolescents at a local YMCA.

Relief is also a common reaction to a loss. You can be relieved because that person's pain and suffering is now over. It is difficult to watch someone you love die—to see them lose strength and weight, to watch them slowly give up the things that once held great importance. It is natural to feel relief for that person's release.

It also is natural to feel relieved yourself. Every illness is a family illness. We all are affected. When someone in our immediate family is dying, our lives change as well. We have added responsibilities and stress. We are often in emotional turmoil. Sleep may be interrupted. When death finally occurs, it is not selfish or wrong to feel that our own suffering is also over. It is natural and it is human.

In unhealthful relationships, there may be other reasons for relief as well. Some individuals can seek to dominate and control others. Their caustic comments can wound. In such cases, it is not unusual that when such a person dies there may be a sense of relief that this unhealthful relationship is now over. Here relief is a feeling of emancipation—that we are finally free of a burdensome relationship. For example, research[4] found that widows who came from highly constraining relationships actually bloom after a spouse's death. They grow and develop new skills and interests.

Some of the emotions we experience as we grieve are even positive. We may have a deep sense of thankfulness that we shared our life together. We may enjoy recalling wonderful moments together or recounting humorous anecdotes of life together. We may feel proud of what our loved one accomplished in life or that we held up so well or took such good care of the person as he or she was dying. "I do not know what is wrong with me," Marge mused. "When my mother died, I thought I would feel this intense grief. I would even think I might feel relief that my mother's struggle has ended—as well as my own. Instead, I feel a strong sense of pride. When will I grieve?"

Marge's pride was understandable. For five years she had been the sole caregiver as her mother developed Alzheimer's disease and then cancer. Marge accomplished more than she ever thought possible. She was able to take charge—arranging respite, addressing her mother's needs, and providing exceptional care. She became active in a local support group, even going to training and becoming a facilitator. In the course of these five years, she discovered new strengths as she developed new skills. She never flagged in her commitment to her mom.

Many people make Marge's mistake and identify grief only with powerful sorrowful emotions. If we are not feeling bad, we think we are not grieving. But like Marge we may have a sense of pride in the relationship or what we accomplished in the circumstances. We may feel a deep, abiding sense of love and appreciation for the gift of time together. When Herb's wife died, he said, "I missed her terribly. Yet, even with the loneliness and the missing, I had a great sense of peace. We had fifty-six years together! How many couples can say that? How many couples can say I loved her more each of those fifty-six years? I felt thankful for all that time."

When a good friend of mine died young, one of my reactions was a deep sense of commitment. I had promised to watch over his young son—my godson. I kept saying to myself, all through the funeral, "That is one promise I *will* keep!" My grief was mixed with a strong sense of satisfaction that my friend would be pleased at my involvement in his son's life.

These positive feelings certainly can be mixed with all the complicated, sorrowful reactions that are part of the journey of grief. The sense of pride and love can alternate with feelings of abandonment and anger. Not everyone experiences such strong emotions. Some of us feel in vivid colors, others in pastels. This is part of the individuality of grief.

Yet because grief is a reaction to a loss, these emotions are a part of the journey. Positive feelings are not a denial of grief but another natural response to loss, offering the promise that the memories and relationship will persist even as the pain of grief diminishes.

These emotions do not follow in any neat sequence. We are a hive of reactions as we grieve. Acknowledge and accept the range of emotions you are experiencing. Your feelings are what they are. You cannot control which appear when; you can only validate and learn how to cope with them. Later chapters will help you more with this.

The Ways We Think While Grieving

Grief also influences the ways you think. When you first experience a loss, you may feel a sense of shock. Even if someone dies after a lengthy illness, you may still not expect the death to occur at this particular time. As my colleague Dr. Therese A. Rando often says, "Most people today die *suddenly*—after a chronic illness." Our initial reaction can be one of disbelief. You feel you are in a nightmare waiting to awaken. Every time the doorbell or phone rings, you half expect it will be that person assuring you it was all a terrible mistake or bad joke.

You may find it hard to concentrate or focus. It becomes very difficult to organize your thoughts. You may feel confused, constantly asking the same questions and forgetting prior answers. You may go into a room looking for something and forget why you are there. Grief impairs your ability to think, so it is not unusual for work or school to be affected. With children and adolescents, these cognitive manifestations of grief may be confused with learning disabilities. In older adults, they may resemble the onset of dementia. As I train counselors and psychologists, I always suggest they begin any evaluation for either dementia or learning disabilities by discussing recent changes, such as losses, in clients' lives so they can evaluate whether what they are seeing are actually the effects of grief.

Your loss may give you a sense of depersonalization—that nothing seems real and you are simply going through the motions. You may get in a car and arrive someplace but have no recollection of the trip. Or perhaps as you prepare dinner, you feel as if you're on some sort of an autopilot. You may take little pleasure in anything you do.

Some people become preoccupied with their losses. They obsessively think about the person who died—wondering *What if?* Intrusive memories may come at inconvenient times. They fall into a pattern of rumination where they constantly review how bad they feel, or become obsessed with the circumstances of the death.

Because our society tends to tell us to focus only on the good sides of a person who died—"Don't speak ill of the dead"—many people tend to idealize the person who died and place that person on a pedestal, making others seem lesser than they are. But idealizing someone who died distorts our real memories of the individual—a living being who had good qualities and some that were not so good. Idealization impairs the grief process, for in grief we have to come to terms with our real loss, which means really we have to deal with both what we like about the person as well as what we did not like—what we miss and what we do not miss. Idealization prevents us from confronting our loss.

Demonizing the person we lost—for example, an abusive parent or spouse—can also impair our coping. Part of dealing with loss is acknowledging the positive moments and qualities even if submerged by so many negative ones. Idealization also complicates life for survivors. One of the problems that surviving spouses often have is that any new partner has to compete with a deceased, now perfect spouse. The same can occur when a sibling dies. The surviving siblings may feel they always have to compete with a dead ghost, as depicted in two films that dealt with such a loss, *Ordinary People* and *Stand by Me*.

Extraordinary Experiences

We may even experience unusual cognitive reactions. Dr. Louis LaGrand calls these *extraordinary experiences*.[5] We may have a sense of the deceased person's presence. I felt that once with my godson's dad. My godson Keith was part of our family's life after his father died; he was a frequent visitor and traveled with us on ski trips and summer vacations. One summer we vacationed at Atlantis in the Bahamas and Keith had the time of his life. One night after dinner, I decided to take a walk on the beach. There was a moment when I felt his deceased father's presence and it seemed like every cell in my body was being hugged—a thank-you for keeping the promise to take care of his son.

Other people feel someone's presence. They may have an occurrence where they seem to smell, hear, see, or feel the touch of someone who died. The first time I ever experienced this, I was a young counselor assisting a young woman, Brenda, whose three-year-old daughter died suddenly. At this point in her counseling, she was struggling with the issue of whether to have more children, and she was highly ambivalent—frightened that her next child might also die suddenly, leaving her again with a grievous loss; but always envisioning children as part of her life. One day she came into my office excited by an experience she just had. One of her favorite rituals with her young daughter was when Brenda would put on her favorite perfume; she would place a dab on her daughter. Her daughter would run around the room, making sure everyone present knew that she smelled just like Mommy. When her daughter died, she anointed her with the perfume, placing the remaining vial in the casket. Later, she switched to a different scent. This morning, Brenda claimed, as she stopped in her daughter's room, it seemed permeated by the old perfume. She felt that it was her daughter's way of letting Brenda know she was safe and happy. Soon after this experience, Brenda completed her therapy and had three more children.

Dreams of the deceased are common and can be very straightforward. One young boy told me that although his grandma had died, she was still alive in his dreams, visiting him as she often had while she was alive. Other dreams can be less clear, more troubling, and full of symbolism. One man recounted a dream where he was traveling on a plane with his wife, who left her seat to use the facilities but never returned. Worried, the man asked the flight attendants to check the bathrooms. The bathrooms were empty—there was no sign of his wife. His wife's sudden death had also been a mysterious disappearance to him.

Sometimes the experience is symbolic. When one woman visited her son's gravestone, a hawk perched on the memorial. Asked if there was any personal significance to the event, the woman replied, "My son's nickname was Hawk."[6] For Charlene, the sight of butterflies is a visible connection to her sister. "They seem to come at moments when I need or miss her the most."

Third-party experiences also can occur—someone else may say or do something that seems to be a message from the deceased. My son Mike experienced this when my mother, his grandmother, died. He was very close to her and at the time was living at her home because his new apartment in NYC was still occupied by the departing tenants. One morning she called him at work—she had misplaced a journal her deceased husband had kept, from which she took great comfort as he constantly reaffirmed how much he loved and treasured her. Mike reassured her that the journal had to be in the house and he would find it when he returned. She hung up confident that the missing journal would be located. Later that day, she had a serious fall. My son found the journal in the folds of an overstuffed chair. He would visit her in the hospital and read to his comatose grandmother from the book. She died a few days later. Mike took some comfort in the fact that she was now reunited with Grandpa. One day, a neighbor called him over. His wife had a dream, he explained to Mike, where she saw his grandparents walking up the street—hand in hand—as they walked through the fifty-plus years of marriage. The story comforted Mike, reassuring him that his grandparents were now together.

Not all experiences may be comforting. A young girl whose father was a raging alcoholic, who died from cirrhosis, would see images of her father beckoning her to dangerous places such as garage roofs or into the street. As we worked on her ambivalent feelings about her father, her guilt over her ambivalence, and her anger at the turmoil the father created, her visions ended.

You may feel troubled if you have not had such an experience, but this is normal, too. We long for such an experience to feel a sense of connection. While not everyone has spontaneous dreams or other extraordinary experiences, you can create virtual dreams. In this exercise, you take about eight to ten minutes to try to construct a sort of daydream with symbols of your loss. You might find a healing message through mentally working with the symbols and constructing a short scene. You can also try writing down the symbols and connecting. Begin by choosing six elements that are symbolic of your loss. Two should relate to a place such as a favorite beach, a forest walk, or a home. Another two should be characters such as a weeping mourner, an angel, or a stranger. The last two elements should be symbolic of your loss, such as an empty bed or chair or an unfinished book. Then try to connect the elements in a dreamlike story. For example, in one virtual dream, Eva, a middle-age widow, envisioned an empty beach (where she had met her husband), a lifeguard (her husband had been a lifeguard when he was younger), a seagull with a broken wing, a mysterious man, tempestuous waves, and an eagle. In her dream, the seagull was struggling in the sea. The mysterious stranger entered the water but disappeared. The lifeguard then rescued the seagull and when the guard lifted the seagull out of the water, the gull turned into an eagle that majestically flew into the horizon. As Eva shared the dream with others, she realized that without her husband, she had to become the eagle—not the wounded seagull she had been.

Once you write your own virtual dream, reflect on the emotions that come up as you read the story, as well as any unresolved or resolved issues that seem to arise. You may wish to share your story, just as you might share a significant dream, with a confidant who may see things in the story that you may have missed. The exercise can often put you in touch with emotions you had not faced or named and give you new insight into all that your loss represents.

Some people seek contact through mediums or spirit guides, but I would caution you first to explore and address the needs underlying the desire for contact, and whether such an experience aligns with your own spiritual values. Of course, some individuals offering these services may be sincere, but it is good to be cautious.

Most of these extraordinary experiences are common, comforting, and reaffirm a sense of connection. Research[7] suggests that almost 60 percent of people report one or more of these experiences. Even so, we know little about them and they occur unexpectedly. Most bereaved individuals find such experiences comforting, yet they are afraid to discuss them, fearing the reactions of others.

A Loss of Spirit

"Go to Him when your need is desperate, when all other help is vain, and what do you find? A door slammed in your face." These dispirited words were written by C. S. Lewis,[8] who was deeply religious. Much of his writing reflects his abiding faith, but when his beloved wife was dying, even Lewis felt abandoned.

Lewis's comment reminds us that while some find great solace in their beliefs, others may be torn by faith struggles and beset by doubts. We can find it difficult to believe in a kind and benevolent world or a merciful deity. We may be angry at the cosmos, or fearful, wondering if this loss was a punishment or a message. Our beliefs seem to be another loss, a casualty of our grief. We may have to search our faith and beliefs to see how they can speak to us in this crisis.

You do not have to believe in a God to struggle spiritually with grief. One of the deepest impacts of loss may be in the ways that it challenges our belief systems. One of the most poignant cases I ever counseled was a man who described himself as a secular humanist. "I don't believe in God," he stated, "but I do believe that everyone has a divine spark within themselves." He saw his role as fanning that spark to help it grow in himself and others. His life was a testament to his beliefs. But when his adolescent daughter was raped and murdered by a homeless man he sometimes employed for odd jobs, it shattered his faith in humanity. "I have come to terms with the death of my daughter," he acknowledged. "I have not yet come to terms with the loss of everything I believed." For him, he had to find a role for random evil in his worldview.

The Ways We Behave With Grief

Grief affects how we behave. Crying can go along with grief, but other behaviors may not seem related to our loss. A number of years ago a secretary in our office, Akiko, had a "sudden divorce." Just like deaths, divorces can be sudden or chronic. Some divorces are like a chronic illness; they follow after a long period of gradual decline and discord in the relationship. Others are unexpected. Akiko was divorced after her husband abandoned her for another woman. Akiko was full of anger, lashing out at all the men in the office. She was soon avoided and isolated—adding to her sense of loss and grief.

Some of us may grieve by immersing ourselves in busyness and activities, hoping to fill our time or bury our pain. Others may wish to withdraw. Dr. Catherine Sanders, a bereaved mother who later became one of the foremost grief researchers and clinicians, spoke of a period of grief she called "conservation and withdrawal." In this period, we look like we are returning to normal—going back to work or school and reassuming our responsibilities—but we are actually just doing what we have to do, which can consume all our energy. We are exhausted and depleted. We go through the motions of daily living but have little energy left for anything else. When we come home we just want to be alone with our grief.

Both withdrawal and overactivity are understandable reactions to loss. You do need time alone to process your grief, but you also need time with others—for respite, support, and to share grief and memories. The answer is to balance time alone and time with others.

Some people cope with loss by using humor. When my dad died, there was that one moment when the family gathered to view him for the last time before the casket was closed. We entered the limousine in a sober silence. The limo fell behind the hearse. It was a busy day at that particular funeral home, with four separate funerals going to different cemeteries. My brother broke the silence; tapping the limo

TYPICAL GRIEF REACTIONS

Emotions

- Sadness
- Loneliness
- Yearning
- Anxiety and fear
- Guilt
- Anger
- Love
- Relief
- Liberation
- Positive thoughts

Cognitive reactions

- Shock
- Inability to concentrate
- Impaired thinking
- Confusion
- Depersonalization
- Idealization
- Preoccupation with the loss
- Extraordinary experiences

Physical reactions

- Headaches
- Muscular aches
- Pain
- Fatigue
- Tightness in the throat or chest
- Shortness of breath
- Oversensitivity to noise, light, or other stimulation
- Sexual dysfunction or menstrual irregularities

Behaviors

- Crying
- Withdrawal
- Angry outburst or acting-out behaviors
- Overactivity
- Humor

Spiritual changes

- Doubts and disbelief
- Renewed or strengthened faith
- Changes in belief

driver on the shoulder, he quietly asked if there was another hearse in front of the one we were following. The driver was a bit confused by the question but indicated that there was only one hearse ahead. My brother answered that it was not my dad's hearse. When the driver panicked, we all laughed as my brother admitted that he was only joking. Conversations started again as we shared stories and memories of our father.

Humor can do that—it can release tensions. It offers an emotional release similar to crying. However, humor can appear callous or insensitive, confusing others and possibly driving them away.

Our different ways of dealing with our grief also may create conflict. For example, some grieving individuals avoid reminders of their loss, while others will seek out those reminders. One person may want the home full of photos while another wants to put away all these painful photographs.

I Am Not the Person I Used to Be

Grief changes us. Some of this is just the way that a loss affects our behavior. It can impair our relations with others, creating conflicts with partners and even sexual dysfunction. Our once characteristic behaviors can change as well. Sometimes this is temporary, as we work with our grief. Other changes are more lasting. We may have to learn new skills to adapt; take on new responsibilities, roles, or behaviors. Ellie always looked at herself as the "fun" parent, enjoying activities and sports with her kids. Yet when her husband died, she had to adjust to becoming more of the scheduler and disciplinarian—roles that her husband once held. Part of her grief was then complicated by the secondary loss she experienced in the changed relationship with her children.

When Grief Is Not Typical

The grief experiences addressed so far within this chapter are common. You are unlikely to have all of these reactions, but likely to have one or some of them. Atypical responses to loss can be "yellow flags" and indicate complications. Other "red flags" clearly indicate that there are problems for which you need professional assistance.

Yellow Flags

Yellow flags signify caution. Often, they simply reflect random changes that may occur as you adapt and change your roles and behavior. However, sometimes they indicate that larger issues underlie your grief.

Taking on the behaviors of the person who died, for instance, may reflect inappropriate identification with the loved one, or it may merely be a common developmental issue or a response to changes in the family system caused by a death. Ellie's becoming the disciplinarian her husband had been was a role change necessitated by her spouse's death. Gavin, once a middle school soccer star, became interested in football following his brother's death. Since his brother had been a football player, his parents worried that he might be trying to replace him. In fact, the reality was less complicated. As Gavin entered high school he decided that he wanted to go out for football since it was, in that school, a far more prestigious sport than soccer. As he noted, "soccer doesn't have cheerleaders."

Other situations are not as benign. Robbie's use of illegal drugs, soon after his brother died from an overdose, involved an unhealthful overidentification with his deceased sibling. To Robbie, his brother was the epitome of cool. Using drugs was not only a self-destructive way to cope with his loss but an attempt to emulate his brother's self-destructive behaviors—to be like him.

It is not unusual to be unable to function well or even speak of the loss without dissolving into tears in the early aftermath of the loss, but the persistence of such behaviors may be a sign that your grief is complicated—that you need professional assistance to help you cope with your loss.

You may experience symptoms similar to the person who died, which can be a result of anxiety that will pass over time. When someone dies, you can become more attentive to your own health and hypersensitive about any perceived symptoms. Nonetheless, if you experience any health concerns, it is good to have them checked out by a physician who understands that you have just gone through a loss. At the very least, it can offer reassurance.

The way we use objects or visit places that link us to the person who died may be another yellow flag. We often have articles that we associate with the person who died—perhaps photographs, jewelry, watches, clothes, or other objects that provide a link to the individual we lost. I began in this field as a student chaplain working with children who had cancer. One of my favorite patients was a mischievous young boy, Johnny, in the final stages of leukemia. The staff threw a party for me on my last day on the unit that included both staff and patients. The staff had chipped in to buy me a few farewell gifts. Johnny felt bad that he did not have a gift for me so he slipped off his medical wristband in order to give me something to remember him. It is still in my drawer forty years later.

There is nothing wrong with holding on to things that are mementos of the person who died. They connect us and comfort us. As you continue your journey with grief, however, these objects may become less critical. Mary told me, after her six-year-old son died in an accident, that she often liked to visit his favorite playground since it was full of memories of him. As time passed, Mary realized that her memories were inside her—she did not always have to visit the playground to relive them. She still visits at times but not as often as she once did.

Linking objects can be problematic when these objects take on a magical quality. In such cases, the object becomes an external expression of the continued relationship that may indicate problems in acknowledging the loss at one level or another. One college student, for instance, could not take a test if he was not using his deceased father's pen, convinced that his dad mystically would help him through the pen.

These objects can interfere with your life or create difficulties for others. I counseled an eight-year-old girl, Lena, whose older sister had died of cancer six years earlier; her relationship with her mother had deteriorated over the past year. In fact, Lena had slapped her mother in public. Her anger was not difficult to understand. The house was a museum to her late sister. Lena's bedroom was Anny's old room—still adorned with Anny's photos, trophies, and toys that Lena was not allowed to move. Quite frankly, I did not wonder why Lena was angry, but I did question that it took six years to come to a head.

Red Flags

Self-destructive behaviors are a sign that you are having trouble dealing with your loss and would benefit from professional assistance. Self-destructive behavior can be subtle—a failure to care. You may neglect your diet, fail to exercise, or stop adhering to a medical regimen.

Sometimes, too, this apathy can be a sign of depression. Sadness is a common response to a loss, but depression is an illness that needs treatment. Major depressive disorders are characterized not by the waves or roller coaster of ups and downs normally experienced in grief, but by a persistent feeling of sadness and hopelessness that is unremitting after more than two weeks. Among the other symptoms may be diminished pleasure or interest in activities, insomnia or hypersomnia, unaccounted increases or decreases in appetite, fatigue, persistent agitation, feelings of worthlessness and low self-esteem, excessive guilt, an inability to concentrate, and recurrent thoughts of death. These reactions can be so severe that they impair your ability to function at home, work, or school. For example, Michelle has found it difficult to concentrate after her brother's death, hindering her ability to do her schoolwork. Cheryl works in a school cafeteria. Every time she sees a child who reminds her of her deceased son, she tears up. Her manager has now placed her on probation. If you are having such reactions, if you have had a prior history of depression, or you suspect you might be depressed, it is essential that you be assessed by a medical professional. The line between a normal grief reaction and depression can be difficult to determine.

Other self-destructive behaviors may mask your inability to cope well with grief. Drinking too much, using illegal drugs, or even abusing prescription medications are common examples of such self-destructive behaviors. Some grieving people may even experience suicidal urges. Seek immediate help from a physician or counselor if any of these behaviors apply to you.

Another red flag is feeling destructive toward others—wanting to inflict emotional or physical pain. Sometimes this anger is targeted at a particular individual whom we blame for the loss. After Rick's son, Charles, died in a car crash, an autopsy showed that he had been driving when intoxicated. Rick blamed Charles's friend, Ron, for allowing his son to drive impaired and for surviving the crash that killed his son. For a long time, Rick rejected any overtures from Ron or his family. When anger defines us, we can drive others away, become isolated, and even self-loathing. This is another red flag that indicates you could use some help coping with your loss.

Most people will experience some of these physical reactions, emotional responses, cognitive effects, spiritual struggles, and changes in behavior. Yet some people have more minimal reactions. With the exception of the red and yellow flag reactions, these reactions are normal responses to loss—even though such reactions may seem unusual to you. You are having these reactions because you lost someone—or something—you loved. You are grieving.

CHAPTER 3

Your Journey with Grief: Understanding the Process

There is an Asian proverb: *Everyone is like all others, some others, and no other.*[1] This is very true as we look at the process of grief. Like all others, we grieve when we experience a significant loss—a person we loved, a job we needed, or a possession we treasured. Like some others, your grief often follows certain processes, pathways, and styles (which we will explore later in this chapter and in chapter 4). But your grief is like no other. It is as unique as your fingerprints. No one grieves exactly like any other person.

Like No Other: The Individuality of Grief

There are many reasons that grief is highly individual. The basic reason is that each of us is a unique person with our own temperament and experiences. As you try to understand your reactions to your loss, you need to ask yourself a number of questions.

What did I lose? We grieve every loss we experience. We grieve the loss of a person, a job, a cherished possession, sometimes even a celebrity or public figure we never met. Yet we grieve each of these losses in our own way. Rabbi Earl Grollman likes to say that when we lose a parent, we lose our past. When we lose a spouse, we lose our present. When our child dies, we lose our future. There is a truth in that, but in reality every loss we experience affects our past, changes our present, and alters a previously anticipated future. The effect of each loss is different, and so is our grief.

How attached was I to the loss? This is a key question. Sometimes the loss of a job simply means the loss of a paycheck, but sometimes it is a dream-crushing event. Grief will be different when you lose a grandparent who was a critical influence in your life compared with a relative with whom your interactions were seldom and remote. The more time you spent with a person, the more you loved that individual, the more intense your grief will be.

Another aspect of attachment that might influence grief is how dependent you were on what you lost. The more dependent you are, the more your life is likely to change with the loss. It is different to lose a parent when you are nine months old, and totally dependent on the parent, than when we are nine years old or when you are twenty-nine years old and independent. For Nora, a stay-at-home mom, her divorce brought multiple changes to her life. She had to move as soon as the house was sold, find a job, balance her work and child, and readjust to a new, lower standard of living after the divorce. All of this complicated her grief over losing her marriage and life partner.

Dependence is not always physical or financial. It can be emotional. The people we love often make us feel valued. They see parts of us that others may not always recognize, perhaps parts that we see only through their eyes. We feel safe around them. We can be ourselves as they understand the totality of who we are in a way that few others can. They bolster our own sense of self-esteem. In their presence, we are not only safe, but special. When they are lost to us—whether by death, separation, or divorce—we still retain these needs, but may not have anyone who can fulfill them.

Every relationship has some degree of ambivalence. We love the person, but things about the person can drive us crazy. Sometimes the ambivalence can be intense. In some relationships, "we cannot live with them—or without them." My aunt had that relationship with her husband. They were on again, off again. Their married life was punctuated by separations and reconciliations. In these situations, grief can be intensified by the anger and guilt inherent in such relationships. That is one of the reasons loss can be so difficult when experienced in adolescence or with the loss of an adolescent. In that time, it is not unusual for relationships with parents to be fraught with ambivalence as the adolescent tests his or her identity and independence.

For instance, Ray's mother died of breast cancer. He had avoided her in the last months of her life, partly out of fear and partly because he had turned more toward his peers. He was highly ambivalent about his mother; although he loved her, he resented her for trying to control his emerging independence as she realized she had no control over her illness. She wanted to keep him close when she sensed her time was limited. As her demands for his time grew, he began to feel she was using her illness to manipulate him. When she died, he struggled with his guilt.

Conflict is often a part of ambivalence. Conflict is an inevitable part of any relationship, yet conflict leaves in its wake unfinished business that complicates grief. It did so for Nancy. The morning of 9/11, Nancy and her husband had a major argument over expenses, which was not uncommon. They often resolved their conflicts during the day by an apologetic text, e-mail, or a phone call. Unfortunately, her husband died during that day and they had not been able to reach each other.

A history of conflict prior to the loss; or lifelong abusive, conflictive, or destructive relationships, also complicates grief, even if there is some reconciliation prior to the death. Kathryn had been married to an alcoholic for most of their marriage. About six months prior to his death, her husband was diagnosed in short order with both lung cancer and cirrhosis. He immediately stopped drinking and reverted to the wonderful man she had married. They enjoyed their last times together, but Kathryn carried a deep sense of anger about the marriage they could have had, if her husband had not given so much time to, as she called it, his "liquid lover." That resentment haunted her grief when he died.

Conflict and ambivalence may have deep roots in relationships. If you had a secure attachment with your parents as you grew, you have a sense of being valued and a positive sense of self. You are likely to enter into secure relationships with others. When you mourn the person who died, you are less likely to have ambivalence and your grief is less likely to be complicated. However, if your parents were ineffective, you may have an insecure attachment style, and you may form highly ambivalent or dependent relationships, or even find it difficult to bond with others. In such situations, anger and guilt may be intense, leading to complications as you grieve.[2]

How did the loss occur? This, too, influences your grief. *Where was I when the loss occurred?* In some cases, if someone dies far away from you, it may be harder to accept the reality of that loss. The circumstances around the loss can really affect your grief. Haley was holding and rocking her young daughter as the daughter quietly died from bone cancer, but her husband, Jeff, was stuck in traffic as he frantically tried to get to the hospital. While Haley's grief was eased by being with her daughter, Jeff's was complicated by the stress, frustration, and unfinished business of missing his daughter's final moments.

Was the death sudden or expected? This is sometimes a difficult question to answer. Even if someone is very ill, we might not expect death to occur when it does. Even a sudden death may not be perceived as sudden. For instance, Ann's son Phillip died after a drug overdose. He had struggled with addiction for a long time, going in and out of recovery. When a policeman visited her house to tell her that Phillip had been found dead, she said that she had expected that one day this would happen.

One situation is not necessarily easier or more difficult than another. They are just different. A sudden loss might surprise and shock you, leaving you with a deep sense of unfinished business—a feeling that you left something unsaid that should have been said, something undone that you had wished to do, or regrets over something you had said or done. With sudden losses we can become haunted by what-ifs. *What if* she did not take the car? *What if* we did not go out that night? *What if* he did not go to school?

A sudden loss may even challenge your sense of safety—reminding you that the world can be dangerous and unpredictable. This can be especially true when a death is violent and traumatic. Depending on the circumstances, a number of factors can complicate grief. First, if you were witness to the event, you may experience posttraumatic stress disorder (PTSD). Symptoms of PTSD can include recurrent, intrusive, and disturbing memories, dreams, or flashbacks of the event. Such symptoms should be evaluated and treated by a mental health professional. Even if you did not witness the event, you can be troubled by images and fantasies of what you imagined happened.

In addition, each type of violent loss—whether an accident, suicide, or homicide—has unique complicating factors. In all there may be a sense of guilt, anger, and blame. Media images may be sensational, compounding grief. There may be legal entanglements, such as police investigations, criminal cases, or civil lawsuits that seem endless and conclude unsatisfactorily. These also pose problems as we grieve.

Expected deaths after a long illness also create issues. As the illness progresses, we can find ourselves torn by the protracted stress of caregiving—simultaneously desiring this to be over, wishing to stay in the moment, and hoping the person will return to health. When death occurs, one of our reactions might be a sense of relief, which also can create guilt and confusion.

Other factors may complicate our relations as well. The individual may be disfigured or emaciated by the illness, creating a feeling of repulsion that increases ambivalence and complicated grief. When Peter was dying of liver cancer, his yellowish, emaciated appearance frightened his six-year-old son, Tommy, who was afraid to hug or even touch his dad. Now in his teens, Tommy still struggles with those feelings. Finally, during a long illness we may have to make ethical decisions such as continuing treatment, allowing artificial hydration and nutrition, or withdrawing or withholding treatment. Later these decisions may be revisited, perhaps complicating grief.

Some losses may be ambiguous. We are not really sure what occurred—possibly even unsure if the person is dead or alive.[3] This was a very complicating factor after the attacks on 9/11. While some persons could clearly be accounted for, the fate of others was less clear. Some were consultants who often had business in the Twin Towers, but surviving spouses were uncertain if they were there that day. They only knew they never returned. Other losses also may be ambiguous. Barbara's son suffers from mental illness. She has not heard from him now in over two years. The last she knew he was wandering and homeless in a city a thousand miles away. She simply does not know whether he is alive or dead—only that he is missing.

Other losses can be complicated because they are disenfranchised[4]—if your loss is unrecognized by others and perhaps not openly acknowledged, publicly mourned, or socially sanctioned. For example, there may be few people with whom we could share the loss of a partner from an extramarital affair. Other losses, such as a death by suicide or a homicide, can carry a sense of shame and stigma that makes us reluctant to seek out support or causes others to be reluctant to address or support our grief. Whether a loss is acknowledged certainly influences your grief.

Did the loss occur in isolation or as part of a chain of losses? It is difficult to grieve one loss. It is far more complex to deal with multiple losses. Sometimes these losses can happen one after another in close succession. This often happens as people get older. Over a short period we may find ourselves dealing with the deaths of a spouse, siblings, and dear friends. As one older woman told me, "Whenever I think it is beginning to get a little better, someone else dies—first my sister, then my husband, now my best friend." Other times multiple losses can happen all at once. For Manny, it was when his wife and daughter were killed in a car crash. Rita's mother died when her mother's home caught fire. She not only lost her mother but also a host of mementos from her past.

While multiple losses are more likely to be experienced by older individuals, other situations such as disaster, terrorism, or war can lead to such losses being experienced at any point in the life cycle—adding another complicating factor. In the early years of the AIDS epidemic, individuals experienced the deaths of many peers—often in young or middle adulthood.

Who you are naturally affects the way you grieve. If you had any prior mental health issues, such as severe anxiety or depressive episodes, you may be especially vulnerable because grief can trigger relapses. Your own history and our family history can influence how you grieve. Families model grief. We learn how to express grief, in part, by viewing how other family members deal with loss. In some families losses are not addressed. We learn not to trouble the equilibrium of the family, not to upset others; we keep our feelings and reactions to ourselves in order to grieve privately. We learn not to speak of our loss. If family members have taught us to stifle any emotions or other reactions to our grief, we may carry this legacy into how we deal with our losses.

In some situations, a significant loss, even generations ago, can severely affect family dynamics.[5] For example, Libby wondered why her mother seemed so emotionally distant until she learned that her mother's interaction with her own mother, Libby's grandmother, had been similar. Libby's therapist suggested that she do a genogram—a sort of family-tree exercise that traced the family's interaction back several generations—which revealed that her great-grandmother's first child had died. From other family members she learned that the death was never mentioned to subsequent children, yet the death still deeply affected the parents and their interaction with their children—and continued to haunt the family.

Certainly your age at the time of a loss will affect you. For example, young children who lose a parent may not fully understand the concept of death, but their lives may be sorely affected by the radical changes that can occur in their routine when a major caregiver dies. Adolescents may find their grief complicated by their emerging independence, quest for identity, and search for intimacy. Adults who lose a parent may find they have lost an important resource, a confidant, sounding board, or friend. For example, Linda counted on her mother's advice, whether it involved making a certain dish or dealing with her children's problems.

There is also an issue of expectation. At various times in our life, we can expect certain losses. When these losses occur "out of order," we may perceive them as traumatic. For example, we do not expect to lose a parent in childhood. Such a loss challenges our assumptions of the world, making it seem less safe, and perhaps making us less trusting of relationships, thereby impairing our ability to bond with others. And even though we expect that our parents will die as we age into middle and later life, such a loss may make us much more aware of our own mortality.

Men and women face different expectations and experiences as they grow, which influence how they respond to crises. One study[6] shows that by preschool, boys and girls already react differently to minor crises such as a skinned knee. Girls were much more likely to respond to a peer's injury by comforting their injured classmate and assisting her in seeking adult support. Little boys were more likely to urge their injured classmate to get up, brush off his knee, and continue playing.

Intuitive grievers respond to loss with intense emotional reactions. Their way of adapting to grief involves the processing of these emotions. They need to examine, analyze, and act upon their emotions. These are "heart" grievers. On the other end of the continuum are *instrumental* or "head" grievers, whose emotional reactions are more muted. They respond to and adapt to loss by thinking and doing. These grieving styles certainly are related to your sex, but not determined by them. Women are more likely to fall on the intuitive end of the continuum, while men are more likely to be on the instrumental end.

Obviously if you cope well with other setbacks and challenges in life, you are likely to handle losses with some resilience. Resilient grievers have fewer losses or other stresses in their lives. Their losses were not sudden; they had a chance to say good-bye. Nor were the deaths or losses so protracted that ethical issues, caregiving stress, or ambivalence added complicating factors. Resilient grievers also tend to have an intrinsic spirituality, good psychological health, and an optimistic mind-set that responded to challenges with a belief that even in facing the worst things, they could learn and grow. Resilient grievers may also have highly supportive families with intimate ties and emotional warmth. When conflicts did occur, they rarely escalated. Or they grew up in conflict-resolving families that were characterized by high cohesiveness and emotional expressiveness. They could fight—fiercely at times—but they could also tolerate differences.

Part of resilience is related to whether you believe you have control over your life.[7] If you think you have little control over your life, that things just happen and you do not see how you can create and resolve problems, you are more likely to simply ruminate about a loss. You will tend to repeatedly focus on the negative experiences and emotions encountered in grief without taking actions to resolve these issues, because you see them as beyond control. Excessive rumination is associated with negative outcomes in grief as well as with depression, so you should work to address this with a counselor or physician.[8]

Some cultures expect and welcome open expressions of grief, while others prefer that inner feelings and reactions remain locked inside. I come from a mixed cultural heritage. My dad's culture was Hungarian Protestant—a sometimes persecuted group in Habsburg Hungary that valued stoicism. My mother's family was Hispanic. Even as a child, I remember Hispanic uncles hugging me at family funerals—encouraging any response. Then my dad's brothers would manfully squeeze my shoulder admonishing me to "be strong."

Beliefs, rituals, and faith community can facilitate or complicate your loss. Beliefs can comfort you—perhaps reassuring you that the person is safe in an afterlife, relieved of all suffering, or left a legacy to be remembered. When Russell's son died by suicide, however, his fears of his son's eternal damnation complicated his loss. An empathetic minister within his faith tradition helped him struggle with that self-destructive belief by pointing to a scriptural verse that indicated Samson's salvation—even though this Old Testament leader was self-destructive and died by suicide.

When others share our grief and offer to support us as we process our reactions, it is easier to cope. People who have support—from family or friends, in work, in faith communities, or in school—are likely to cope better than those who lack such support.[9] Today, however, almost everyone can find support with grief counselors or bereavement support groups.

Your grief reactions will not be like anyone else's. Each journey will have a unique and distinctive quality because we all are different, each loss is unique, and we cope in different ways.

Like Some Others: The Processes of Grief

While each of us will have our own unique pattern to grieving, there are things about the process that we do share with others. Coping with grief actually involves two distinct processes.[10] First, we have to cope with the loss. We mourn the loss. Yet, second and simultaneously, we also must learn to live life now in the face of this loss. We may have to learn new skills and begin new experiences. Life is different now.

Successful grievers oscillate between mourning and coping. So grieving often has this uneven process—a feeling of constant moving back and forth, good days and bad days that can be unsettling. Shanice illustrates that. In one session she prided herself on her competence in dealing with a car problem, and felt good that she was now able to diagnose the basic issue and negotiate a good price. Yet when she saw me the next week, Shanice noted that if her husband were still alive, she would never have had to deal with such a problem. This moving back and forth in our grief is, in fact, normal and healthful. Focusing only on the past can lead to chronic, or never-ending, grief, and centering only on the future can delay or inhibit grief.

Grief involves a stepping backward and forward. Earlier we spoke of grief as a roller coaster—full of ups and downs, highs and lows, good and bad days. But grief may also come in waves—again moving you backward or forward. Some waves you see coming and others will take you by surprise. Some days will seem easy while others may be more difficult.

Your journey may begin with deceptive ease. You receive cards, calls, and letters from those who care, but when this support turns elsewhere, you are left alone with your loss and grief. You may be resilient in this next stage, but many people feel the full force of their loss once the shock, support, and busyness recede. It is not unusual that six to eight weeks after the loss, you may feel worse than you did at the very onset of the loss. This is a normal trajectory of grief.

Some days simply will be more difficult. Perhaps an event reminds you of your loss or vulnerability. Perhaps you saw someone on television or something on the street that triggered a painful memory. You may not even be conscious of why this day is more difficult than others. Todd told his grief counselor that when he woke in the morning, he felt relatively good, but his mood plunged when he started his car. The counselor and Todd—whose daughter had died—explored without success this change in mood. Only when he returned home did Todd realize what had happened. As he parked, he smelled the aroma of lilacs. His daughter's favorite perfume had a lilac scent.

Any number of factors can trigger a surge of grief by stimulating memories—smells, songs, or photographs. Reading about losses similar to your own, or seeing things like cars or clothes, or sharing in an experience we associate with the person we grieve, can trigger an upsurge of grief. When Josiah participates in a pickup basketball game at a local park he is reminded of his brother, with whom he often played. Life changes such as retirement, or transitional rituals such as graduations or weddings, may prompt memories and a sense of grief. Times of personal crises may make us long for the presence of the person we grieve. Lynnette found her forty-seventh birthday extremely troublesome. In counseling she realized that her mother had died at forty-six years of age. Lynnette became aware of all the events her mom had missed. Lynnette's story also reminds us that there is no timetable to these grief surges—they can occur years after a loss.[11]

Certain times during our journey can be expected to be tough. On significant days—holidays, birthdays, and anniversaries—your grief can become intense. You may even have private "special days" when your loss looms large. For Donna, it was not only the anniversary of their wedding that troubled her after her ex-husband Cameron's death but other, as she called them, "secret holidays," such as their first date, or the day Cameron proposed.

If you suffered a loss, for example, in the early summer, you may be reminded of it by everything from summer sales to graduations, from warming weather to Fourth of July celebrations. Each day can be a distinct reminder of each moment of loss. We may remember the day the illness took a turn for the worse, the day the individual died, and the day of the funeral. We may be troubled that we are feeling worse just at a time we may believe we should be doing better. After all, we think we made it through the year.

The holidays are particularly hard. They are centering moments in our lives, full of memories. We remember the Thanksgiving the oven broke down, the Hanukkah or Christmas gifts we received or gave to the person we miss so badly now, or the Mother's Day barbecue that was invaded by wasps.

Holidays in November and December can be especially difficult. Television specials and movies celebrate families, reunions, and reconciliations that accentuate our loss. Holiday tunes churn your memories. Cards may arrive from businesses or distant acquaintances still addressed to the person who died. As you shop, you may find an ideal gift for someone, if only he were still alive. Winter holidays are full of so many tasks and, when grief depletes your energy, this can be worrying. You might feel so out of step with the season—your sadness seems magnified against the seeming joy of others. In the midst of winter, you may also feel more isolated and alone, the deepening darkness and increasing cold a reflection of your own inner being. The very lack of sunlight may contribute to sadness.

The spring holidays such as Easter or Passover, as well as events such as weddings and graduations, can bring unexpected plunges in mood. In these centering moments, too, losses are all still keenly felt. Some like Mother's Day or Father's Day may especially sting if you are dealing with the loss of a parent or child.

That is why it is essential to plan. This does not mean that you need to spend a great deal of time thinking of holiday menus or planning the perfect gift or card. You need to plan how to get through the holidays.

The danger is drift. It is easy in the stressful times of the holidays to surrender your decision making to well-meaning others—such as the sister-in-law who will not take no for an answer. The result is that you find yourself drifting into activities that are stressful, tiring, painful, or do not meet your needs.

The first thing you need to do is to *choose*. Prioritize. What are the activities you really want to do? What activities do you need to do? What does not need to be done, at least for this year? You might decide that this year you will not send cards or host a large dinner.

For those activities you choose to do, it is critical to find the best way to accomplish them, consistent with your own needs and wants. For example, if you decide that you do wish to give gifts, consider how to do this. Can you simply send a check, shop from the Internet or a catalog, or shop with a friend?

Most important is the critical question: With whom do I wish to spend the holidays? Who can be present with me as I grieve? Who can tolerate and understand that I may not be my usual self?

Sometimes it is a choice not to make a choice. The holidays can be tough and unpredictable. Toni-Ann understood that. So she decided that she would keep all her options open till that very morning. She would spend some time with her late husband's family but would wait until that day before committing to a particular schedule. You can create some flexibility and freedom. David decided to take his own car so he could leave when he was ready, rather than be obligated to wait for others.

Once you have made your choices, *communicate* those decisions to others. Part of that communication is listening to others, which may add a third *c* to your holiday plans—*compromise.* The first Mother's Day after her mother died, Isabella had little desire to celebrate, but she realized that her children and grandchildren needed to honor her—even more so after the death of their nana.

Rituals can sometimes help. When I was a child, one of our rituals on Mother's and Father's Day was for my parents to place flowers on the graves of their parents. After that we would have a family meal—a celebration of our parents. It was an effective model to help us to handle our loss: looking backward to what is lost while still looking forward to the present and future.

There is no single right way to experience the holidays. While for some, the holidays are difficult and stressful, others may welcome the diversion and find comfort in the bustle of activity. Getting together with family can ease a sense of loneliness and sharing of memories and reminiscences can comfort. After my father died, my mother noted that she found her first Christmas "surprisingly reassuring." The shared stories of our dad made her feel closer to him and reassured her that her children and grandchildren would always remember him. That was very comforting.

There is one other critical point to make about the journey of grief. For many of us, grief's journey is lifelong. We live with our loss and carry it with us through our life. This does not mean that we live in a state of perpetual pain. Rather, we accommodate the loss—integrating our loss into the rest of our life. This means that, over time and with work, the pain of our loss lessens. For some that might happen in the first year, but for others, the second year can be just as difficult as the first. After a time, though, we can function similarly to the way we did earlier. Some may even function better—mastering new skills, appreciating emerging strengths, or developing deeper insights as a result of the loss. However, you still may feel surges of grief as you continue to remember the person at varied points of your life—even at different moments in a single day.

Dr. Catherine Sanders,[12] the grief therapist, writer, and a bereaved mother, spoke similarly of grief. To Sanders, in the early phases of grief, pain was intense. Later in the process, pain still existed—but to a lower degree. After a while, you may function in your roles at work and in the family, but you may feel at first as if you are going through the motions—without any real joy or pleasure. Many of the bereaved people Sanders interviewed spoke of a turning point—a moment when they realized this was not the legacy that honored their loss. As one mother put it, "I learned to live again."

The intense pain of grief will not be forever, but grief is not something you get over. It is a process that becomes part of a new, meaningful life. Certainly the pangs of pain will continue. But you need to be mindful that, over time, it is not helpful to the deceased for you to live in a state of chronic loss. Nor is it a useful legacy.

If your grief becomes disabling—inhibiting you from working effectively or impairing your relationships with others, self-destructive, or destructive of others—you need to understand that your journey has gone off course, and seek counseling.

The Tasks of Grief

In one aspect of grief, you are "like all others" at least in one small way. We all have to deal with a common set of issues or tasks.[13, 14] There are five major issues you need to address as you grieve. As with any set of tasks, whether cooking, driving, or organizing, some individuals are good at some tasks and need help with others. Approach these tasks in your own unique way and work through them in your own time.

1. Acknowledging the Loss

A crucial primary task is acknowledging your loss—moving past the initial sense of denial and disbelief. In the beginning grief seems unreal—a nightmare from which you hope to wake. Part of you continually expects the person who died to reappear. As you tell the story of the loss and participate in the rituals that surround it, however, you begin to acknowledge that hard reality. Unacknowledged losses, such as a layoff or divorce, can be complicating because the stigma associated with the loss may make it difficult to discuss with anyone but the closest of confidants, and there are no consoling rituals associated with them. There are fewer opportunities to openly address and acknowledge the losses, or for the community to come together.

2. Coping with the Pain of Loss

You also have to deal with the pain of loss and cope with complex and multilayered feelings and reactions. In chapter 2 we explored the many emotional reactions we can experience as we grieve. There are three actions you should take to deal with emotions. First, you need to name and identify what you are experiencing—anger, guilt, sadness, or some other emotion. Second, you need to own or validate your emotional reactions. Most of these reactions are normal expressions of grief. Recognizing that simple fact often helps you deal with these emotions. Finally, you need to explore these emotions. What are the reasons for your anger or guilt? What can you do about or with these feelings?

Yet dealing with ambivalence can be particularly complex. Ambivalence is a natural and normal part of any close relationship. The people we love also are the same people who sometimes anger and annoy us. Jane's relationship with her teenage son Marty models that ambivalence. Like most adolescents, Marty at times bristled against Jane's authority so much that Jane once confessed, "I always loved him, but there were times I did not always like him."

Sometimes ambivalence is not so much a part of the relationship as it is a circumstance of the loss. Just as there are *secondary losses*, there are *secondary gains*. You may receive, as a result of a death, a large inheritance or a legal award for damages. This, too, can increase a sense of ambivalence. While many families may welcome the award as just, they also can feel disquiet from receiving a benefit from such a tragic event. When Marty died as a result of a car crash, Jane sued the driver of the car that killed her son. In Jane's mind, this was an act of justice, because that driver had been texting when the crash occurred and had driven through a stop sign, crashing into the passenger's side where Marty sat. Jane felt that the other driver should be held accountable for her fatal negligence. So did the jury, which awarded Jane a considerable sum of money. The lawsuit that resulted from Marty's death did much to ease the financial pressures of Jane's mortgage, and it would provide well for Jane's younger son's eventual needs. Still, Jane felt highly ambivalent about the lawsuit because it felt like she was benefiting from this tragic event.

You also may have unfinished business—things you wished to have done or said as well as things you regret doing or saying. Adeline and her husband had their rough times in their many years of marriage. Only years later in therapy did Adeline write a letter to her deceased husband that afforded her a sense of both granting him forgiveness and accepting his pardon.

3. Learning to Live without the Person

Whenever you experience a loss, your life changes. Sometimes these changes are relatively minor. You grieve, but the day-to-day pattern of your life remains the same. When my mother died, I missed her greatly but little changed within my life. Holidays were now different as Mom was missing and missed. Many times I wished I could call—to share some news or just say hello. Nevertheless, the everyday pattern of my life was much the same.

In other cases, though, change can be profound. In many losses, we have to "relearn the world."[15] If you lose someone intimately connected with the pattern of your life, everything changes.

You must make any necessary adjustments as you advance into a future you never desired or dreamed of. We take on new roles, learn new skills, cook, maintain a car, or balance a checkbook. Your ways of life, your choices, even your relationships change after a loss. Brian described these changes poignantly after the death of his young son. "Not only did I lose my son, I lost all his friends as well." Surviving spouses may find their friendship networks change.

Other relationships may change, too, even familial relationships. Joan's relationship with her sister-in-law seemed to remain strong after her husband's death—at least until the second year of her loss, when she began dating once again. At that point, her sister-in-law began to become more distant and disengaged.

Other changes are more subtle and may surprise you. Lewis, an older widower, missed breakfast banter and washing dishes together. Dr. Thomas Attig, a philosopher who has written about grief, describes this as "relearning the world."[16] What was once familiar no longer is. You may have to relearn skills previously neglected, engage in tasks that you once could ignore, or gain knowledge in areas you had never known to exist. But most important, you now have to *learn* to live again in a world without the individual you now grieve.

You have to be careful in managing change, and cautious of changing too much too quickly. In the time immediately after a major loss, you might not be thinking clearly and respond out of immediate emotions. You are already stressed, and too-rapid change can add more stress. Moreover, it can remove you from significant sources of support when you need that support most. That support is not only family and friends; it also includes members of the community who know of the loss. A number of years ago I watched a woman have a significant meltdown at a dry cleaner's about an order that was not yet ready. I was moved by the patience of the store owner who sympathetically responded to what seemed to be an irrational customer. When she left, he apologized to the witnesses and explained that the woman was generally quite kind, but now was going through a difficult time after her daughter's death.

Do your best to pace changes. While there are no rules to grieving, you should try to avoid significant changes for six months to a year after a major loss. Sometimes, interim or partial solutions can offer time for more serious consideration. When James's wife died, his work no longer seemed to offer the same challenge and satisfaction, so he considered retirement, but instead decided to take a leave. At the end of that leave, he was anxious to return to the routine, structure, and stimulation of work.

I once received a frantic call from a well-meaning daughter concerned about her newly widowed mother. Her mother had reluctantly moved to Arizona after her husband's retirement. Her husband enjoyed outdoor activities such as golf and tennis, and relished the opportunity to play year around. Her mother was more ambivalent about the move. Her family lived close by in Connecticut. She had a strong relationship with her church and was actively involved in her parish. She counted many friends in the area. After the sudden death of her husband, her mother decided to move back north. The daughter was fearful and felt she should wait—based on what she had heard me say in a lecture. But I did speak with her mother and, in this case, the change made sense. While she would encounter the stress inherent in any relocation, she was moving *to* rather than away *from* support.

It is important to manage the stress of change. Good self-care is essential here. Adequate sleep, good nutrition, and exercise empower you to deal with the ongoing stress you're experiencing. Accept that in the immediate aftermath of loss, you have limited energy and may not accomplish all that you wish. You also can delegate or put off tasks that might not have to be done right at the moment. Finally, you can do whatever you find helpful in building your ability to withstand stress—such as breathing exercises; listening to music; prayer; meditation; massage; a walk in the woods—whatever helps you cope in difficult times.

As you adjust to life after loss, you may find it helpful to mark and acknowledge varied steps in your journey. Whenever Adeline found she had moved to a different place in her journey with grief—getting through a year of learning new chores, or marking the first time she traveled on her own—she felt it helped to mark it with a small ritual of transition.

It helps to name these changes. Sometimes they occur so quickly that you do not even realize how much and how fast your life has been altered. Once you are aware of all that is now different, you can assess how well you are coping with your now changed life. What changes are creating difficulties—with what are you struggling? What changes are you coping with well? The last question is particularly important because you can learn from your strengths. As you analyze your successes, you are reminded of the strategies that have worked for you at other times in solving problems.

Good problem solving is important, too. You need to be proactive and assess situations that might be difficult. Jacky, for example, worried about how she would manage the outdoor responsibilities that her husband so enjoyed. She realized that she could not take these on, so she hired a young adolescent neighbor to do the yard work and shovel snow. Deborah, a surviving spouse, came into my office and expressed her anxiety that summer was approaching and she had no idea where her husband had stored the air conditioners. She suffered from asthma—a condition that tended to worsen for her in hot, humid weather. We began to problem solve together. When I asked Deborah if her husband used any help, she recalled that a neighbor's adolescent son had assisted him the last few years. She contacted the boy. He knew that the air conditioners were stored in the crawl space. She paid him and his friend to install them, solving the problem.

Beyond these general principles, you will have to manage the transition to that new life in your own way. Dr. Catherine Sanders[17] suggested three questions that can guide that journey:

1. *What do I want to take from my old life into my new life?* Perhaps there are memories you want to retain, or even objects that remind you of the person. You may want to recapture the joy and confidence you had. Perhaps there are relationships that you want to preserve and carry forward.

2. *What do I want to leave behind?* As you adapt to a new life, there will be pieces of your old life you do not wish to bring along, such as anger or guilt. Perhaps there are memories or images that you want to explore and release; or relationships that no longer seem significant, meaningful, or constructive.

3. *What do I need to add?* As you move into a new life, you need to develop different skills in order to survive. You may need to develop new relations, interest, or support.

I would like to add one other question to these three:

4. *What have I learned and how have I grown in my journey with grief?* Some people not only cope with grief but actually grow as they journey. You may develop new insights, find a deeper spirituality, strengthen relationships, or make other significant changes in your life. It is often useful to pause as you journey to reflect on these changes. These, too, are a legacy to your loss.

Even in grief, you do have choices. But ultimately the choice is, Can and will you choose to survive, and perhaps even—as difficult as it seems now—thrive in this new life?

4. The Continuing Bond

Roller coaster rides end; grief does not. We live the rest of our lives with our loss. For example, at her son's wedding, Kendra deeply missed her ex-husband, even though he had disappeared from her life many years earlier after a bitter divorce. When I work with clients, one of the things I ask them to do is to think about the times in the future—often milestones such as weddings, births, or graduations—when these surges of grief are likely to occur. Knowing that there will be such surges may not make those moments any easier, but at least they become a bit more predictable.

You never lose your connections completely. Individuals you loved and were attached to remain part of your life symbolically rather than physically. With some forms of nonfatal loss such as divorce, you may have continued contact, awkward or friendly. You even maintain connections in death. You may dream of the person, have experiences where you think you hear or glimpse the person, believe in some form of spiritual connection or reunion, retain memories, and even recognize the ongoing legacies—and liabilities—you still carry from your association. Any attachment to a person, position, or property is part of your own biography. Despite my age and career, to some friends I will always be "Dot's kid brother." In short, one of the tasks of grief is to relocate the loss, deciding how you will live and honor your memories of and associations with that person. This is a critical concept. You need not hold on to grief, fearing that if you lose the pain of it, you will lose any connection, and memories will fade.

In fact, as the intense pain of acute grief recedes, we are often able to revisit these memories, reveling in moments shared. The good memories or life lessons that a person left us create a legacy that now lives with—and within—us. Sometimes this happens naturally. In other cases, we may have to work on revisiting and restoring these memories. This can be especially true when someone has died of a long illness, or after a lengthy dementia. Here the memories of the illness may crowd out remembrances of life before.

Many hospices or grief programs offer summer camps for grieving children and assist young campers in memory work—creating memory boxes, photograph albums, collages, and scrapbooks. These can be useful tools for adults as well. Deborah's husband died of a long, debilitating illness that emaciated him. Her final memories of her husband were of the long, difficult period of caregiving, and of his skeletal appearance. Later Deborah decided to do a biographical photograph album. The album reinforced her memories of the good times they shared, as well as images of the handsome and fit man she married.

The critical question is not *if* but *how* you will remember the person. On cold, rainy, and depressing days, Deborah likes to wear her husband's old flannel shirt. You may carry things—perhaps a watch or a ring that reminds you of that individual. You may recapture memories by putting together photo albums or DVDs of your life together. Rituals of continuity, such as remembering birthdays or anniversaries, also offer focus on days in which memories center on your loss.

You may retain mementos of the person you lost. I still treasure, for example, my dad's watch—a gift from his company on his retirement. It reminds me of his loyalty—not just to his work but to all, including family, that he held dear. When my mom died, I retained a gift I had once given her—a small sculpture of a mother holding a child. It reminds me of her caring presence throughout her life.

For some, the memento may be a song or symbol—perhaps even connected with the time of death. When Al was notified that his only sibling, a beloved sister, had died, "Hang On Sloopy" was playing on his oldies channel. To Al, it almost seemed a message from his sister—to hang on even in the tough days when his grief swells.

However, we may also carry liabilities—unhelpful connections that impair growth. Sometimes, for example, "the ghost" rules. Out of a sense of misplaced loyalty, we continue behaviors that are no longer helpful or try to fulfill promises that are not meaningful and perhaps never were. Anya swore to her dying husband that she would never marry again. Now she regrets a promise that seems to relegate her to a life of loneliness. In other cases, we may emulate problematic behaviors as a way of connecting to the deceased. Though Robbie had a brother who died from a drug-related death, he continues to experiment with drugs, searching for a way to connect with his brother's adolescent experience.

Legacies and liabilities can include mannerisms and gestures, how we speak and how we feel, what we do and how we behave, and even our sense of self, our values, and our beliefs. As you journey with grief, examine these imprints to decide which ones you wish to keep and cherish, as well as to leave behind. Managing these continuing bonds is one of the tasks of grief. Yet it is important that you do so in a way that allows the person within you into your new life. You do not want to stay mired in your past. After all, the greatest legacy your loved one can offer are the memories and life lessons you can take from them as you learn to live without their physical presence.

5. Rebuilding Your Faith and/or Philosophy

In chapter 2 we noted that a loss may challenge all our life's assumptions, our very sense of spirituality. We must inevitably consider the question *What do I believe now?* in the face of this loss. Damian deeply felt that issue as he watched his young wife die of breast cancer. He wondered why the world seemed so random and unfair. As we cope with the reality of loss, we have to reexamine our faith. Whether it's a reaffirmation of a closely held belief or a complete reversal of years of assumptions, grief forces us to ask, *What do I believe* now?

In fact, faith, philosophy, beliefs, and rituals can be essential sources of support. It always helps to ask yourself: *How does my faith or philosophy speak to me in my grief?*

Sometimes, though, you do not find a ready answer to that question, and faith is deeply challenged. *How can the world be fair or God just, for such a loss to occur?* Or you just feel that your beliefs somehow seem distant.

One of the most difficult tasks in grief is reconstructing your beliefs in the face of loss. And one of the biggest mistakes you can make during this period is to isolate yourself from your beliefs. You need instead to share your struggles within your faith community. This is a time to identify those within our faith communities who can journey with you, who are comfortable in hearing your struggles and sharing their own. Sometimes you may have to search to find those people.

When Judy's son died, she tried to share her own questions and conflicts with her minister. Her minister, however, could not seem to relate to her struggle. Instead, he seemed to offer only platitudes and empty reassurances. Judy found another minister who was willing to engage in serious discussions about her concerns. Together they studied and conversed. Judy felt her faith was strengthened as they struggled together.

Maintain your own spiritual discipline, whatever that is. Prayer, meditation, ritual, and readings are all ways to connect with our faith traditions. Each spiritual tradition and every philosophy has encountered death and loss. Each has writings that speak to that encounter.

CHAPTER 4

Your Style of Grieving

There are four major patterns of grieving—*heart grievers, head grievers, heart + head grievers,* and *heart v. head grievers.*[1] These styles of grief exist along a continuum; that is, it is extremely rare to observe either a "pure" heart or a "pure" head pattern of grief. Many people experience and express grief in ways common to both patterns. But most grievers are "more heart than head," or "more head than heart." You may also have a different response to different losses. In other words, you may be "more head" in your grieving earlier in life and become "more heart" in grieving over time.

None of these approaches is necessarily better than any of the others, but they can help you recognize how you cope with loss, to understand what might best help you given your style, and to understand how your way of grieving may create issues as you deal with others, who may not have the same patterns. These patterns also tend to be consistent not only with the ways you cope with loss but with the ways you cope with life. If, for example, you respond to most crises with intense emotional reactions, you are likely to respond the same way to a significant loss.

Identifying Your Pattern

You might want to do this brief exercise to see what your style is.

Grief Inventory

Please respond to each of the following statements using the key below. If appropriate, choose the response that best describes you in the past two weeks.

KEY
A = Always
U = Usually
S = Sometimes
R = Rarely
N = Never

Please circle the best response for you.

1. A U S R N I am more emotional than most people I know
2. A U S R N It is easy for me to cry and show my feelings to others
3. A U S R N Even though I have returned to my normal routine, I still have strong and painful feelings about my loss
4. A U S R N Even though I feel like crying, I do not cry in front of others
5. A U S R N Although I am grieving in my own way, others may think me cold and unfeeling

6. A U S R N I don't seem to get as upset as most other people I know

7. A U S R N I feel overwhelmed by feelings of grief

8. A U S R N I appreciate when others encourage me to share my painful feelings with them

9. A U S R N I avoid highly emotional or "touchy-feely" situations of any kind

10. A U S R N It is important to me that others view me as being in control

11. A U S R N I have been told that I am avoiding my grief even though I don't think that I am

12. A U S R N I have been controlling my painful feelings by drinking or using prescription or nonprescription drugs

13. A U S R N I believe that a bereavement support group is (would be) very helpful for me

14. A U S R N I worry that I am not as upset by my loss as I should be, and feel guilty that I don't have more intense feelings

15. A U S R N I resent efforts to get me to show feelings that I don't have

16. A U S R N I *think* more about my loss than *feel* things about my loss

17. A U S R N I believe it is very important to be aware of, and in touch with, all of my feelings

18. A U S R N I find that solving problems associated with my loss helps me

19. A U S R N Although I can sometimes control my painful feelings, they usually return and overwhelm me

20. A U S R N Since my loss, I feel like I'm just pretending to be strong in front of most people

21. A U S R N I find that I can't stop my grieving by thinking of other things

22. A U S R N I have taken deliberate action to honor the memory of my loved one, even though I have not been as upset as most others who are grieving my loved one

23. A U S R N Others seem surprised by my recovery from my loss

24. A U S R N Although I took care of things immediately after my loved one's death, I was surprised when I eventually "crashed" and began to have intense and painful feelings

25. A U S R N I would describe myself as more intellectual than emotional

26. A U S R N If I am upset or sad, I don't like to show it for fear that I will be seen as weak

27. A U S R N It does not usually occur to me to deal with my pain by talking about what is bothering me

28. A U S R N It is easy for me to put my feelings into words and discuss them with others

29. A U S R N I usually respond to the question of "How are you feeling?" with what I am not feeling (e.g., "not too bad")

30. A U S R N I don't see the value of talking about feelings that I don't have in the first place

SCORING YOUR PATTERN

The Grief Inventory contains items with response choices ranged along a continuum: always, usually, sometimes, rarely, and never. What follows are brief descriptions of many of the questions and the pattern suggested by a positive response.

1. *I am more emotional than most people I know*
   The basis of the patterns lies in the individual's customary choice of feelings over thinking and vice versa.
   POSITIVE = INTUITIVE

2. *It is easy for me to cry and show my feelings to others*
   A willingness to disclose feelings is associated with the intuitive pattern.
   POSITIVE = INTUITIVE

3. *Even though I have returned to my normal routine, I still have strong and painful feelings about my loss*
   POSITIVE = INTUITIVE

4. *Even though I feel like crying, I do not cry in front of others*
   This is the first of six questions where a positive response could reveal a tendency toward a dissonant response.* Although this would usually point to an intuitive dissonant response, it could include instrumental grievers who have no other outlets for expressing whatever degree of feelings they experience.
   POSITIVE = DISSONANT

---

* This began with work that Dr. Terry Martin and I did on gender differences in grief. We found a variety of coping styles that were related to, but not really determined by, gender. We originally called these styles *intuitive*, *instrumental*, *dissonant*, and *blended*. Soon after, the Oregon Center for Applied Science began to adapt them for use in their employee assistance program. Rather than using the technical terms that we developed, they asked if we would be willing to let them use terms such as *head and heart* that would be more easily understood. We appreciated their suggestions, as they did lead to greater clarity for the ideas of these grief patterns, or styles of grieving, that we were trying to develop.

5. *Although I am grieving in my own way, others may think me cold and unfeeling*
   Instrumental grievers are often perceived as lacking feelings.
   POSITIVE = INSTRUMENTAL

6. *I don't seem to get as upset as most other people I know*
   POSITIVE = INSTRUMENTAL

7. *I feel overwhelmed by feelings of grief*
   POSITIVE = INTUITIVE

8. *I appreciate when others encourage me to share my painful feelings with them*
   While this could measure a griever's tendency toward introversion, it is most likely an example of intuitive grieving.
   POSITIVE = INTUITIVE

9. *I avoid highly emotional or "touchy-feely" situations of any kind*
   Instrumental grievers rarely choose to place themselves in situations designed to elicit the experience and expression of feelings.
   POSITIVE = INSTRUMENTAL

10. *It is important to me that others view me as being in control*
    This is especially important for intuitive grievers who may become image managers in the wake of a loss.
    POSITIVE = DISSONANT

11. *I have been told that I am avoiding my grief even though I don't think that I am*
    POSITIVE = INSTRUMENTAL

12. *I have been controlling my painful feelings by drinking or using prescription or nonprescription drugs*
    POSITIVE = DISSONANT

13. *I believe that a bereavement support group is (would be) very helpful for me*
POSITIVE = INTUITIVE

14. *I worry that I am not as upset by my loss as I should be, and feel guilty that I don't have more intense feelings*
Penitent instrumental grievers feel unusually guilty about their lack of pain.
POSITIVE = DISSONANT

15. *I resent efforts to get me to show feelings that I don't have*
POSITIVE = INSTRUMENTAL

16. *I* think *more about my loss than* feel *things about my loss*
POSITIVE = INSTRUMENTAL

17. *I believe it is very important to be aware of, and in touch with, all of my feelings*
POSITIVE = INTUITIVE

18. *I find that solving problems associated with my loss helps me*
POSITIVE = INSTRUMENTAL

19. *Although I can sometimes control my painful feelings, they usually return and overwhelm me*
POSITIVE = INTUITIVE

20. *Since my loss, I feel like I'm just pretending to be strong in front of most people*
POSITIVE = DISSONANT

21. *I find that I can't stop my grieving by thinking of other things*
POSITIVE = INTUITIVE

22. *I have taken deliberate action to honor the memory of my loved one, even though I have not been as upset as most others who are grieving my loved one*
POSITIVE = INSTRUMENTAL

23. *Others seem surprised by my recovery from my loss*
POSITIVE = INSTRUMENTAL

24. *Although I took care of things immediately after my loved one's death, I was surprised when I eventually "crashed" and began to have intense and painful feelings*
Even strongly intuitive grievers can sometimes manage certain post-death activities before being overwhelmed by their feelings.
POSITIVE = INTUITIVE

25. *I would describe myself as more intellectual than emotional*
POSITIVE = INSTRUMENTAL

26. *If I am upset or sad, I don't like to show it for fear that I will be seen as weak*
POSITIVE = DISSONANT

27. *It does not usually occur to me to deal with my pain by talking about what is bothering me*
POSITIVE = DISSONANT

28. *It is easy for me to put my feelings into words and discuss them with others*
POSITIVE = INTUITIVE

29. *I usually respond to the question of "How are you feeling?" with what I am not feeling (e.g., "not too bad")*
POSITIVE = INSTRUMENTAL

30. *I don't see the value of talking about feelings that I don't have in the first place*
    POSITIVE = INSTRUMENTAL

Suggested guidelines for interpreting a griever's scores:

KEY

A = +2
U = +1
S = 0
R = −1
N = −2

Intuitive Pattern:

Questions 1, 2, 3, 7, 8, 13, 17, 19, 21, 24, 28

SCORE:

16–22 Profoundly intuitive pattern
11–15 Moderate intuitive pattern
6–10 Blended intuitive pattern
−5–+5 Blended balanced patterns

Instrumental Pattern:

Questions 5, 6, 9, 11, 15, 16, 18, 22, 23, 25, 29, 30

SCORE:

16–24 Profoundly instrumental pattern
11–15 Moderate instrumental pattern
6–10 Blended instrumental pattern
−5–+5 Blended balanced pattern

Dissonant Responses:

Questions 4, 10, 12, 14, 20, 26, 27

Each dissonant response should be evaluated separately; that is, each response indicates why you may have this conflict of head v. heart.[2]

Heart Grievers

You may be more *intuitive* in your grief—that is, you tend to experience, express, and cope with grief more emotionally. As a heart guided griever, you have strong feelings of grief. Grief comes over you in waves of emotion—yearning, sadness, anger, guilt, loneliness. Especially early in the grief process, these waves may be strong and persistent, so powerful that you may find it difficult to focus or think clearly. You may forget things or become distracted for short times. The intensity of your emotions may be so strong that they seem to consume you.

If you are a heart griever, it is critically important to understand the ways that grief may affect your health. You easily become emotionally exhausted, feeling tired with little energy. Routine activities, such as self-care, work, school, or family, may be more difficult to complete. Because you are so focused and consumed by your grief, you may neglect your health—failing to maintain your health regimen, eating poorly (by not eating, eating too much, or eating the wrong things), failing to exercise, or struggling with insomnia.

Your expression of grief mirrors inner feelings. You grieve from the heart—tears may come very easily, sometimes in unexpected moments. The smallest event can evoke an emotional response. Responding to waves of loneliness and sadness, you can become withdrawn, or you respond to the feelings of anger by lashing out at others around you.

Heart grievers tend to benefit from opportunities to express and explore emotions. You may find it useful to write in a journal, attend a support group, or seek counseling. Kiara's grief manifests intuitively. She is a heart griever—profoundly so. Kiara has felt a persistent sadness every day since her mom died. Often when she watches her children play, she is overwhelmed by sadness, by the fact her mother will never have the opportunity to see these children, her mother's grandchildren, reach critical milestones. As she begins to verbalize these feelings in a supportive group of "motherless daughters," she is reassured that her feelings are a natural reaction to her loss. Somehow this helps.

Like Kiara, you may find strength and solace from other grievers. You may do this with selected confidants or sometimes seek out larger groups, especially those with similar types of losses. For heart grievers, a grief shared is often grief lessened. Heart grieving is more common in women, though many men may also share this style of openly expressing and sharing feelings.

As a heart griever, you may find counseling helpful in order to have your feelings and responses validated as being part of a normal grief process, and to offer you new strategies to deal with the intense feelings you are experiencing. In fact, your characteristic of being in touch with your emotions and feelings, together with the willingness to discuss your feelings, works well in both grief groups and counseling.

Counseling and support groups also might help in another way: Sometimes your grief can be experienced so intensely, and the need to share is so overwhelming, that you drive others away—depriving you of the support you need. You can become perceived as so needy that others minimize their interaction. In support groups and in counseling you can find others who truly know and understand and are willing to be there in this difficult time.

Head Grievers

Head grief is *instrumental*—experiencing, expressing, and adapting to grief in more cognitive or active ways. If you are a head griever, you are more comfortable in dealing intellectually with your losses. Thought and action are the primary ways you deal with your grief. One of your strengths is that you may have a different worldview that emboldens you with a sense of control, a belief that you can eventually master even this crisis. You may perceive your loss as more of a challenge than a threat.

Tom, like many men, grieves instrumentally. Tom even wonders if he grieves at all. He is troubled that he hardly cried when his son died in a car accident. Yet he thinks of him often, while not recognizing that his constant replay of memories is his reaction to the loss, is his way of expressing grief. Tom's son had been a new driver, and he lost control of the car as he turned the corner onto their street. The car had overturned, rolling through a neighbor's picket fence. On the same day that he buried his son, Tom began to fix the neighbor's fence. The neighbor, an elderly woman, came out to reassure Tom that he need not worry about the fence. "You don't have to do this," she repeated. "No, I do," he replied. Tom later told me that fixing the fence was the most therapeutic thing he did. It was the only part of the accident he could fix. He needed to fix it. Like most head grievers, Tom handled his grief by doing and thinking. Yet like most head grievers, he at first couldn't recognize his actions and thoughts as legitimate expressions of his grief. Because his feelings were muted, he wondered what was wrong—why he could not seem to mourn his son. Since head grievers' grief comes out mainly in their thinking, it should come as no surprise that many of the most initially troubling aspects of grief involve impaired cognitive activity. Confusion, disorientation, an inability to concentrate, and disorganized thought may be difficult issues for head grievers.

This is not to suggest that, as a head griever, you do not react emotionally to your losses—you do. You share common feelings experienced by other grievers such as sadness, anxiety, loneliness, and yearning, but you may not cry or even feel a need to cry. However, you may be more comfortable in expressing anger than other feelings, because by being angry you do not feel like you are losing control of other emotions.

If you are a head griever, you may find it useful to return to work relatively soon after the loss. The familiar activity and the rhythms of work may offer a necessary diversion from your grief. You may choose to "dose" your grief—finding appropriate times to reflect on your memories. Sometimes, for example, after my dad died, I would choose to put on a 1940s channel from satellite radio. The music, some of his favorites, would spark warm memories. You may choose to engage in activities that memorialize the person. One colleague enjoyed sculpting as a hobby, and after his son was stillborn, he expressed his grief through carving a memorial stone. Others have engaged in corrective actions to prevent deaths or other memorial activities such as fund-raising events. Sometimes the activities may not be directly related to the loss, but simply allow you to expend your emotional energy in some physical way. Even if the connection may not be immediately apparent, you can usually acknowledge the connection once it is brought to your attention.

As a head griever, you may not find support groups to be helpful—especially those that emphasize sharing feelings. In such grief support groups, there is often a rule of reciprocity—"I will tell you my feelings and you will tell me yours"—that may make you uncomfortable. Though you may confuse others with your lack of strong emotional responses, you also are unlikely to make them feel uncomfortable.

Head grievers often find that their social networks remain pretty much the same after the loss. Other people find you emotionally stable and less needy than some heart grievers, so you are still invited to social occasions and other events. You do not drive away support or have an emotional meltdown.

Counseling approaches such as cognitive behavioral therapy—which centers on thinking and reflection—may work well for you. Reading books about grief, and other forms of educating ourselves about grief, may appeal to your mind and allow you to "dose" your grief. A book after all can always be put down for a while. Activities such as journal writing or other creative acts may provide a useful outlet for your grief. Eric Clapton, for example, wrote the song "Tears in Heaven" as an elegy for his dead son, while John Gunther memorialized his son Johnny's lost battle with cancer with his book *Death Be Not Proud*.

Heart + Head Grievers

Heart + head grievers have both types of reaction to grief but move back and forth between the two. Just as you are unlikely to be solely a head or only a heart griever, you are unlikely to have a perfect balance of both. However, you may be able to move from heart ways of responding to more cognitive or head ways. Gene prides himself on his ability to lift himself from his sadness and take care of the business of raising a family since his partner's death. He feels very in touch with his emotions, but "When I need to, I can put them aside and do what needs to be done."

Dawn remained calm and objective as she cared for her mother during her mother's long battle with breast cancer. Although she was distressed, Dawn coped well with the illness, even taking pride in her ability to be there for her mom. She arranged the funeral and even delivered the eulogy. During the eulogy she was a bit tearful, but even told some warmly humorous stories. Everyone noted how well she did.

Two years later, when Dawn's sixteen-year-old niece died in a car crash, Dawn's response worried her family and friends. When she was notified of the death, she felt shocked and numb; afterward, she often felt confused and disoriented. Taking care of her two young children seemed a struggle. During the funeral Dawn burst into tears and rushed out of the church. In a support group she was finally able to share how unfair she thought the death was, as well as her awakened fears for her own children in a world that seemed so unpredictable.

If you are a heart + head griever, you can benefit from a wide variety of sources of help. Support groups can be useful, especially if they respect the wide variety of reactions you experience in grief. It can be difficult to respond to both the emotional and cognitive currents that are sweeping around you. You may be discomfited by the fact that you can seem to put your emotions aside, and confused by moving between heart and head. But whichever you feel with *this* loss is normal.

Heart v. Head

This may be one of the more difficult patterns. Here you clearly experience grief in one way, often in a very heartfelt way, but for many reasons you feel constrained about expressing grief in that way. In therapy, we call this a *dissonant* pattern—there is a dissonance or disconnection between how you experience and how you express your grief. Here you are expressing grief differently than you are experiencing it.

You may experience this style for a number of reasons. Sometimes it is a way to adapt temporarily to a difficult situation, or to the immediate needs of others. When Tina's mother died, for example, she felt pulled in many different directions. Her kids were close to her mother; she often babysat them. Her dad was an emotional wreck. Even though Tina had deep feelings for her mother, "her best girlfriend," she felt she needed to be there for her children and father. She put aside her own grief. But over time, her grief became more intense. Each day she seemed to feel worse.

The longer you put aside your reactions, the greater the toll it can place upon you. Try to find time sooner than later to attend to your own feelings. There is an ancient Chinese proverb: *Expression of feelings leads to momentary pain and long-term relief; suppression leads to momentary relief and long-term pain.*

For other head v. heart grievers, it is not a temporary response to an overwhelming situation—instead it is a lifelong pattern. Many men may fall into this pattern. Their need to express and share feelings is overshadowed by a rigid definition of manliness. Here, unlike the true head griever, the experience of emotion is intense, but they feel it must be suppressed. Jerry experienced strong emotions when his sister, Carole, died. Now in his thirties, Jerry has worked hard at restraining the deep grief that he feels. Jerry was brought up in a home with the rigid rule that boys should not cry. Even when he was young, any show of emotion would draw a strong rebuke from his dad: *Keep bawling and I will give you something to cry about.* The result is that Jerry has long learned to repress his emotions. This pattern is especially common in older generations—or traditional cultures—where stoicism is a sign of masculinity.

Sometimes this can work the other way, too. You may be ashamed that you are a head griever—feeling disconnected from your feelings because they are more muted. You may wonder what is wrong with you—even feigning emotions as a way to fit in with others and normalize your grief. Here you resonate with the words of Anthony Newley's song "What Kind of Fool Am I?" The lyrics well express the discomfort of the heart v. head griever, who feels empty and alone, disconnected from emotions. Women who are heart grievers but have had to suppress emotions may doubt their own grief. They may become withdrawn or, worse, abuse alcohol to try to elicit a sense of emotionality.

Being at odds with your feelings has its consequences, since perpetually suppressing feelings becomes a way to avoid the reality of the loss as well as a way to avoid these feelings. This can often lead to more complicated forms of grief that can benefit from counseling. With head v. heart, you need to learn strategies such as dosing your emotions that allow you to know that you can both express and control your feelings. It may help to explore your style with a therapist, or within a group that feels safe, so that you can explore the factors that inhibit your expression of emotions.

Grieving Your Own Way—But Together!

Whatever your style of grieving, it is yours and you need to own it. Yet you rarely grieve alone. The way that you experience, express, and cope with your loss may be different from that of others around you. It is not unusual for different styles to exist within a family, which can cause confusion. Heart grievers may worry that head grievers are repressing their feelings—or mistakenly believe that the head griever did not love the person. Head grievers may find being with the heart griever overwhelming, and even worry about the individual's ability

STYLES OF GRIEF

Heart

- Often experiences grief as waves of emotions
- Expresses grief emotionally—cries easily, gets angry or sad, and withdraws
- Finds it helpful to express and explore emotions

Head

- Grief is often experienced physically or cognitively
- Grief is often expressed in reminiscences or in active ways (developing memorializing activities, etc.)
- Adapts to grief in ways that involve thinking and doing

Heart + Head

- Shares characteristics of both heart and head grievers
- Often responds to different losses differently—perhaps more emotionally to some and more cognitively to others
- Can benefit from a wide range of strategies depending on the reaction to loss

Heart v. Head

- Disconnect between the ways grief is experienced and the ways it is expressed
- Frequent repression of emotions may make it difficult to speak about loss
- May need help in learning techniques, such as dosing to deal with grief

to cope with the loss. As a result of different grieving styles, you can grieve in isolation without the support of family, to which we usually look for support; or find your differences a source of conflict.

However, having similar grieving styles does not necessarily mean that you always find support. Sometimes your own grief can be so devastating that you have little to offer others, or they have little to tender us. Here the very similarity of the way we grieve can isolate us. Karen and her partner Terry's child died. Both are heart grievers. Throughout their grief, they have tended to avoid each other. As Terry stated, "Whenever I see her cry, I start to tear. My tears spark hers, so we generally engage in innocuous activities and conversations avoiding the ghost of grief that haunts us."

Other times, you may see your differences as a source of strength, which they certainly can be. You respect that the differences in the ways you grieve are not differences in the ways you loved. An episode of the TV show *Home Improvement* illustrates this well. In that episode, the father of Jill, the spouse and mother in the series, dies. Jill's grief is somewhat complicated since her relationship with her father had some ambivalence. Her husband, Tim, responds beautifully—getting her to the airport, taking care of the kids, and shepherding them to the funeral. Jill reminds Tim that she often would prod him to be more in touch with his feelings. But at the end of the episode she affirms, "What makes it so wonderful is that I can count on you when I need you the most."

It is also important to realize that even children will have their own grieving styles. You need to respect these as well. Some children are simply less emotional than others. Others really benefit from opportunities to explore and express the ways that grief is affecting them. George has two sons, eleven and twelve years old. When his wife died, Evan, the eldest, found it useful to attend a local grief support group for children. George's younger son, Brennan, decided after one meeting he did not want to go again. George was concerned that Brennan was not dealing with the loss. He spoke with his brother-in-law, Mark, Brennan's favorite uncle. Mark recounted that on every outing, Brennan reminisced about his mom and delighted in hearing stories of her childhood. As long as there are no reasons to worry—such as substantive or especially self-destructive changes in the child's demeanor, grades, or behavior; signs such as acting out; or regressive behaviors like bed-wetting, you should respect the child's own way of grieving.

Should conflicts become problematic, it might be useful to seek family counseling. Counselors can validate these different styles and offer insights as to how these styles develop.

Resources that can assist you as you cope with loss include therapy and self-help literature. The Internet provides spaces to memorialize our loss, information about grief, and even online support. Grief support groups—some general, others focused on a particular kind of loss—are accessible in most communities. Counselors specializing in grief are readily available.

Yet you need to find the resources that would be most helpful to you—most suitable for your unique path. This is critical, as new research on grief indicates that utilizing the wrong resource may do more harm than good. Intuitive grievers such as Evan may benefit from self-help groups that allow them to ventilate and explore their emotions, while instrumental grievers like Brennan may be best helped by groups that are more focused on solving the practical problems associated with loss. Similarly, resilient grievers may benefit from self-help books or informational lectures that validate their pattern, but other grievers may want to be actively involved in some form of support group. This chapter will explore how different self-help resources are best used once we understand our own path.

Rituals make us confront reality. That is why funerals and memorial rituals can be so valuable, and the lack of ritual—as in divorce—problematic. Sharing our story helps, too. Sometimes we find the more we tell the story—however painful it is—the more real it becomes. We can do the sharing in many ways. For intuitive or emotional grievers, support groups offer opportunities to tell the story. For instrumental or head grievers, journaling or other expressive approaches may work best. After her husband's death and throughout her own chemotherapy for breast cancer, Beth Nielsen Chapman found solace in performing "Sand and Water" both as an elegy for her husband and a statement of her own belief in immortality, which sustained her in her illness.

As you speak with others who are grieving, it can help if you are open—however painful it might be for you—to hear their stories.

You should avoid euphemisms in speaking about the loss. Questions such as *How are you doing since his death?* reinforce the reality and signal that you are ready to hear that story. Listening is the gift you can best offer. Trite phrases or helpful reassurances do not take away the pain of the loss. The message you can best give is that you can be present for grieving friends or family—walking beside them, tolerating their pain, and supporting them.

Expressing and exploring your emotions can be a long process. It took you time to develop a relationship with the person you loved. It takes time, too, for you to examine the layers and levels of that relationship. In some ways it is like peeling the layers off an onion. As you explore each layer and how your relationship changed and developed over time, different emotions come to the fore. And like peeling an onion, the exploration can be tearful.

This exploration best takes place in a nonthreatening, nonjudgmental environment—a place where you feel safe. It may be in a support group, with a counselor, in speaking with a good friend, or perhaps even as you express it in your own writing. Find someone to listen as you explore. But you do not need someone—however helpful the person is trying to be—to tell you that you should not be feeling what you are, in fact, feeling.

Accept your feelings—do not hide from them. Resentment, anger, or guilt may be uncomfortable, but when you accept your feelings as natural and normal reactions to grief, you can then explore them. *Is my guilt realistic? Are there times when my anger or loneliness seems to be especially high?* Often as you explore your emotions, they become more understandable and less troubling. Some even fade away as you review them.

There is much you can do to help yourself. There are many resources available. Thinking of grief as a set of tasks reminds you that whatever you do, you have to do it in your own way and your own time. If you are experiencing more complicated long-lasting reactions to grief, you might reflect on what tasks are creating the most difficulty, and what barriers seem to impair your abilities to surmount these tasks. This is best done in counseling.

Using Resources Wisely

Getting Support from Friends and Family

The best support often comes from those closest to you. Mourning individuals who can rely on a close network of support generally do much better than others.[3] But if those you rely on most are grieving as well—and grieving in their own ways—they may not be able to offer the support you need.

Sometimes you may feel you are not getting support when, really, you are asking people for support they cannot offer. It is good to remember that some people are good listeners; others are doers, while still others offer respite—or time off from your grief. Use your support system wisely.

If you are not getting the support you need, you should examine why that support is not available. In some cases, it may be that everyone is dealing with their own grief in their own way—with little energy left to deal with others' grief. Here you may have to seek support in a wider circle—perhaps in a support group or with a counselor.

In other cases, you may be giving mixed messages—saying you are all right when you really can use support. You cannot expect people to read your mind and guess your intentions. If you need others' support, you have to ask for it. Only then can you know if it is available or not. Others may simply not know how to provide assistance. If they are offering help, it is best to offer specific suggestions on how they can help. Sometimes people may offer help so generically—for instance, saying "Call me if I can help"—that you really do not know that they are willing to follow through with their offers. If someone offers to help, ask them for something tangible, such as bringing a meal or driving the children to school, or simply listening.

You will also have to acknowledge that not everyone in your circle is helpful. Sometimes, people say cruel things unintentionally. You may have to educate them—kindly remind them that a comment such as "At least you still have two other children" does not compensate for the loss of the child who died. Sad to say, there are some people who are destructive and consistently try to bring us down. Here you simply need to minimize contact, or even avoid such people entirely.

Self-Help Books

Information can be a powerful tonic in grief. Since you have to create your own road map for your grief, education helps. As you experience grief, you can doubt yourself—wondering if your reactions are common to others. Books reassure you that your feelings are normal and allow "dosing." That means simply that you can put the book down for a while and walk away if the feelings and reactions to what you are reading should become so intense that they make you uncomfortable—something that is more difficult to do in a support group.

Yet you have to choose print materials carefully. Doctors do not send patients to a drugstore with advice to just grab something that sounds good. They select the best drug possible. Self-help books should be as carefully selected. For example, there are two excellent books that document spiritual struggles—C. S. Lewis's *A Grief Observed* and Harold Kushner's *When Bad Things Happen to Good People*. Both ask the question of how a powerful and loving God can allow horrible loss to happen. Yet their answers are very different. Lewis ponders the question and, after wrestling profoundly, concludes that he still struggles with accepting the mystery. Kushner's conclusion is that God has created the world and now allows it to operate by the laws of nature—yet, to Kushner, God remains to offer comfort and support. If you believe that there must be a reason for your suffering, Kushner's book may be less satisfying. And if you do not believe in God, neither book may be helpful. The point is that you want a book that speaks to where you are—and who you are—as you grieve. Book services such as the Centering Corporation (centering.org) and Compassion Books (compassionbooks.com) specialize in resources for individuals who are grieving.

The Internet as a Source of Support

Through the Internet, we can locate local and national self-help groups, counselors, and retreats. There are even online self-help groups and counseling. This can be of great value, especially in areas where groups may not be available or we are not mobile. Online groups can offer the ability to be available at all different times, as well as anonymity and the opportunity to "dose," to take from the group what we need to take and remove ourselves when we find the experience too intense. This can be very helpful, particularly for individuals who grieve in a head-on instrumental style.

There are downsides to Internet support as well. We lose the opportunities for personal support, the warm touch that may be available when groups are physically together. There may not be opportunities for the group facilitator to adequately screen members. Some comments may be cruel.

Take care. In periods of grief, you can be vulnerable. There are many supportive services available at no cost, low cost, or on sliding scales. You should begin your search for help with trusted resources within your community.

The Internet can also be a place to memorialize. Every person likes to leave a legacy, a reminder that their life counted, a place to visit and remember. That is one value of cemeteries. However, in a mobile society, cemeteries may no longer have that same role. Cyberspace can. It can be a "place" where one can leave tributes and condolences, share memories, and validate life. Many sites such as MuchLoved (muchloved.com/gateway/muchloved-charitable-trust.htm), Virtual Memorials (virtual-memorials.com), or Legacy.com (memorialwebsites.legacy.com) provide opportunities to create memorial sites. Some are free while others charge fees. This, too, can be one more gift of a technological age.

Self-Help Groups

Self-help groups can be a godsend when you are grieving. They allow the tangible and physically present support of others who share a similar loss. Groups offer validation—reminding us, through the testimony of others also coping with loss, that the reactions we have as we grieve are shared and understood. Support groups also model or demonstrate how others have coped with all the daily difficulties of grief. There is no one solution to loss, no clear path of how you should or should not grieve, but support groups can offer a range of alternatives. As you hear the stories of how others coped with a particular problem, you can find the solution that might work best. Support groups also provide respite and opportunity to be with others who understand. They can offer an afternoon or night away—a break in the loneliness, isolation, and the boredom that also is a part of grief. Support groups offer hope. In the midst of your grief, they provide models that reaffirm that you can survive loss.

There is a hidden benefit as well. As you help others, you find you help yourself—raising your own sense of self-esteem and self-efficacy. It is little wonder that support groups are a long-established, time-tested method that has helped people struggle with all sorts of difficulties.

Support groups are not magic, however. There are no words that can be uttered within a group setting that can make your grief disappear. They are places to work—and work hard—together to support one another. In a group, you give as well as take. That is an important consideration. Sometimes you can be so needy in your loss that you have nothing left to give. Here individual counseling might be the best approach.

Yet all groups are not equal. Some types of groups better meet the needs of intuitive grievers, while other groups might meet the needs of more instrumental grievers. For example, instrumental or head grievers may be attracted to groups that impart information or engage in advocacy, such as Parents of Murdered Children (POMC), rather than simply process grief. If you are struggling with complicated grief, you may benefit more from a group facilitated by a therapist.

Poorly structured and led groups can simply expose you to hours of shared anguish when the sole focus of the group is on sharing feelings. In such groups, it can seem like each member tries to top the other with his or her story of woe. Effective groups will help with the ventilation of feelings, but will also focus on the ways you can best cope with your reactions: Adjusting to a life without the person you loved; finding healthful ways to maintain a continuing bond with that person; and reconstructing your sense of faith, philosophy, and meaning after your loss. A group may not be right for you if they insist there is only one way to journey with grief.

Using Expressive Arts

You can use your talents and interests as you journey with grief. Whether it is writing poetry or prose; painting; singing; photography; or any other method, you can use these approaches to help yourself express your grief. Earlier, I mentioned how John Gunther memorialized his son in *Death Be Not Proud,* and Beth Neilsen Chapman composed and wrote "Sand and Water" as a tribute to her late husband, Ernest Chapman. Fourteen-year-old Brianna Reynolds memorialized the young students massacred in a neighboring school district with her poem "Meaningless Bullets."

Expressive approaches work because they are natural. You are simply using a common activity to express what you are experiencing. These approaches are reflective—allowing you to explore fully your reactions. They are cathartic—releasing pent-up energy as you engage in the activity. They draw from your inner self—connecting you to your culture, background, and beliefs. Finally, they work—in their own way. Intuitive grievers can express their emotions, while more instrumental grievers recollect and reexperience memories.

Journal writing is often used in therapy. In one approach, grieving individuals struggling with a loss were asked to write two entries, in the first person, on the circumstances of the deaths, expressing their thoughts, fears, and sensory perceptions. In the next two entries, they were asked to write about one troubling, intrusive memory, again noting thoughts, fears, and senses. In the second phase, they were instructed to write two entries as a letter to an imaginary friend who experiences a similar loss. The first letter should express common feelings, and not any guilt, worrisome behavior, automatic and intrusive thinking, and unrealistic assumptions. The second letter should offer advice on new roles, helpful rituals, lessons learned, and resources. The final entry was a letter to someone (possibly, yourself) about the deceased. It should reflect on memories, the ways the loss changed the writer, and how the griever will cope now and in the future.[4] This approach may offer you some ideas, should you wish to journal.

The point is that the way you have been creative in the past can assist you as you cope with your loss. It may be painting a picture of the person you loved, symbolically portraying your loss and grief, building a photographic collage, describing your grief in poetry, writing a story, journaling your grief, exploring your journey in a blog, or sharing our memories or emotions in a song. We all have creative talents that offer resources as we journey with grief.

There is never a good time to experience loss or to grieve. We now live in an age when our journey with grief is as difficult as ever, but you have many more resources available to you than in earlier times. We can do much to help ourselves—using our own personal strengths, effectively using the support offered by family and friends, and even engaging our own inner creativity. While there is an inherent loneliness in your journey with grief, you do not have to journey alone. A counselor can help you explore the ways that your grieving styles inhibit or facilitate the ways you interact with and support one another. Counselors also can assist you to assess realistically what support they can reasonably expect from others in the family, given these different styles, and assist you in finding other sources of support. Most important, counselors can remind you that your grief is the price you pay for love, but how you grieve is not necessarily a measure of that love.

PART 2

The Many Losses in Life

Each loss creates unique issues for grief. In any marital relationship, one partner is likely to survive the loss of the other. Reconstructing life after the death of our spouse can be difficult—even daunting. The loss of a child—whether in childhood, adolescence, or as an adult—can be psychologically devastating. Though we do expect to eventually grieve the loss of our parents, the expectation does not necessarily ease our grief or prepare us for all the subtle ways our life may change when our parents die. Most of us fail to realize that the longest relationship we have in our lives is likely to be with a sibling. They are generally there before we have spouses and children and after our parents die. Yet often when a sibling dies, we may find our experience of grief discounted and ignored. These chapters explore grief reactions that we may experience in such losses, as well as ways to cope with our loss and reconstruct our lives. Later, in part 3, we explore other such losses that are disenfranchised by others.

CHAPTER 5

When Your Spouse Dies

Deborah is surprised at how her life changed after her husband's death. Some of the changes were relatively minor and expected. She has had to assume tasks, such as managing finances, that were once her husband's job, which was relatively easy because they had planned for this. Other changes were more subtle. For example, when she watches TV, Deborah still turns to her husband's empty chair to make a comment—only then reminded that he is no longer here. Even sleeping alone in their king-size bed seems so different after seventeen years.

Deborah also finds her relationships with others have changed. Deborah's mother calls more often now, worried about how Deborah is managing. Yet her former in-laws barely call at all. Her mother-in-law mentioned how difficult it was to see Eli, their oldest child, since he is an image of his dad. Deborah's kids both miss their paternal grandparents and feel angry at their absence.

Friendships have changed as well. A few relationships

with couples they knew have cooled. Yet some casual friends, Deborah noted, "have really stepped up to the plate—offering friendship, support, even a shoulder to cry on." Deborah has a new set of friends—widows that she met in her support group.

Her relationships with her children have changed as well, since she is now a single parent. Deborah is more of a disciplinarian now that her husband is not there. Her relationship with her adolescent son became very different. "Our relationship became far more intense. There was no one to bounce off—no one to say, 'You deal with him tonight.' "

Major lifestyle changes occur when a spouse dies. Home life is different, as are relationships with parents, in-laws, and friends. Even relationships with children can change. Like Deborah, you may have to adjust to a life that is now different both in subtle and very evident ways. Yet each experience is unique because every relationship is different.

Your Unique Relationship and Marriage

Relationships differ. Some spouses retain considerable independence and maintain separate activities and friendships along with those they share. Other relationships' interactive style may be companionate; spouses enjoy the same activities and friends but are not highly interdependent or dependent. Deborah and her husband did a great deal together—from going out with friends to attending their children's activities. Aside from work, they spent little time apart, but when one was on a business trip, or when the competing claims of children forced them into separate activities, they also enjoyed their time alone.

In every marriage, there is some degree of mutual dependency, but the highly dependent and interdependent relationships are most likely to complicate grief.[1] Often we get into such relationships because of earlier issues in our life. Vibba, for example, never felt approval from her dad as she was growing up, as her dad always seemed to favor her brothers. When she married, she constantly sought reassurance from her husband.

When dependency is high, we often feel alone as we grieve. Our resources to deal with the crisis of our loss seem limited, and we may have little confidence in our competence to effectively deal with our loss. We may be terrified that we cannot even function in a world without our protector. Even if our partner was the dependent one, our grief may be complicated. So used to being the protector, we may be tortured by guilt that we somehow failed—that there was something we still could have done. If you had such a dependent relationship, you may find it helpful to seek counseling if you are struggling with issues of dependency or excessive guilt.

Grief is complicated by the way you interact with your spouse as well as the way you feel about him or her. Perhaps none of us ever quite makes the "happily ever after" promised by fairy tales, but some relationships are more happy than not. In such relationships your grief is readily understandable. You have lost a life companion.

Yet the more troubled relationships, the ones wrapped in considerable ambivalence, can cause the most difficulty. Ambivalence is a normal part of most relationships. We love a person, but can become easily angry at a perceived slight or annoying habit. We cannot live with or without the person. A sense of guilt, regret, and unfinished business can trouble our grief.

Deborah's relationship with Gil, who suffered from ALS (Lou Gehrig's disease), was ambivalent. They constantly bickered—over whose car to take, over finances, the children, or any number of reasons. The fights were never important, even big, but they were constant. They loved each other but somehow annoyed each other often over little things—Gil would leave the toothpaste uncapped, Deborah might forget to record a check. Even during Gil's illness, Deborah and Gil would struggle with the strains of caregiving. While generally mutually supportive during this time of medical crisis, they did argue about such things as Gil's incontinence. After Gil died, Deborah regretted that their relationship was, at times, so uneven. She wished she could take back some of the things she had said in anger.

When your spouse dies, as Deborah realized, your life changes dramatically. In some cases, the role of spouse may be core to your identity, and your very sense of self is challenged. I have often worked with the widows of clergymen. In one particular denomination they do not ordain women and the wife often takes on the role of a co-minister—presiding over the women's auxiliary and having a central role as the "first lady" of the congregation—which many find meaningful. When their husbands die, these women often experience multiple losses simultaneously. They not only lose their spouse but their role in the congregation. They may have to move from their home—especially if it is the church parsonage.

Even if your loss is not that extreme, you struggle with other losses. You may have lost a financial provider, a sexual partner, a homemaker, a calendar keeper. You have to take on new roles that were once done by your partner and do things alone that you once did together. In some cases, you may be required to move or change jobs as your responsibilities or finances change. Relationships may change as well. You may now have to raise your children alone, intensifying those relationships. You may find, as Deborah did, that relationships with friends, families, and in-laws now are different. Some of the changes may seem small but can still be significant. When Gil died, Deborah found that all their holiday rituals—from cutting the Thanksgiving turkey to Mother's Day breakfast—changed as well.

After the loss of a spouse, you can benefit from understanding and assessing what the relationship meant to you and what losses have occurred as a result of the death. Sometimes it helps to put your relationship in perspective by examining where you were months prior to meeting your spouse. I asked Deborah the question *Where were you six months before you met Gil?* Her answer surprised both of us. She had been engaged to a fireman, Sergio, who died in a car crash. She realized that Sergio's ghost had unwittingly haunted her marriage to Gil—that part of her ambivalence was due to the fact that she idealized the relationship she fantasized she might have had with Sergio. Your answer may not be as dramatic, but it may help you understand just what the relationship meant to you at the time in your life when it occurred.

One of the critical tasks of grief is adjusting to a life without your spouse—a life that is now very different. It can help to name those changes. Naming does two things. First, it validates—reminding you of all the ways that life has changed. Second, it allows you to problem solve—to figure out what you can have control of and which changes you may simply have to accept. You also need to assess your own strengths and weaknesses. How have you adapted to change and loss in the past? What did you do well? What are some of the problematic ways you have coped in the past that you might now want to avoid? Who can you count on to help?

Surviving the Death of Your Spouse: Different Times, Different Issues

Another factor that differentiates experiences of losing a spouse is when that loss occurs. You face different issues when you lose a spouse in your thirties or in your seventies. We do not expect to lose a spouse early in life—at least for most people in North America and Europe. We expect to grow old together. The loss of a spouse early in life may be perceived as traumatic—it challenges our assumptions about life and the world. Our world no longer seems safe and predictable. When Gil was diagnosed, it tore apart his and Deborah's images of life together. They had dreamed of retiring in New York's Adirondack Mountains—a plan that now would never find fulfillment. Deborah became far more conscious of her health and worried about the health and safety of their children.

When we are younger we are more likely to exist in a world of couples. The death of our partner may make us feel like a spare in the world of pairs. Even friends may look at us as possible rivals and competitors. Deborah found that some of her once good friends seemed uncomfortable in continuing to include her in activities—

one friend even became agitated when her husband offered to drive Deborah home. At the same time Deborah resented the sexual innuendos of some of her male friends.

When you lose a spouse early, you have to raise your children alone. You no longer have a spouse with whom you can discuss issues or share responsibilities and discipline. This may become a particular issue for male spouses, who may have not had as large a role in the lives of their children prior to the loss. The Harvard Bereavement Study, a major piece of research on the grief of children who experienced the loss of a parent, found that many men benefited more from groups focused on single parenting than grief support groups.[2]

Your children are grieving as you cope with your own grief. The Harvard Bereavement Study found that the single best predictor of how children dealt with the loss of a parent was how well the surviving spouse coped with the loss.[3] If you are struggling with your own grief and are understandably too overwhelmed to deal with your children's loss, you may wish to engage a larger network of family and friends. Deborah turned to her brother, who provided major support to Deborah's sons in the years after the death of their dad.

Yet you also have compensatory strengths when you experience the loss of a spouse at a relatively young age. Your own health is likely to be good. You usually have the ability to work should you choose or have to do so. You are likely to have support from your own family, in-laws, and some of your friends. In short, you have the resources—both external and internal—to assist you as you deal with this traumatic loss.

When you are older, you have different strengths and different issues. You are no longer alone with your loss—the spare in a world of pairs. You are less likely to be shunned or feel ignored, and you may find that many of your peers are struggling with similar issues. You may find that you have a natural support system.

As we age, we become accustomed to the rhythms of grief. By the time we are older, we have experienced the deaths of others we loved—parents, grandparents, relatives, friends, and mentors. You know grief now; you understand how you cope with loss. And while each loss is different and calls forth a different response, you are not surprised by your reactions or the periodic surges of grief that follow—even though you still may experience them deeply. You are a grief veteran.

Moreover, you have developed an awareness of your own finitude. As you age, death is no longer a distantly troubling thought. The writer Muriel Spark captured that in her book *Memento Mori*—the moment of death as one of her octogenarian characters addresses its nearness. "We survive amongst the dead and dying as on a battlefield."[4] Even our language acknowledges the reality of death. As my mother aged well into her eighties, she would no longer tell my son, "I cannot wait for your wedding." Rather, she began to say, "I hope I am there for your wedding." This means that the death of another person at that age is not totally a surprise, even if it is sudden. As I consoled a neighbor on the sudden death of her husband from a heart attack, I said, "It must have been quite a shock." She replied she was more surprised they had both lived so long as a couple. In these cases, our assumptions of the world are supported, rather than challenged, even while we grieve the loss.

When you are older, you face different issues that might complicate your grief. Your own health may be more fragile. Grief is bad for your health. Grief is stressful because you are less resilient to stress as you age, and need to monitor your stress and take active steps to reduce it. Older bereaved spouses have both higher rates of illness and disease.[5] Older people are more likely to die of chronic diseases such as cancer, or cardiovascular diseases that are affected by lifestyle factors such as diet or smoking. Spouses often share the same lifestyle.

When a spouse dies, you may stop your healthful lifestyle habits. Perhaps you once walked every night with your partner and no longer do so. You may no longer eat as well as you once did. You may begin coping chemically—using alcohol or excessive medications to ease your pain. So if you are older, you need to be especially careful about maintaining your health. Find ways to address the inherent stress of grief—even simple things like a walk, a hot bath, or listening to music may help. You also need to monitor your lifestyle. Are you getting enough sleep? Are you exercising? Eating healthfully? While these questions are important for everyone grieving any loss, they take on special importance with the inherent fragility of age.

Older relationships with spouses can be more interdependent—each compensates for the other's weaknesses. Josephina and her husband, Hector, could function well together, though Josephina had mobility problems and Hector had developed severe vision issues. They would even joke about being "one and a half" persons—describing how she would guide him to pick out the groceries she needed to cook. When Hector died, Josephina could no longer live independently and she soon moved to an assisted living facility—another loss as she gave up her beloved home and many possessions that would no longer fit in her more limited space.

You are more likely to experience multiple losses and may be grieving, in short order, the deaths of a spouse, sibling, and a good friend. Not only are we overloaded with grief, but you may be bereft of the very people who helped you adapt to earlier losses.

While older surviving spouses may suffer social isolation, other groups, too, might find social support problematic. Some widowers, especially older men who were raised when traditional gender roles were sharply defined, and may be less ready to assume all the roles that a wife may have traditionally played, now find it difficult to deal with all the household demands such as cooking, cleaning, and doing laundry. Traditionally, women are the family's "keeper of the kin" and "social secretary." The wife sets social events—inviting adult children or relatives to dinner and making social plans with neighbors and relatives. When the wife dies, the widower may not have the connections, knowledge, or skills to maintain these connections. My uncle George experienced this when his wife, my aunt Peggy, died. He complained that there was little to do—friends and family had deserted him. Yet he never reached out to them—even to his own children to invite them over. He seemed to lack the social skills to maintain these relationships. I encouraged my mother to call and invite him over. He answered the phone with a "Jesus, Jay, you always seem to call me when I am in the middle of a show!"

This was hardly a response to encourage further contact. However, men do have more opportunities to reengage if they are healthy and interested. The odds are good. Over sixty-five years of age, there are six widows for every widower.

Surviving spouses of childless marriages also may be at greater risk for isolation. They lack the usual support system naturally offered by adult children. Childless couples may have had a strong couple orientation—focusing on highly interdependent or companionate relationships that offered little space for others. Children are often great "connectors," building bridges to other parents and neighbors—bringing you into relationships you otherwise might not have had. Another factor operating especially for older childless widows is a support paradox. Neighbors may be less inclined to offer support when they believe themselves to be the sole source of support. When there are children—even living away—they have the sense that they can and will step in and provide help if needed.[6]

This may be an issue for same-sex couples as well. Same-sex marriages are relatively new, so there is little research on the issues that the surviving spouse faces when a partner dies. Much of the research that exists focused on gay men in the midst of the AIDS epidemic when same-sex marriage was generally not recognized, the death toll was massive, and young and middle-age men often were victims. Vicky Whipple, in her study of lesbian widows, noted that many of these widows were disenfranchised in their grief—that for much of their world, their grief was invisible.[7]

This is what Antonio faced after his partner, Julio, died. They had been together for thirty-five years—marrying only a few years prior, when their state legalized same-sex marriage. Antonio found solid support within their gay community. Family support was more limited as some of his siblings recognized the relationship and others did not. In fact, one of his brothers encouraged him to "marry for real"—invalidating the long supportive relationship that he and Julio shared.

If you are socially isolated and unsupported as you grieve, you need to examine the reasons why. Are you putting off people—

conveying a brave front that belies the support you crave and need? Are you giving mixed messages? Like my uncle George, Thad, an older widower, recognized that was exactly what he was doing. His kids would call constantly—asking how he was doing. He would be abrupt: he was doing fine, and they need not constantly worry and call. Soon the calls ceased. If you need help or even wish support and contact, you may have to make your needs clear.

In other cases, you may overwhelm your support system. Sometimes neediness can drive away other people. Then you may need to seek out new support from counselors or grief support groups. You may be expecting too much from those around you. Or you may not be using your support as well as you can.

This simple exercise is helpful to evaluate available support. I ask my clients to compile a list of all the persons they know who have promised or are likely to offer support. As we examine the list, we are likely to expand it. I often ask questions here such as: *Is there anyone else we should include such as people at work, in your faith communities, or other neighbors or friends?* Once the list is complete, and clients are often both reassured and surprised at how extensive the list is, I ask clients to put an *L* next to all the persons on the list who are good listeners. Next, I request that they put a *D* next to the names of doers—people they really can count on to complete a chore or errand. Finally, an *R* goes to people who offer respite. These are people who may never ask how we are doing and seem to avoid any discussion of the loss or grief. Nonetheless, they often can provide "respite" or time away from grief—laughter and distraction. After all, grief is hard work—like any hard work, we need time away from it.

This exercise often accomplishes three things. First, it often reassures that the bereaved persons have extensive informal support. Second, it allows assessment of whether or not support systems are being used effectively—asking the doers to do and the listeners to listen. Third, it validates the idea of respite and the role that such persons offer in their support.

Certainly there may be times when your support system is simply not adequate. As with Deborah, others may be threatened by our new status. Or you may have recently relocated—perhaps for a job or school—and your support system is geographically distant. Or if you are older, you may no longer have a viable support system. In these cases, grief support groups or senior clubs and centers can be particularly helpful as they offer a network of individuals in similar circumstances—perhaps allowing us to reconstruct, over time, a new network of friends.

Surviving a Spouse's Death: The Immediate Aftermath

Funerals and Memorial Services

Rituals have the power to help you along your journey with grief. Funerals or memorial services can be highly therapeutic, especially when they are personal. You may wish to consider, for example, different ways to exhibit photographic images either through memory boards or computer-generated slide shows. It can be especially important after a long illness and dementia to remember the images of the person and the activities we shared before the deteriorating effects of disease. You can also personalize ceremonies with eulogies, readings, poems, music, or hymns that have special meaning. Family and friends can participate in the reading or music, or serve as pallbearers or ushers. One older woman shared with me how meaningful it was to her to see her four-year-old great-grandson solemnly hand out flowers for a graveside ritual. It was a reaffirmation of the continuing cycle of life within her family. Naturally, clergy and faith communities may differ in what opportunities for participation exist and what they allow within a religious service, but rituals do not have to be limited to religious services. There is no reason you cannot set aside another time for such remembrances beyond the funeral.

Most faith traditions recognize that mourning is a continuing journey. Catholicism, for example, encourages anniversary masses. Judaism marks the first anniversary of the death with a ritual called *yahrzeit*; others mark the anniversary with an unveiling or dedication of the memorial stone. You can create your own rituals and traditions to mark varied points in your grief journey including holidays or birthdays. One widow visits her husband's grave, near the anniversary of his death, to recount what has happened in their family.

Dealing with a Spouse's Clothes and Other Personal Possessions

Deborah mentioned to me that it was hard to cope with "all the stuff." At first, I thought that she meant all the emotions and other reactions that are part of grief, but Deborah actually was being literal. She meant the physical stuff—all of her husband's possessions and clothes, all the things that were in closets, drawers, and the garage; the bits and pieces of her husband's life that bore a mute witness to her loss.

You always have to deal with the "stuff of grief"—especially when a spouse dies. Each time you look at it you are reminded of your loss. You receive so much advice—friends tell you to get rid of it, to clear everything out lest you are constantly reminded of your grief. Others may even make requests subtly, or not so subtly, requesting items. Yet you can do it in your own way.

The first rule in dealing with the stuff of grief is that there are no rules. Make your own decision on what you choose to keep or what you choose to give away. One man in my support group shared that, for him, opening an empty drawer that once was full with his wife's clothes would be far worse than seeing her things. As in other situations of grief, there is no one way to cope.

There is no timetable for when you should choose to deal with such "stuff"—you may never choose to deal with it. You should not feel pressured to do this at all, certainly not in the first week, months, six months, or year. You should do it when it seems right, when you are ready.

If you do decide to clear out some of the possessions of the person you lost, you may need to consider whether you should do it alone.

Again, there are no rules. Some people need to do this at their own pace—slowly—stopping at times as they confront memories. Others may welcome the support and assistance of family or friends.

When and if you do it, it helps to create systems. Deborah's husband, Gil, had saved everything. The basement was full of boxes that included World War II ration books given to him by his dad, and every check Gil ever wrote in his life. When Deborah decided she was ready to tackle the task, she divided everything into five categories.

The first were things that clearly could be discarded. These items had no value—symbolic or otherwise. She quickly discarded the ration books, except for one sample her son wanted for a possible class project. A second category was for things that she was unsure about, and that she felt she should discuss with her children or Gil's siblings. For example, there were athletic trophies from high school that their children might want, and photos of his family of origin. Once she got the family's feedback, she made decisions to discard or transfer them.

A third category was simply "not now." With these items, Deborah was not ready to decide what to do, and she simply needed to wait a while so that she could make the best decisions. There were many 45-rpm records with songs that were part of the soundtrack of their lives together. True, she had also purchased many on iTunes, and now that they were on her iPod, she had long discarded her turntable. But she still could not part with these vinyl reminders of her past.

A fourth category was for things she would donate or give to other individuals who would treasure them. Deborah knew a good friend, for example, who had often fished with Gil, would appreciate foraging through Gil's tackle box.

The last category was for things that she wanted to keep. Even though we never lose our memories, it is nice to have items that hold those memories and comfort us. For Deborah, it was Gil's old flannel shirt that he had since college. She had often suggested to Gil that it was time to toss it out, but he never had. Now there are days when it comforts her to wear that shirt.

Coping with Insensitive Comments

Dealing with the loss of a spouse is bad enough, but you often face the additional difficulty of coping with the remarkably foolish things people say to comfort you as you grieve. Such comments are more likely to occur in the immediate aftermath of the loss, but they can happen at any point in your grief. Many of these fall into the category of "false cheer" or the "silver lining" (that every cloud is supposed to have). These are comments like: *You are young—you will marry again. You have to be strong for your children. It was his (or her) time. Everything always happens for the best.*

At best, these comments are insensitive. At worst they can be destructive—corroding relationships, your sense of self, or even your faith. For example, a comment such as *God will never send you more than you can bear* can create doubt and even anger toward God. These comments may alienate a bereaved person from seeking support from others.

Erin Linn, in a wonderful book entitled, *I Know Just How You Feel: Avoiding the Cliches of Grief,*[8] offers a sound strategy for dealing with insensitive remarks. You ask yourself three questions:

What was the person trying to say? Most of our friends and family are not intentionally cruel. In most cases, they are trying to convey support and comfort. When you ask yourself this question, you reaffirm their concern even as you deplore their comment. You can recognize the goodness of their intentions even as you understand that their expression of support was poorly chosen.

Why did the comment hurt? Most insensitive comments hurt because they invalidate our grief. Whether you will marry again is irrelevant to your sense of grief now and does nothing to resolve it. You will always mourn the loss of your mate.

What can you say in response? You may never have the opportunity to respond, but just thinking about what you could have said reaffirms a sense of control and empowers you not to be a victim again. You can answer comments like *At least you have your children* with a simple *It is a great comfort to have them, but I will always miss that*

Terry will not be with me to raise them. A reply to *Everything always happens for the best* can be *I will never understand how the loss of my wife could ever be "best."* Responses such as these reaffirm your grief and perhaps teach others how to be more sensitive.

Other troubling comments may come in the form of unsolicited advice such as, *You should move out of that big house right now.* In such situations, try to remember two points. First, trust your own instincts. Everyone handles loss differently. What worked for someone else may not work for you. You need to listen to yourself.

Second, give yourself time and space. In the beginning you might not know what you want or should do. While there are no rules in grief, try not to make any major decisions for at least six months to a year.

The best support in grief is often the quietest. A friend need not say much beyond *I am sorry* or *How can I help*. It is often manifested in caring actions—the meal that is delivered or the chore that is done. One woman shared that at the funeral of her husband, a neighbor, herself a widow, pressed a key into her hand. "It will be lonely sometimes," the neighbor shared. "There will be times you may not wish to be alone. You have my key. Come over." That level of quiet caring is always welcome.

Returning to Work

You may need to resume work soon after the funeral for a variety of reasons, but it can be difficult to grieve in the work environment. The work world is structured, full of responsibilities and expectations. Little allowance is made for the difficulties you can face as you cope with grief. There will be days you function well and other times when it is difficult to cope.

It helps to accept your grief. You cannot simply turn it off when you go to work. Acknowledge to yourself that some days may be more difficult than others. Flexibility is important. When you have a rough day, you may not be able to accomplish all that you wished. Other days will be more productive. Be gentle with yourself.

Be gentle with others as well. They simply may not know what to say. It helps if you are clear about your loss. You can share your grief with those who can offer support. Coworkers, even supervisors, may need guidance about the ways they can best help. Utilize the resources that work can offer. Human resources or employee assistance programs may offer information, support, counseling, assistance, and referral.

Coping with the Tasks of Grief When Your Spouse Dies

Acknowledging the Reality of Your Loss

When a partner dies, it can seem like a bad dream. You may not wish to believe it. You may pretend that the person is at work, on a trip, or perhaps shopping. Whenever the phone rings or you hear footsteps, you may wish it were that person. Even as you shop for groceries, you may still have in mind what you would purchase for him or her.

In the beginning, the shock of the loss insulates you from the new reality of what has happened and is still happening. But slowly that reality begins to emerge—eroding that shock and initial denial. The funeral ritual itself is a reminder, a reaffirmation, of your loss, as are the sympathy cards and condolence calls.

Most people, over time, acknowledge the death and gradually no longer expect their spouse to return. The reality of the loss slowly seeps into your consciousness. Bit by bit, your behaviors adjust to the new reality. You no longer look from the television to the empty place. Your hand no longer reaches to the grocery store shelf for the once-requested item.

Exploring and Expressing Emotions

There are few emotions that you do *not* experience as part of grief. The first step in dealing with your feelings is to acknowledge them. They are a natural part of the process of grief. You really have little control over this experience of feelings and need to explore them. Ask yourself, *What are the circumstances and times that trigger these emotions? How am I dealing with these feelings?*

While you cannot completely control *what* you feel, you can control *how* you deal with your grief. There are constructive and destructive ways to deal with emotions. Constructive ways to deal with anger may include exercising, punching a pillow, screaming at an empty chair, fantasizing, or directing your anger to create change. A destructive way to deal with anger is lashing out at those around you, which drives others away and limits your support; avoid or minimize this behavior.

Sometimes you can explore these feelings on your own by taking time to work through them or journaling about them. At other times it may be helpful to examine these emotions with a close friend or confidant, within a support group, or perhaps with a counselor or clergy. Support groups and counseling can be particularly helpful if your feelings are intense or complicated. Here counselors or support groups are valuable since your strong need to share feelings, as well as the lengthy time struggling with your grief, may exhaust friends and family.

Adjusting to the New Reality of Life without Your Spouse—Dating Again?

There may come a point in your life when you might be open to considering new romantic relationships. Even as we age, we still retain psychological, social, and sexual needs. You can decide when (if at all) it is time for such a relationship, based on your needs and readiness, rather than be pushed into relationships by well-meaning friends and family. You will need to have integrated your earlier loss into your life so that you are ready to make a new commitment to someone else. Head grievers may run a special risk here, as they may see another relationship as a way to resolve problems such as loneliness even though they are still extensively coping with their grief over the loss of a spouse. At best this is unfair to the new partner. Any new relationship or remarriage has a certain complexity, and there is always an inevitable comparison with a deceased spouse, who becomes sort of a third person in the room. If you have not yet integrated your grief, you may always be comparing that new person with an idealized vision of your deceased partner.

If you have children, it is critical to introduce the new partner slowly into your relationship with them. Dr. J. William Worden, in the Harvard Bereavement Study, found that many children considered parental dating and remarriage a mixed blessing.[9] Some children welcomed it as it reduced parental loneliness and the child's anxiety about the parent, but others acted out and resented the new person—particularly within the first year of the relationship. Worden found that children were generally more accepting by the second year. While Worden's research focused on children and adolescents, some of my own clinical observations would suggest this even holds true for adult children.

Continuing the Bond

You maintain a relationship with your partner even after death. That bond continues in many ways—in the memories, in the legacies that are left, and in the spiritual connections and experiences that we have.

Memories are natural, even unavoidable. You can no more control what you remember than what you feel. In fact, as the pain of your loss eases, your memories become more vivid. Memories are often comforting, bringing the individual closer, if fleetingly. Memories also connect you with others who are living. I love my mother's shared stories of her courtship with my dad, which revealed another side to my father. His sensitivity and love came through in a different way than I knew as his son. These stories complemented our own, leading to a richer understanding of the man, not just the father, that he was. Even funny and amusing stories have their role, providing respite to our grief and reminding us of the joys of relationships. Such memories are the home fires that warm the chill of loss. You may wish to evoke memories by visiting the cemetery, viewing photographs or videos, or engaging in private family rituals and remembrances. You may also need to confront painful memories. Only when you fully explore them can you truly understand and find ways to release them.

Your spiritual beliefs may offer connections to your spouse—even occasions to memorialize. For example, many temples, synagogues, and churches offer opportunities to dedicate flowers or other items in memory of your spouse.

You may even choose ways to celebrate your spouse's legacy. When Richard, a state trooper, was killed in the line of duty, he and his wife Nadine had infant sons. Every year Nadine sponsors a fund-raising run in his memory. The run supports the trooper auxiliary and also keeps Richard's memory alive. Each year many of his fellow troopers return and share stories of Richard. It gives his two sons a sense of their father, whom they barely remember.

Rebuilding Faith

Elliot deeply mourned the death of his wife, but her death did not shake his faith. She died after a fullness of many years, physically frail but mentally intact. She died surrounded by family of many generations.

Some deaths, however, will shatter your beliefs or cause you to question them—however deeply held. You may find it hard to believe that there is any meaning to the universe or any point in life. The circumstances of the death, the age of the person who died, or the extent of suffering may make it hard to believe in a benevolent God or universe. You may feel lonely and abandoned. Your faith may seem to offer little comfort.

One of the tasks of grief, then, is to rebuild faith or philosophies that have been challenged by your loss. One of the biggest mistakes you can make during this period is to isolate yourself from your beliefs. Instead, share your struggles within your faith community. This is a time to identify those within your faith communities who can journey with you, who are comfortable hearing your conflicts and sharing their own. Sometimes you may have to look hard to search out and find those people—people who are willing to listen and engage in honest discussion rather than simply offer empty reassurances and platitudes.

Do not isolate yourself from your faith community or your spiritual practices. You may find value in reading about the struggles of others to remind yourself that difficulties are natural and normal in the journeys of belief and grief. They may also offer insight and suggestions on how to best cope and how to restore hope.

The loss of a spouse is disruptive. Your life inevitably changes when your spouse dies. However, your basic choice is to survive—and perhaps even grow—even though it may be painful. Survival is, perhaps, the most fitting legacy.

CHAPTER 6

When a Child Dies

Brian is grieving the loss of his eight-year-old son, Shay, who developed a brain tumor and did not survive the dangerous surgery necessary to cure him or give him more time. Brian thinks of Shay often and lovingly plans an annual carnival in his young son's memory—a fund-raiser for Little League, which Shay loved. But his wife, Marla, worries that Brian has not grieved because he's never cried or talked about his feelings. She pressures him to join her support group, but he attended a few sessions and did not find them helpful, calling it a "pity party." Brian worries about Marla as well, because she easily breaks down whenever someone speaks about Shay, even two years after Shay's death.

Shay's siblings feel ignored. Shay's twin brother, Scott, feels he is living in Shay's shadow. The day before, while playing in Little League, he hit a game-winning triple. After the game, his dad told him that when Scott was up to bat, Dad had asked Shay to guide his bat. His dad thought this was a compliment, but Scott felt hurt that he wasn't recognized

> for his own achievement. Scott also has a hard time with his own fears. He wonders if he, too, will develop a tumor, and obsesses about it whenever he gets a headache. Meanwhile, their older sister, Heather, feels that her own problems are minimized by her parents and told her guidance counselor that nothing seems important to her parents other than illness and death.

Whether the child is twelve years old or fifty-two years old, we do not expect our children to die before us. The death of a child challenges our sense of a just and predictable world and can shake our faith to the core. It is little wonder that the death of a child, in and of itself, is considered a risk factor for more complicated grief.[1]

The deaths of children test you. They affect your relationship with your spouse and your other children. Few deaths affect a support system as much as the death of a child. Parents, siblings, grandparents, and other relatives all struggle with their own grief, which make them need support, too, and might make them less available to help you. Friends and neighbors can seem remote. Other parents may be reluctant to extend invitations to you to parties or events marking their own child's milestones, knowing you have lost your child.

Siblings may feel neglected—even invisible—as the family struggles with a child's death. It is easy for parents to idealize a child who died, which makes the surviving siblings feel they have to compete with a perfect ghost—an image of a child who was flawless. For instance Landon never knew his brother Lee, who had died of cancer two years before Landon was born, but his life was haunted by his brother. Pictures of his brother adorned the house, and his mother's vanity license plate read "I LUV LEE."

In other cases siblings may be scapegoated for the death. Latoya's surviving daughter, Nicki, always felt her parents blamed her for the death of her younger sister, Toni, who had asked her for a ride that night because she was reluctant to drive on wet roads. Nicki was too busy with her homework and annoyed that even though she had her own license, Toni still looked to her for a lift.

The death of a child may mean you will have to give up treasured activities or associations you once shared. Brian, for example, used to coach his twin sons' Little League team—a valued activity that he has now stopped as too painful. Marla no longer watches those games even though they connected her with other parents. Scott feels that he not only lost his brother but his mom and dad as well, and Scott wonders why his dad does not coach anymore. Did his father care about just Shay?

Parents often carry a continuing sense of the child as they continue through life, retaining an image of how the child was but also how he or she might be now if still alive. We remain very aware, even years after death, that a daughter would be making a first communion this year, or that a son would be graduating from high school. Children remain our children even as they age and even when they are adults; we do not expect them to die before we do.

Yet especially with adolescent children, relationships can be volatile and highly ambivalent, and some deaths may be the result of self-destructive actions that further complicate grief.

Our Experience with Grief

The death of a child at any age complicates grief. It is a most difficult loss. We expect to watch our children grow and develop, marry and have children of their own, before we pass from their lives. Whenever a child dies, we lose not only that child but also our assumptive world—our beliefs about what the world should be like.

I cannot explain such a loss; I don't believe anyone can. But I can offer ways to cope. Your reactions and responses to the death of your child are shared by other parents. This may not make you feel any better, but perhaps it will make you feel less alone in your feelings and reactions. Grief can be isolating because it is a highly individual process. There is no single right way to feel, or to act, as well as to cope with your loss.

This chapter offers hope for your healing in the shared stories of the many parents who have experienced the indescribable pain of losing a child. Many parents, even as they live with their loss, are able to find continued meaning in life. Their lives have become living legacies to their child. Dr. Catherine Sanders was one such example.

One Labor Day, Sanders was on shore watching her fifteen-year-old son, Jimmy, water-ski, when another boat crossed Jimmy's tow-line, causing Jimmy to crash into the other boat. Sanders had just returned to college, and after Jimmy died she changed her major to psychology, focusing on the study of grief—in many ways to help her understand her own grief. Sanders has contributed to understanding the phases of grief that many parents go through as they cope with the death of a child.

Many parents naturally experience a deep sense of *shock* when their child dies. Even in cases where the child has a terminal illness, we still never truly expect our child to die before us. In the days immediately after the death you can feel as if you are in a haze or a bad dream. Everything may seem confusing or unreal. You may deny or disbelieve the loss. You may feel that you go through the motions, never quite believing the horrific reality. One of the values of funeral rituals is that they help us face that terrible truth and adapt to the new reality.

Next many parents become *aware of their loss.* As the shock begins to fade, you are likely to experience grief intensely. After all, grief is the natural and normal response to loss. And it will affect you at every level—physically, emotionally, cognitively, socially, and spiritually.

Grief can make you feel unwell. It is essential to monitor your health carefully in the period following a death. If problematic physical symptoms continue, go to your doctor. You may get a range of aches and pains—headaches, backaches, muscular pain, digestive difficulties, or exhaustion. Sometimes the pain may even be symbolic of the loss. Some parents describe chest pains and a feeling of emptiness that feels like "a hole in the heart."

Besides periods of deep sadness, intense yearning, and even moments of profound loneliness, you may be unprepared for the anger you feel—shocked that your temper seems to run so short. Anger is a natural response to loss. You may direct that anger at those you feel are responsible for your loss. Sometimes you may direct your anger at those closest to you, or you rage at God for allowing your child to die. You may be angry that your child died when other children who engage in self-destructive acts or delinquent behaviors are unharmed. While anger is a normal reaction in grief, it can be unhealthful if it turns into blaming, or drives others away and thus deprives you of support, separating you from those you most need in your journey with grief.

Sometimes your anger may be directed inward—at yourself. Guilt is a common response to grief. Parents often place unrealistic expectations upon themselves and may think that they could have somehow protected a child from death. You may feel *role guilt*—a sense that you might have been a better, more caring, more responsible parent. Ruth felt that when her seventeen-year-old daughter died. Just before her sudden death, they had argued—the normal kind of disagreement parents and teenagers often have. But after the death, Ruth felt awful that their last interaction had been so negative. There is also *death causation guilt*—a feeling that we had some role in the death. This is very common when a child dies of a genetic disease, but parents feel it in other circumstances as well: *I should have made him go to the doctor sooner, not let her get into the car, or watched her cross the street.* Parents and siblings may feel guilty they are still alive. You may feel a *moral guilt* that this loss is some form of cosmic punishment for something you had done or not done. You may even feel guilty that you are doing too poorly—or too well—in your grief.

You cannot control the onset of guilt feelings. Guilt does not have to be rational for it to feel real, which is why it sometimes helps to move outside of yourself—to ask others if they would see you as guilty. Know that guilt is a common response, but that it is based on an unrealistic expectation that you, as a parent, can control everything that happens to your child.

After a child dies, parents may feel increased anxiety and fears.

The world feels unsafe, as if anything can happen. It may be difficult to let surviving children engage in normal activities. It is easy to become overprotective.

You may even feel jealous of others who still have their children. Jealousy is normal but also disturbing. You may find you have less patience with parents who have the normal problems of raising children—bad behavior, poor grades, or other factors that now seem like minor complaints. You may even feel a sense of being different; perhaps even a sense of shame, feeling that other parents now see you in a new way.

If your child suffered with a disease or lived with agonizing injuries, you may experience a sense of relief that his or her pain or discomfort has now ended. At other times, you may feel a renewed appreciation of the role your child played in your life. These emotions are normal, too.

There is no order to these feelings. It is not unusual to experience many conflicting emotions at the same time. Prayer, meditation, support groups, and grief counseling are all ways that you can help yourself through these feelings. However, feelings and emotions are only part of the grief experience.

Grief also influences the ways you think. You may find it difficult to focus or concentrate. You may be forgetful and easily distracted. You may repeatedly think about your loss—constantly going over painful details in your mind and wondering if it could have turned out differently. You may dream frequently about your child. Events or comments evoke a sense of your child.

Your behaviors may change. You may cry a great deal, at times uncontrollably, or you may be confused that you cannot seem to cry. You may feel lethargic and apathetic. You may withdraw and seek lots of time alone that was not typical before your loss. Or you may constantly seek the activity and company of others as a way to distract yourself from your pain. You may avoid reminders of the child who died. It may be too painful to view photographs or watch activities that bring the child to mind. Or you may seek these reminders and find them comforting. Some parents create activities that affirm the child, such as an annual memorial event, a gift in the child's name, or a fund. Any of these very different reactions are normal.

Grief often affects you spiritually. You may find great strength in beliefs and find your spirituality deepen—attending services, praying, or reading scripture even more frequently than in the past. Or you may find your faith threatened. It is easy to feel the death of your child is not the way it should be, and you may feel abandoned by your faith. You may struggle with anger at God and doubt prior beliefs, searching for some way to make sense of this unfathomable loss.

During this phase, which can be described as *conservation/withdrawal,* grief is full of ups and intense downs, highs and lows. On some days, you may feel that you are doing well—only to plunge into a deepened sense of grief. Some of these low periods are unsurprising. Holidays and birthdays may be difficult, but there is no predictability. Sometimes little events—seeing a child who looks or dresses similarly, clicking past your child's favorite television show, hearing a song, seeing your child's friends on the street, or even seeing a favored toy or game—evoke intense grief.

There is no timetable to this intense period of loss. Over time, the intensity of emotions usually begins to lessen. You may be forced back into living life by the demands of family or work, even as you still cope with your loss. After time passes, the world around you may seem less patient with your grief. You may feel that you are putting on a mask as you go through the motions of living.

In many ways, this phase is one of the longest and most difficult in the grieving process. Your grief continues, perhaps at a lower level of intensity, but it is still acute, and you have less social support. Family and friends may underestimate or fail to understand your continued grief and need for support.

In this period, it may seem to take all your energy just to cope with the demands of life. Physically, you may feel fatigued and need even more sleep to meet the ongoing demands of life. The continued stresses of grief can weaken your immune system and make you vulnerable to illness.

Some people have trouble ever leaving this phase of conservation/withdrawal. One mother whose only child died felt that experiencing any joy would be a betrayal of her son. This kind of difficulty warrants exploring with a counselor. But many parents experience a *turning point* in their grief. In some cases it arose as they began to reengage in activities, or as they recognized the needs of their other children, or even as they became involved in activities that were their child's legacy. These parents reach the phase of *renewal*. They choose to move forward, to live a meaningful life despite the loss. They find a meaning that makes their lives a tribute to their child.

Renewal is learning to live with the loss. You have an empty space in your heart, but you have learned how to live with that empty space. Over time, the roller coaster of emotions begins to slow down—the bad days are less frequent, less intense, and do not tend to last as long. As the pain ebbs slightly, your energy and previous abilities return. Grief becomes less disabling. You begin to function at a level similar to the one prior to the loss. In this period, you still may experience some down times, especially at anniversaries, birthdays, or other special events. But you will never lose your connection to, or memories of, your child.

Marla made it to that point after a powerful experience that her therapist recommended. "My counselor asked me to talk to an empty chair—to imagine it was Shay—and to tell him how my life was now. I did—crying how miserable I was. After I regained my composure, the counselor had me sit in Shay's chair and imagine what Shay would say to me. He started out saying how sorry he was, but then I heard myself saying that he did not want me to be so sad—I realized how much Shay enjoyed every minute and how much my sadness must weigh on him."

It is important to remember that there is no single, right way to experience grief. Nor does grief have a timetable. Your experience of grief is what it is and comes from who you are. You cannot compare your loss to the losses of others, or your reactions or responses to those of others. Differing experiences of grief have little to do with how much you loved or cared about your child. Each child, relationship, and the circumstances of the loss are unique. Grief will be different as well.

Particular Cases of Child Loss

Pregnancy Loss

There was a time when losses in pregnancy were unacknowledged and the parent's grief unsupported. Any counseling was often limited to a doctor saying, "You are young and healthy—get pregnant again." There was even an assumption that if the mother never saw the deceased baby, she would feel little attachment and her grief would be limited.

We now understand how wrong and how harmful such beliefs were. Years prior to getting pregnant, most women have fantasies of how many children they want and what their children will be like. Even as a child, you might have thought of names for your future kids. Bonding with your unborn child strengthens during pregnancy. Today we recognize a mother's grief at losing a pregnancy, but we also need to acknowledge that fathers, siblings, grandparents, and other relatives will grieve as well. All who would celebrate the birth mourn the death.

Siblings, especially younger ones, might have more complicated grief reactions over a parental pregnancy loss. Though excited by the birth of a younger brother or sister, they may also have some ambivalence, feeling jealous of the attention and excitement generated by their unborn sibling and anxious over their role in the family. Younger children often exhibit magical thinking—believing that their wishes and thoughts might be responsible for the pregnancy's end. You will want to reassure them that whatever occurred was not their fault, and that their feelings are natural and normal.

After pregnancy loss, one of the first decisions you may have to make is whether you wish to see or hold your baby. Some hospitals may offer opportunities for keepsakes such as a photograph or a handprint or footprint. Jane Nichols, a pioneer in the issues of pregnancy loss, used to teach hospital staff to allow mothers (and fathers) to see and hold the baby. When she found out that this advice was being interpreted as a directive, in later years she would recommend that nurses "allow the parents to see or hold the baby *or not*"—stressing the individuality of grief, that no one experience fits all. I agree but would also recommend that the medical staff retain some memento of the birth, such as a hand- or footprint, in case the parents want it down the line. Parents may not be ready to see it at the time, but may change their minds. You can choose to have a ritual—at the time of the loss or at some time in the future.

Whatever the circumstances of your loss or wherever it occurred in the pregnancy, or even after sudden infant death syndrome, you need to grieve in your own way. If you are not getting the support you need from your own circle of friends and family, or if you wish to connect to families that have had similar experiences, there are support groups, such as the Compassionate Friends (compassionatefriends .org), or Share (share.org), that can offer information, resources, and connections to local and online support groups.

Only Children, All Children

The death of a child is a devastating event, but the presence of other children in your family often offers comfort, as well as motivation and incentive to get up each day. The loss of an only child or—in cases of genetic diseases or traumatic events—all your children is especially horrific. In these cases, your secondary losses are extensive as well. You lose any future grandchildren, sons-in-law or daughters-in-law, and the possibilities of weddings or other rites of passage such as bar mitzvahs, confirmations, or graduations. You have no one to remember you on Father's or Mother's Day.

In short, it is not the future we imagined. There is no one to tell your stories to—to leave treasured possessions or pass on family heirlooms. You may fear aging alone. You wonder if you can still identify yourself as a mother or father when you no longer have children.

With the loss of children, grief is complicated. Counseling and support groups may be helpful. The Compassionate Friends deals with all situations of the loss of a child, and specialized Web-based resources or support groups such as Alive Alone (alivealone.org) or GriefNet (griefnet.org) focus on the loss of an only child or all children.

When an Adult Child Dies

> If he were twelve, everyone would understand my grief. Why can't they understand it now? Even though he was forty-two years old, he was still my son.—Sonya

Other parents who have experienced the death of an adult child often echo Sonya's comment and feel a lack of support. Part of that may be because sympathy and support are focused on other survivors—the child's spouse or children. Part may occur simply because there is little recognition of the powerful bond that exists between parent and child once that child is independent. Whatever the reasons, the grief of the parent of an adult who dies can be disenfranchised.

The death of an adult child often comes as the parent is aging. This loss may be one of the many losses that the parents are experiencing that complicates their grief. They may be mourning other losses of family or friends, or intangible losses such as relinquishing cherished roles or activities.

When an adult child dies, you may lose a critical source of support in your own life, someone on whom you depended. The child may have provided emotional, physical, or even financial support. You may have experienced a sense of vicarious achievement in your child's successes, or feel a deep sense of sadness that the adult child never accomplished cherished goals. Sonya, for example, was distressed that her son never had the opportunity to watch his own children grow or to achieve a long-sought and nearly attained promotion. The death of an adult child can also affect other relationships. Relations with the widowed spouse or grandchildren may change. Even family events are different now.

You may feel a lack of control that complicates the loss because you have little or no control over the funeral or memorial. If you had little control over the funeral rituals or if these rituals were not meaningful, you may wish to gather your own friends for a ritual. Sonya did that. Her son died two thousand miles away. While she attended the service, her friends who had known her son could not. They had been part of his life as they had been part of Sonya's. To Sonya, it was important that they gather with her to mourn his death and celebrate his life.

The very term *adult child* is an oxymoron, yet it captures the paradoxical relationships that may exist when both parents and children are adults. We as parents often continue to give advice or counsel to our adult children. As we age, our adult children may offer their own recommendations and suggestions. At times we may resent these, even as we appreciate their underlying concern. This ambivalence can complicate grief as well.

It is critical to validate your grief, to recognize that the death of a child, regardless of age or circumstances, causes great suffering. Support is critical. You may want to seek counseling or join a support group. The Compassionate Friends offers local support groups for parents who are grieving the death of a child at any age or stage in life.

Self-Destructive Deaths

Children—whether adults, adolescents, or even younger children—may die from self-destructive causes such as suicide, drug-related deaths, criminal activity, or gang violence. In some cases, the child may have had a history of mental illness, drug use, or delinquent activities leading to complicated relationships with parents. Such deaths can intensify emotions including blame, guilt, and anger. Research has suggested that parents in such cases are more likely to suffer from physical and mental illnesses including depression,[2] in part because these deaths are often stigmatizing and disenfranchised. It is difficult to receive support from other friends and family who may come across as judgmental. Such deaths can be frightening to other parents, and one of the ways others may cope with their fears is to place blame unfairly on parents. *It cannot happen to us—we are more attuned to our children,* they think. That leads us to become secretive about the loss, and hide our grief.

We need to make sense of the death—to try to understand what happened—but our spiritual beliefs may not offer us the comfort that other parents might find. We may need to create, at least in our own minds, a coherent story that explains both our child's life and death. Specialized support groups such as suicide survivor groups, or general support groups, or counselors and clergy are a significant source of help as parents struggle with such a loss.[3] Some of these bereaved parents rated psychics as helpful, while other bereaved parents did not. This reliance on psychics may help the parents because their perceived contact with this deceased child offers an opportunity to repair the bond ruptured by self-destructive behaviors and death. Nonetheless, I would advise you to be cautious in seeking out psychics. It is important that you are clear about what questions you are really seeking to find answers to, and it may be helpful first to explore that with a therapist, clergyperson, or confidant. You want to avoid any financial exploitation by a psychic or, for that matter, by any helping relationship.

Coping with Grief

The Power of Ritual

Funerals play many roles for surviving family. This rite of passage provides a sense of structure and support in highly stressful times, and a safe venue for the physical and emotional expression of grief, because the ritual contains that grief and guides its expression. Funerals offer a chance for family, friends, and the larger community to come together in support. Rituals evoke memories that help you find meaning in the life of the person who died.

Funeral rituals are especially therapeutic when they are personal.

You can display photographs of your child, showing that your child's life—however short—touched the lives of others who share your grief and memories. You can suggest readings, poems, music, or hymns that have special meaning to clergy or other celebrants. If your child was older, perhaps friends can play a role—serving symbolically as pallbearers; giving readings from scripture, poetry, or song that had significance to your child. Many years ago I attended the funeral of a young adolescent girl who had died in a bicycling accident, and whose friends participated in the funeral as ushers and readers. The junior choir and the school glee club both sang. It reaffirmed to the parents how much friends and classmates loved their daughter.

You can also create private, family rituals such as lighting a candle on the anniversary of the death. Marla and Brian place gifts such as a video game system under the Christmas tree, and another family purchases a wrapped gift in memory of the child, which the family donates to a children's shelter. Rituals give voice to feelings of loss that might otherwise remain silent, and permit family members to share their memories and grief.

Legal Issues

Issues of liability may occur in any loss, but they are more likely to occur when a child dies. Issues of liability can arise due to medical malpractice or some form of personal negligence that resulted in death. Clearly some cases cry out for a sense of justice, and a lawsuit may lead to a beneficial change that may spare other parents or individuals the horror we experienced. In other cases, a lawsuit may stem more from a desire to blame someone for something that cannot be controlled, or to find a cause or meaning for a death. You need to be clear about your motives and expectations and recognize that lawsuits are lengthy, uncertain, and expensive. Even if a lawyer is working on contingency—that is, for a percentage of the award granted—there are many other expenses. A court case can also create secondary traumatization. First, you will hear in great detail about the death. Second, in an adversarial legal system, it is likely the defense will attempt to shift blame to you.

A lawsuit will not bring closure to your grief—there is no closure possible after a significant loss—but it may bring a sense of meaning to the death, if the result is a change in medical practice or safety procedures that will benefit others. That may be reason enough to bring suit.

Acknowledging the Reality of Your Loss

In the beginning, the shock of a loss insulates you from the new reality of life after your child, but slowly that reality erodes that shock and initial denial. The funeral ritual itself is a reaffirmation of loss, as are sympathy cards and condolence calls. As you talk about your loss and grief with others, perhaps even in a bereavement support group, you begin to feel the full extent of your grief. Gradually you no longer expect your child to return. Bit by bit, your behaviors adjust to the new reality. You no longer look in the room to see whether your child returned.

You may struggle to answer simple questions such as "How many children do you have?" There is no correct answer. Some parents will answer "three but one died" or "two living," while others will simply answer "two"—not wishing to explain at that time or in that situation. Follow your own instincts and do what is comfortable.

Exploring and Expressing Emotions

When shock recedes, you may struggle with many difficult and complicated emotions such as loneliness, sadness, yearning, guilt, or anger. The first step in dealing with your feelings is to acknowledge them. They are a natural part of the process of grief. You really have little control over this experience of feelings. Recognizing your feelings is the first step in dealing with them.

Explore these feelings. What are the circumstances and times that trigger these emotions? How are you dealing with these feelings? As you examine your emotions, you may discover that you are holding yourself responsible for things or events you simply could not and cannot control. Sometimes when we really examine and face difficult emotions, they will shift and fade.

That often occurs with guilt. As parents, we feel responsible for anything that happens to our child. But when you carefully examine your specific guilt feelings, you realize that you are not and could not be responsible for your child's death. You cannot always see all possible consequences, control all actions, or maintain perfect relationships. As you examine your feelings, you can learn to forgive yourself.

There are constructive and destructive ways to deal with emotions. Avoid lashing out at those around you, driving others away—limiting support. Constructive ways to deal with anger include exercising, punching a pillow, screaming at an empty chair, fantasizing, or directing your anger to enact change. Liam's parents became involved in MADD—Mothers Against Drunk Driving—and actively lobbied for greater drunk driving enforcement so as to prevent the deaths of other victims like their son.

The death of your child may make you think the world unsafe. You can also use your fear and anxiety as a force for change. When Ryan was killed crossing a street near his school, his parents fought for a crossing guard to prevent more children's deaths, a constructive way to deal with their anxiety about the safety of their other children. A more problematic way would be to insist that their other children stay within view every minute as they walk to school, inhibiting their children's development and emerging independence.

You may regret something you did or said, or something left unsaid or undone. Once you recognize the unfinished business, you may find a way to complete it. Some parents share a final comment at graveside, write a note in a journal or a letter to their child, or create a small ritual.

Take time to work through your feelings or journal about them. You may find it helpful to examine your emotions with a close friend or confidant, within a support group, or with a counselor or clergy.

Adjusting to the New Reality of Life without Your Child

When a child dies, changes in your life are both profound and subtle. The house may seem strangely quiet. Activities that once had meaning—cooking or watching television together—no longer have the same significance. You may miss the activities that you shared with your child. If your child was an adult and had a spouse or children, relationships with in-laws and grandchildren may be affected. The death of a child may create these and other secondary losses. Relationships with other parents may no longer be the same. You may miss seeing your child's friends, who no longer come by the house.

One of the critical tasks of grief is adjusting to how a life changes without your child. It helps to name those changes. This does two things. First, it validates what you are going through—reminding you of the ways that life has changed. Second, it allows you to solve problems—to figure out what you can control and which changes you may simply have to accept.

When Shay died, his parents struggled with the fact that relationships with neighbors, many of whom had children the same age as Shay, seemed different. Talking with these neighbors eased some awkwardness and discomfort. His parents developed a new network of support through their involvement in the Compassionate Friends group.

Assess what changes are causing you the most difficulties. What can you do about them? Assess the situations, times, and events that are challenging for you. Then you can decide how to adapt to these changes in the way that is best for you. For Lacy and Martin, mourning the death of their toddler, the most difficult times were in the early evening. They loved the ritual of putting their youngest child to sleep—hearing her prayers and tucking her in bed. Once they recognized that, they began to consciously develop other evening rituals with their two older adolescent children.

Assess your own strengths and weaknesses. How have you adapted to change and loss in the past? What did you do well? What are some of the problematic ways you have coped in the past that you might now want to avoid? Who can you count on to help?

Get help when needed. If the family is not functioning well after the death of a child, you may need to draw upon extended family, friends, or professionals. If you have other children, how well you function will have a major influence on how they cope with the loss. Your surviving children need what every child needs—love, support, consistency, and structure. If the intensity of your grief is impairing your ability to meet those needs, draw upon the strengths of others.

When Anna Lee died, her mother, a single parent, found it tough to cope simultaneously with her own grief and the demands of raising her two surviving children. Her sister moved in for a month to give the children the attention they needed while their mom struggled with her loss.

Recognize, too, that change adds stress to your life. Taking good care of yourself—eating nutritious food, getting adequate sleep and sufficient exercise—as well as doing whatever you can to manage stress, which prepares you to cope more effectively with your now changed world.

Give yourself the gift of time. Try to make interim solutions, rather than final ones. In this stressful time, you may not always think things through clearly. It might be better, for example, to put away your child's toys and belongings—if that is what you wish to do—rather than to immediately dispose of them or give them away. Later, you may be more attentive to the items you wish to retain.

Remembering Your Child

The end of grief is not the end of memory. Words like *closure* have little significance in grief. Even in death, you always retain a bond with your child. Time or death can never break that connection. That bond continues in many ways—in your memories, in the legacies that he or she left, in the spiritual connections and experiences that you have.

You always carry an "inner representation" of your child. This means that when a child dies, you will be constantly aware of the age the child would be now. You will recall that this is the year your child would graduate from school, have a bar mitzvah, or join Little League. This inner representation is natural—another example of the bond you retain with your child.

Memories themselves are natural, even unavoidable. You can no more control what you remember than what you feel. In fact, as the pain of your loss eases, your memories become more vivid and less painful. This is often one of the first positive signs in your journey with grief.

Memories are often comforting, bringing your child closer, if even fleetingly. They are an affirmation of the life and love you shared. Some memories can be painful, too, reminding you of tough or troubling times or difficult relationships. You may ruminate over certain memories, reviewing the illness or death, or even actions or words you regret, or actions you wish you had taken, or words you wish you had said. You also need to confront these painful memories. Only when you fully explore them can you truly understand them and find ways to release them. Brian struggled with one such memory. One of the first signs of Shay's brain tumor was that Shay—an excellent athlete—began to have difficulties with motor coordination. One day after Shay flubbed an easy catch in an important moment of a game, Brian barked at him to be more attentive, which caused Shay to cry. Troubled by this memory, Brian wrote a letter of apology to Shay that he read at Shay's anniversary carnival.

You will find it helpful to engage in activities that allow you to continue your bond with your child. Scrapbooks, photo albums, special events and rituals, even remembrances such as scholarships or contributions in the child's name are natural and helpful ways to reaffirm your child's continued presence in your life.

Some people may be uncomfortable with your grief and believe that any mention of your child—even years after the loss—can only upset you. This can deter you from sharing your memories and can lead to an intensification of your grief; you may feel that others are forgetting your child. It might be helpful to share this sentiment with others. One holiday dinner Marla shared with her family, "I find it so comforting when we share memories of Shay—even if I tear up—I never want us to forget him."

However, it is important that your memories are not so idealized, or the bond become so strong, that your other children feel they are always second to the child who died. Marla and Brian's daughter, Heather, read the vanity license plate they had made to memorialize Shay—"SHAY'S #1"—and asked if she or her other brother Scott were number two or three.

Rebuilding Faith

Sometimes your faith can offer comfort, or at least a sense of support, in your grief. In other cases, the death of a child can challenge your beliefs—making it difficult to comprehend how there can be a loving God or any fairness in the workings of the universe.

This can be the case even when your beliefs are not theistic or religious. Belinda and Greg both described themselves as agnostic, but in truth religion was unimportant in their lives. But they did believe that the world was benevolent and just, that if you worked hard, were ethical, and sought to treat others as you wished to be treated, things would go well. Then the death of their daughter, a delightful, deeply caring young woman who aspired to a medical career, from meningitis while she was away at college, deeply challenged that sense of a good world.

Jan described himself as a secular humanist. Core to his beliefs was an idea that each human had a divine spark that should be nurtured—in oneself and in others. Jan lived his beliefs. In addition to his work as a lawyer for an advocacy group, he regularly volunteered at a homeless shelter. Jan believed that work was redemptive. He would often employ individuals he met at the shelter to do odd jobs around his home—paying them a good wage and treating them, if the family was in the midst of a meal, as an honored guest. One of the men he befriended brutally raped and murdered Jan's adolescent daughter. Jan's comment when he came years later for counseling was that "I have come to terms with my daughter's death—I have yet to come to terms with all I believed."

One of the tasks of mourning is to rebuild faith or philosophies that have been challenged by loss. One of the biggest mistakes you can make during this period is to isolate yourself from your beliefs or your faith community. Find people within your community with whom you can discuss your faith struggles.

One bereaved mother shared that after her teenage son drowned on a family vacation, her minister met her plane on the family's return. All her anger and frustration poured out on him when she saw him as she exited the plane. "Don't you dare talk to me about a loving God," she fumed. He merely hugged her. "Right now," he added, "I am pretty angry with Him myself." She knew she had found someone who could be present with her in her faith struggle.

Sometimes it helps to read how others wrestled with their faith. Rabbi Harold Kushner wrote *When Bad Things Happen to Good People* as he struggled with the death of his young son. Such writings remind us that losses come to all, and that it is natural to feel as if we are at the bottom of a deep valley of grief, while at the same time hoping that we can go on and learn to cope.

Grieving as a Family

Effects on Marriage

The loss of a child not only affects you, it also affects your spouse. Yet that does not mean that you will grieve in the same way. We each grieve in our own way. You cannot and should not compare your reactions or responses to those of others. Differing experiences of grief have little to do with how much you loved or cared about your child.

The death of a child can add tension to the marital relationship, but it is a destructive myth that many couples divorce after the death of a child. *This myth is simply not true.*[4] The divorce rate in couples who have experienced a death is not higher than the rate in the general population. A child may have died, but the love that you shared for that child remains. The same skills—open communication, understanding, and mutual respect—that saw you through other relational crises can see you through this one as well.

As discussed earlier, people have different grieving styles. Some people are *intuitive grievers* who experience grief much as Marla—as waves of emotions—loneliness, sadness, anger, and guilt. Their expressions of grief will mirror these feelings—for example, crying uncontrollably at times. Their emotions are vivid—easy for others to see. Others know when these grievers are angry or sad.

On the other end of this continuum are *instrumental grievers* whose feelings tend to be more muted, or they are not as clearly accessible or evident to others, perhaps not even to the griever. This grief is experienced more in thoughts, or perhaps physically in the body. They may find it easier to express grief in what they do. For example, when his son died, Brian found solace in using his executive talents to create an annual memorial event in Shay's memory.

Some people are more in the middle of this continuum and find that their grieving style blends traits from both. Others, often at great difficulty, may try to act in ways different from their inclinations. For example, they may hide their emotions and tears to spare a partner.

Recognize and respect that your partner may grieve in different ways than you do. This does not mean your spouse loved your child less or more. It simply means that he or she is different. These differences can be strengths. Marla, for example, learned to appreciate the fact that her husband found solace from his grief in keeping active and assuming a more active role with their other children. This was especially meaningful to her since her grief often left her fatigued.

You may have to take responsibility to meet your own needs. The way you find it helpful to deal with grief may not be helpful to your spouse. Remember, for example, how Marla wished to attend a support group. Since Marla realized that she needed someone to attend with her, she asked a sister who also found it helpful to participate in the group.

Communicate your concerns. The dimensions of how you grieve may affect every aspect of your relationship—including your ability to relate to each other, your ways of supporting each other, even your level of intimacy. Sexual intimacy is an aspect of relationships that can change as a result of loss. For some, sexual activity is relational—a way to offer affection and support. Yet for others, it has a close association with procreation and may remind them of their loss. Stay open in discussing your sexual needs, feelings, and frustrations. While sexual relations are likely to change in the immediate aftermath of loss, most parents do rediscover a new equilibrium. It is important to talk about the ways that you cope as individuals, as a couple, and as a family.

Parenting and Grieving

You may have other children who will also grieve. Their grief may come out in many different ways—physically, emotionally, cognitively, behaviorally, and spiritually. Some reactions such as sadness or crying are recognizable as grief. Others, such as changes in behavior, acting out behaviors, or even changes in interests or grades may not be immediately seen as grief. As parents, you need to be attentive to the ways that your other children may be dealing with the loss. Again careful observation and open communication are essential. If any of the children begin to behave in ways that are destructive to themselves or others, counseling may be helpful.

After a loss, children need love, caring attention, and structure. Studies have shown that the best predictor of children's outcomes in grief is how well the family continues to function.[5] Yet it is extremely difficult to both parent and grieve at that same time. For some parents, the presence of other children is a lifeline—one that gives meaning even in this time of loss. For others, it is an additional burden, complicating their grief.[6] Sometimes the best thing to do for your children is to make sure you have the help you need to work well as a family. That help may mean counseling, or relatives or friends who can assist with your children as you cope with your loss.

Shay's twin brother Scott, for example, began to feel that he perpetually lived in Shay's shadow. He felt that every good achievement was attributed in some way to Shay, and he felt guilty that he did not seem sufficient to keep his parents' minds off his deceased twin. He even felt constraint from his parents in being allowed to move things around in the bedroom he once shared with Shay. Scott began to act out. In counseling he confessed his frustrations, and in family therapy, the therapist helped Marla and Brian realize they had crossed a line in their memorializing of Shay and were making their other children feel marginalized. They were able to acknowledge both Scott's and Heather's individuality and need for attention.

Even as you honor the memory of the child who has died, you should do so in a way that is sensitive to the ongoing needs of your other children.

Others' Grief for Your Child

Your child's death will affect not only your spouse and children but also other relatives and friends. Your parents have lost a grandchild; your siblings grieve the death of a niece or nephew. Neighbors, coaches, teachers, and friends all experience that loss. Their own ways of dealing with that loss may influence their own abilities to offer support. Some may be extremely supportive—sharing their own stories of your child and their grief. Others may find it too painful and withdraw.

Single Parents, Noncustodial Parents

If you are a single parent or noncustodial parent, the death of a child may be even more complicated. On one hand, you may be able to grieve alone—without attention to the way your spouse is dealing with the loss. Yet there are considerable disadvantages. If you are the custodial parent with children at home, you may have to parent alone. Your support systems may be more limited. In cases where the noncustodial parent is involved, increased conflict and blame over the death can arise. In other cases, the common loss may put other issues in deeper perspective, perhaps opening opportunities for mutual support. In any case, you need to be especially careful to take care of yourself and find support, whether in your own network of family and friends or in other resources such as counselors or support groups.

Transforming Loss

You had no choice about your child's death. You have no choice about your grief. That grief is the result of the attachment and love you felt for your child. You may always carry an empty space in your heart for that child.[7]

But you do have choices within your grief. You could choose to live your life in perpetual mourning for your child. Or, as difficult as it is and may seem right now, you can choose to live a now different life—but to live it fully, keeping alive the memories of your child and lessons that, however long or short your child's life was, you gleaned from your child. Living your life in that way will be a tribute to your child.

CHAPTER 7

When a Parent Dies

Jemal was never close to his dad. His earliest memories are of conflicts and arguments with his father. No matter how hard Jemal tried, he could not seem to please his father. His father expressed disappointment that Jemal never achieved the athletic prowess that his dad, an athlete himself, viewed as his birthright. Jemal's grades were solid Bs—not the higher grades his father expected. After Jemal's parents divorced, his father was absent more than present, and when he and Jemal were together they soon bickered. When Jemal chose a college out of state, he let his relationship with his father lapse. They would share some hurried time at Christmas but little beyond that. Even Jemal's wedding was a source of conflict. He invited his father and stepmother, but his father was angry that they were not officially recognized at the ceremony or reception.

When Jemal's father developed pancreatic cancer, Jemal made dutiful visits to the hospital and even provided some caregiving when his father returned home from hospice care, but they really didn't talk. His dad's last comment to Jemal criticized Jemal for naming his son "Jordan." "I guess he just needed one last shot—I even asked him what was wrong with the name and he just turned his head in disgust. Maybe he thought I should have named Jordan after him."

Despite this difficult relationship, Jemal was surprised by his own grief, and berates himself for not actively trying to repair the relationship in the waning years of his father's life.

When I first started as a grief counselor, I was surprised by how many adult children came to see me or joined a support group when a parent died. I had expected widows, bereaved parents, and even young children whose parent had died. But having had my own parents die, I am no longer surprised. Most people will have to face the deaths of parents. The death of a parent may be our first significant loss as an adult, so we may have no sense of grief or how to grieve.

Deaths of parents can bring their own difficulties and challenges. You may have to comfort or assist the surviving parent; your siblings; or, in the case of a parent-in-law, your spouse. You may have to support your own children even as you grieve. If, as in Jemal's case, your relationship with your parents was complicated, your grief may be complicated as well.

Parents always leave their legacies. Some are tangible, if there was a material or financial inheritance. However, far more important are the intangible inheritances—the habits, coping techniques, values, and beliefs that parents inevitably impart to their offspring. Some of these are positive and help us as we cope with our grief. Other legacies, such as Jemal's, may be liabilities—regrets or lowered self-esteem. Even though losing a parent is a near universal loss, we are never fully prepared for the effects a parent's death can have on us. We can be orphaned even as adults.

A Parent Dies

Chronic Illness, Caregiving, and Death

I am often asked whether it is easier to lose a parent after a long illness or a sudden event. I am supposed to know, but my answer is that both are miserable ways to lose a parent. My own dad died in hospice care of cancer. My mom died a decade later after falling down a flight of stairs—never regaining consciousness again.

My dad died at home after his earlier cancer recurred and metastasized to his liver. Approaching eighty, my dad initially was hopeful that chemotherapy might buy him a few more good years, as it had the first time. Within a few months, though, the goal of care became palliative and we arranged for home care through our local hospice. My mother, also near eighty years of age, was too frail to care for Dad. Fortunately for them, all three of us siblings lived close enough to share caregiving responsibilities.

Sometimes a sibling is involved in caregiving. This can create issues with siblings who feel they are unfairly burdened, or conflicts between the siblings directly involved in caregiving and those offering opinions from a distance. The dirty secret of caregiving is that not only is it difficult to offer, it is equally hard to accept. Few adults want to be dependent on others, especially their children, for the most intimate actions of bathing and toilet. Everyone experiences tensions in such situations.

In cases of slow decline, caregivers and adult children feel their lives are on hold. We are reluctant to make plans, not really knowing what the future holds. Some adult children are sandwiched between their responsibility for parents and other responsibilities such as jobs and family. For instance, I needed to negotiate my caregiving responsibilities with occupational duties and the needs of my adolescent son.

Caregiving is physically exhausting. Like many terminally ill patients, my dad was bedbound. Most nights he woke me up to ask me for a bedpan or some other help. Stress due to the extra work and the lack of sleep can create conflicts that subsequently generate feelings of guilt and regret. This, too, can be compounded when there are conflicts between caregivers.

My siblings and I were able to fulfill my dad's wish to die at home—in large part thanks to the help we received from the hospice. But many adult children face inevitable and necessary care transitions such as nursing home placement, which generate guilt. When I begin working with individuals struggling with caregiving, I often ask them to indicate when it might be too difficult to continue home care—to draw a line in the sand. I do this for three reasons. First, it helps them acknowledge that there may come a time when it is too difficult to offer care. Second, it assists them to clarify what situations may create insurmountable burdens. Finally, most of them go beyond whatever they initially believe to be the line, which gives a sense of satisfaction rather than failure.

I also want to emphasize that even if you do place a parent in a facility, you still remain caregivers. Your caregiving role now is one of advocacy.

Incontinence or immobility adds to the sense of caregiver burden, as does dementia. It can be difficult to see an individual with dementia as the person we once loved, or to retain a relationship or connection with the person who once was. The burdens of care are excessive and the joys are largely absent. There are no opportunities to reminisce about better days or even receive thanks for the endless toil. This was extremely difficult for Adriana. Her mother would often complain to Adriana and others that Adriana had not fed her when, in fact, Adriana had. Moreover, despite their once close relationship, Adriana's mom never called her by name or even seemed to acknowledge that she was her daughter.

While factors such as incontinence, dementia, and immobility add to a sense of caregiving burden, they are eclipsed by another factor—past relationships. This made caregiving difficult for Jemal. He deeply resented caring for his father, questioning why he should be taking time away from his family and his job for a father who, when he was present in his childhood, always berated him.

In addition to caregiving, you may also struggle in negotiations with physicians and other medical professionals, and medical institutions and insurance companies. This can be complicated when there is not a consensus between the patient, family, and medical staff on the goals of care. When my dad was in hospice care, the oncologist and radiologist both suggested another round of treatment. When I questioned the radiologist about how this would be palliative, the radiologist suggested that this might shrink some spinal tumors that were causing my father discomfort. We agreed. The oncologist could not really explain how another round of chemotherapy would offer any palliative benefit. His response was simply, "It is what I would do for my father." In the absence of any viable explanation, we opted for not doing it for ours. While my dad and family discussed and concurred with the choice, these types of negotiations, whether care decisions or end-of-life ethical quandaries such as withholding or withdrawing treatment, can create conflict and discord within families. They can also engender regrets even when you have done everything you could to make your parent comfortable and well cared for. All these situations also complicate our grief.

As you watch someone you love decline slowly, you may grieve each and every sense of personal diminishment that you witness—the inability to walk, the loss of consciousness, or lapses of memory. Each decline generates another loss and fresh grief. As death approaches, you may be torn by ambivalence—wishing a peaceful release, wanting your parent to return to what he or she once was, wishing to stay in the moment with the dying person, and simply wanting it to end so you can go on with your life. These mixed feelings, too, can complicate your grief.

There is not too much of a distinction between grief at a sudden death or grief at a death that comes after a chronic illness. Even in chronic illness a death can seem sudden or be sudden. Perhaps the final decline was much more rapid than expected. Many older parents have multiple chronic illnesses that make death difficult to predict. With a long, slow decline, we assume he or she will make it to Thanksgiving, a birthday, or when a relative is returning to home. Sometimes, however long the illness and predictable the death, we are simply not ready for our mother or father to die.

When a Parent Dies Suddenly

Sudden deaths occur from accidents, suicides, homicides, heart attacks, strokes, or other acute illnesses. Each cause can have complicating factors. Suicides can generate blame, guilt, shame, and stigma. Homicides are complicating factors in their violence and trauma. We may even experience secondary loss or vicarious trauma as we try to envision—or encounter intrusive imagery—of our parent's last moments. We may be angered or distressed by media accounts of the death, or be frustrated by the pace of investigation or by our experience with the criminal justice system. We may feel some of the same reactions if our parent died in an accident where death was caused by the actions of another, even unintentionally.

Sudden loss is likely to create a sense of shock, disbelief, and unreality that slowly diminishes as we journey with grief. It is always difficult to believe that someone who seemed so well the day before is now deceased. The nature of traumatic death also creates a sense of feeling of being unsafe—the world no longer seems predictable or secure. We may feel fearful and anxious. Our grief may also be complicated by unfinished business. We didn't get to say a good-bye. We may feel guilty about things that we said or left unsaid.

Even when death comes more suddenly, we still may struggle with varied ethical issues at life's end. When my mom died, she had been transported to the hospital unconscious after her fall. We hoped that once the swelling in her brain lessened, she would regain consciousness or even make a full recovery. She was placed on a respirator. After a few days, it became clearer that she was unlikely to recover. We struggled with whether to remove her from the respirator. We decided we would give her one more day. The sad blessing was that she died within hours of our promised decision.

The Effects of a Parent's Death

Our First Journey with Grief?

For many people, the death of a parent is our first experience with grief. The intensity of our reactions and their complexity often surprises us. We are often a jumble of feelings, experiencing many emotions simultaneously, such as sadness, loneliness, anxiety, jealousy, guilt, anger, and even perhaps a sense of relief. Even as an adult, you may feel that your world is emptier, less safe without your parent. Naturally, your relationship with your parent will be a big factor in your grief. For Nina, her mother was her best friend and confidante. They talked daily, many times. Nina depended on her mother for advice on everything—children, husband, cooking. Her mother's death left a great void in her life, a loneliness that even her husband and children could not fill. In other cases, such as Jemal's, the death of a parent removes any opportunity to resolve the complicated, ambivalent relationship that existed. In this instance, guilt and anger can prevail.

As with other losses, you first need to understand what the relationship meant to you, what you actually lost, so that you can identify and understand the emotions that you are experiencing. Then you can decide how best to deal with these emotions. Nina found that her loneliest moments were during the days when she was alone doing chores, so she began to call her sisters during this time and share memories of what their mother might have said about things going on in their lives. Jemal found it useful to share his reactions with a childhood friend, and he also found that a hard game of basketball often dissipated his anger.

You may have varied physical reactions such as emptiness in the stomach or aches and pains—these often accompany grief. You may find it difficult to concentrate or think straight. You may even reach out to your parent—for a moment, thinking he or she is still there for us. For months after her mom's death, Gerry found herself picking up the phone to ask her a question—even beginning to dial her mother—before remembering the loss all over again.

Your behaviors can change, too. Gerry found that at the oddest moments she would sometimes become tearful as she remembered her mom. You may have different spiritual reactions as well—perhaps a sense of comfort from your beliefs, while at other times you may feel alienated and doubtful.

You may be shocked at the length of the grieving process. Some people who have not experienced a significant loss before expect grief not to last much longer than the funeral. But any journey with grief may be long, with many ups and downs. On some days grief is intense, and on others you may function well. The smallest event—a call from a sibling or a peek at a photo—can create a surge of grief. Holidays may now be both different and difficult. You are journeying on unfamiliar ground.

Awareness of Mortality

The loss of a parent may sharpen your own awareness of mortality. By seven or eight years of age, we have learned that people die. We know what that means. We understand the nature of death—that it is universal, unpredictable, and inevitable. We comprehend that the dead do not function. We know it is irreversible. Even at a young age, we know something of the causes of death and have begun to explore beliefs about any afterlife.[1]

There is a wide gap, though, between knowing in the abstract that *people die* and personalizing it to knowing that *Someday, I will die*. Some of my professional work has been on just that—the awareness of personal mortality. For most of us, this sharpened and personal awareness of mortality begins sometime in midlife,[2] when four ideas generate this awareness. One is that we can no longer "double our age"—reminding us of the finiteness of life. When I am twenty-five, I can reasonably wonder what life will be like when I am fifty years old. But once I hit fifty, it becomes difficult to imagine life at one hundred!

A second is that we see our own aging. We become aware of the increasing limitations of age. There are things we no longer can do.

By forty, most people will need glasses. We recognize that we no longer have the energy we once had. Third, we may experience the deaths of friends—not from accidents or suicides but from disease—which increases our own sense of vulnerability.

Fourth, and perhaps the most important realization for the awareness of mortality, is that our parents now are more likely to die. As long as our parents live, we have a sense, however illusory, that we are safe. It is in the natural order of things that they pass first.

A friend of mine tells a story of a family funeral for the last of the parental generation. All the cousins noted that the only times they seemed to get together was at funerals, and they thought they ought to begin to schedule family reunions. At that moment his eight-year-old son piped up that the next funeral was going to be for "one of you guys."

This awareness of mortality has both positive and negative aspects. As we become aware of our mortality, our anxiety about death may increase. This may be one reason that when we are in midlife, we are likely to have higher death anxiety than when we are even older.[3] We may begin to more actively prepare for death—writing a will and advance directives. We may have increased concern about our health, and schedule annual physicals. We may revisit our spirituality, showing renewed concern about what occurs after death.

Some aspects of the awareness of mortality can enhance our lives. We may take stock of our relationships and appreciate the shortness of life, decide to nurture the relationships that we value and shed those that are toxic.

We may even find a renewed zest in life. For Jemal, the death of his father reinforced his desire to build a positive relationship with his son. Now that he realized his time was limited, Jemal stopped delaying experiences and activities that he wanted to share with his son.

The death of a parent then may very well change your orientation to death—and to life.

Changes in Relationships

Families are systems whether they are fully functional or not. The roles that family members play, the interactions between kin, and the ways they behave toward one another all fit together. When we remove one part—one member of the family—that system has to change and adjust. So when a parent dies, we may find that all the relationships within the family now are different.

Certainly your relationship with the surviving parent is likely to change. Your surviving parent has to adapt to the loss of a partner and may undergo many personal changes. Some might become more independent—finding strengths they never knew existed. Others may be crippled by the loss and have difficulty in grief. All of these changes affect you. You may become worried about how your surviving parent reacts to the loss and you want to keep an eye on him or her. Are they taking their medications? Have they lost significant weight or gained it? Are there signs of depression—does Mom get up and get dressed, or does she who was once meticulous now seem unkempt, or is the house untidy?

Sometimes the problem may be yours. Frank's mother, Geralyn, spent the last five years caring for his dad. She was a devoted caregiver, and Frank had deep respect for her commitment and dedication. Yet, within months after her husband died, Geralyn seemed to come alive in a way Frank had never seen. She became active in a group of seniors and took day and weekend trips. At her party for her seventy-fifth birthday, Frank felt anger that his mother seemed to be flirting with some of her male friends. While his siblings did not have any difficulty with it—even rejoicing in Mom's new life—Frank could not shake the feeling that his mother was disloyal to his dad's memory. In counseling, Frank realized that his image of how his mother should be—in some state of perpetual mourning—was not only unrealistic but unkind.

You may have to take on new roles with your parents. When my dad died, my sister took responsibility for paying the bills—a task

Dad had jealously guarded when he was alive. Others find that parents may become increasingly needy, calling for every small repair or minor problem. While you wish to help and to be there when you can, you also have to realize your own limits. If dependency needs are real, you need not do it alone. See what help is available within your own family as well as within community resources. You may even wish to seek the help of a professional such as a care manager, who can both assess the needs of an aging parent and connect you with the variety of services that are available.

You may find your relationship with a surviving parent becomes close. When my dad died, I loved to hear my mother's stories of their courtship—sentimental stories that would have embarrassed my dad while he lived. Dad was an excellent student and when they first started dating in high school, my mom feared that her new scholarly boyfriend would break up with her when he heard about the low grade she received in history. Dad found her crying. When he heard the reason, he simply laughed, kissed her, and told her that he did not care what her history grade was—after all, he did not want to study history with her; he wanted to make history with her. These stories gave me a new appreciation of both my parents and a new sense of closeness with my mom.

On the other hand, the loss of one parent may lead to an estrangement with the surviving parent. This can deeply complicate your loss as you find yourself dealing with not one loss but two. There can be a number of reasons for such an unfortunate estrangement. In some cases, the deceased parent may have served as a buffer, smoothing relations with the other parent. Amanda had that role. Her husband, Terrell, could be curt and judgmental, but Amanda could always reason with him—easing ruffled feathers with the children. When Amanda died, Terrell quickly alienated his kids.

In other cases, the stress of grief can exacerbate tensions and engender conflict. We each deal with grief in our own way even when we share the same loss. Sometimes the ways we cope may not make sense to, or may even conflict with, another person's perspective. Some of us, for example, may wish to avoid conversation while others seek to share memories. And however we cope with loss, grief is stressful. When we are stressed, it is easy to lash out at those near us. When a parent dies it often places new demands on and generates new issues for the children. These arising demands and issues can be a source of confrontation and estrangement.

Your relationships with your siblings may change as well. In some cases your shared grief and experiences may forge stronger relationships. In addition, shared responsibilities for caregiving of the surviving parent can foster communication and engender stronger relationships. Yet the same factors can increase conflicts. You may have different reactions and patterns than your siblings do, which may cause misunderstanding and miscommunication. Grief—even as you anticipate the loss—and caregiving are stressful, and it is easy in stressful situations to lash out at those closest to you. Caregivers may resent siblings who are perceived as critical or are not helping enough. Parents can be mediators—helping you negotiate your relationship with a sibling. When that parent dies, the common focus offered by the parent, and the role the parent played in mediating these conflicts, is no longer available. Typically, if the relationship with a sibling was generally good, it will remain so—perhaps even become closer. However, if it was poor prior to the death of a parent, the loss can increase conflict.

Other relationships may change as well when a parent dies. Your relationship with your spouse may now be different. The relationship may strengthen as you deal with your loss and find new appreciation in the support you received as you coped with loss. Or you may have a new commitment to your relationships and new priorities due to your emerging awareness of your own mortality. Jemal found that his relationship with his wife Alyssa became much stronger. Alyssa was supportive as Jemal shared with her his grief and his struggles with his father. She gained insight into Jemal and was touched by a sensitivity he had not shown so openly. Alyssa appreciated the renewed commitment he had to his own children so he would not repeat his own father's mistakes.

Sometimes the changes in the relationship may not be as positive.

The strains and stress of caring for a parent may create conflict as it becomes difficult to manage their needs as well as the needs of your spouse and children. While some spouses are supportive of their mate's grief, others may become impatient with your reactions and the intensity and duration of your grief, especially if they have not experienced loss or have a different pattern of reacting to loss. You may have some responsibility here as well—perhaps your anger about the loss or about the lack of support may make you short-tempered.

You may have lost a safety valve. It is not uncommon to vent to parents about the conflicts experienced with a spouse. Your parents may offer advice or sometimes just an opportunity to blow off steam safely. Without that counsel and that safe place to vent, your relationship with your partner may be affected.

Your own children's grief, as they deal with the loss of a grandparent, may be intense. The loss of the grandparent as a caregiver, and any mediating influence and advice he or she offered, can significantly change your interaction and relationship with your child.

Children can also resent the time and effort you spent caregiving for your parent. They may be ambivalent at the death—missing the grandparent but pleased to have parental attention again. Or they may become anxious as they try to understand your grief—frightened perhaps by their "strong" parent becoming tearful.

Some children grieve the absence of a meaningful relationship with a grandparent—perhaps due to physical distance or simply the poor relationship of the grandparent to the parent. Grandparents' relationships and access to their grandchildren are heavily influenced by their relationship with their adult child. When the parent-child relationship is poor, grandparents may have a limited or nonexistent relationship with their grandchild. Jemal's eldest son, for example, grieved the fact that he never really knew his grandfather.

Even relations with others—such as other kin or ordinary friends—can change. The death of a parent may loosen bonds with other members of your extended family. You may draw closer to friends you find supportive and more distant from those who seem to have little patience with you as you cope with your grief.

And, of course, some people may experience little change in any of their relationships. Your family and friends may be supportive as you expected and needed. Or your own resilience maintains stability in your relationships even as you cope with loss. For many people, the death of a parent is, however painful, an expected event. We may find that our work and family responsibilities both comfort and divert us from being overwhelmed by our grief.

Orphaned in Adulthood: The Death of Both Parents

A Developmental Push

The death of your second parent may create some additional issues. Some people may describe themselves as *adult orphans*—emphasizing that they are now parentless. Others may find such a label meaningless. The deaths of both parents, however, have some subtle and obvious effects. As long as your parents are alive, they continue to have roles in your lives. You remain, as oxymoronic as it sounds, adult children. You may look to them as sources of unconditional love and security. Their homes may remain your last refuge. They still may be your cheerleaders, vicariously proud of each achievement. You count on them for permission and advice. You may even depend on them for practical tasks—loans, child sitting, perhaps even pet care. Whenever I was stumped in trying to balance my checking account, I could always count on my dad—a financial whiz—to find the hidden error.

When your parents die it creates a *development push*.[4] We now become the eldest generation in the family. There is often no one to lean upon any longer. You take on new responsibilities as you become even more autonomous—perhaps more mature.

Parentless Parents, Motherless Daughters, Fatherless Sons

If you are not an adult orphan, you may very well be parentless parents, a motherless daughter, or a fatherless son.[5] Grandparents may play a significant role in the lives of their grandchildren and also have a vital role in your life as you parent.

Around one in ten grandparents is highly involved in raising grandchildren, offering free child care or sometimes obtaining temporary—or even permanent—custody. Other grandparents are significant support for their adult child, babysitting on occasion, picking up a sick child at school, subbing for parents at sports events or recitals, or simply offering respite from the ongoing demands of a young child. Even grandparents who live at a distance may still provide such service. For example, one mother would schedule her New York visits between her grandchild's school and camp. Others take the child on vacation or for an extended visit. Many might offer financial assistance, quietly picking up tuition or camp bills, or buying those special extras.

Beyond these tangible contributions of time and money, grandparents may offer considerable advice and validation—a powerful intangible asset that may be incredibly important as we struggle with our own demanding roles as parents. *Jack isn't walking yet; I'm worried.* Comments often calm with the simple wisdom of experience. *You did not walk till you were thirteen months—all children are different.* Whether your child is eleven months or eleven years, you count on your own parents for perspective.

You may count, too, on the presence of grandparents at significant milestones such as graduations from kindergarten or college. It is powerful to share those moments and feel the respect that flows between generations. There is something special about simply sharing the day-to-day triumphs and tragedies with someone who shares your love for your child.

It is tough, then, to be a parentless parent. It may affect you more than you sometimes even know or realize. Pavel experienced that. His dad died at the age of forty-seven when Pavel was a senior in college. As Pavel's daughter was approaching college graduation, Pavel began to have anxiety attacks. In counseling, Pavel realized that his own father's premature death haunted him—creating a lifelong but unacknowledged fear that he would never live to see his own children graduate.

Whatever the effect that a parent's death has on your own parenting, you need to understand and acknowledge it. Think about the ways parenting has now changed—in both very practical and emotional ways. Understanding those effects is the first step in adapting to the loss.

Share your thoughts with those around you—a simple comment that "Grandma would have loved this" may allow your own children to acknowledge and share their grief.

See if there is a way to fill voids. Is there anyone else in your life who can offer advice and counsel? Is there someone who would welcome the opportunity for involvement? That person cannot replace the bond now changed by death, but may help fill a critical empty space.

It is important to acknowledge that the role of every parent/grandparent is not always so positive, or the relationship so helpful. In situations where the relationships were more complicated, grief may be more complex as well. You may struggle with unresolved questions, continued resentments, or unfinished business. In such situations you may need to seek out counseling, or other forms of support, as you cope with this new loss.

Secondary Losses

The death of a parent or even both parents can generate either estrangement or a new closeness with other members of your family of origin. The death of both parents is likely to lead to a gradual fragmentation of your family of origin. Parents serve as a centering element in families. We come together to celebrate holidays, birthdays, and anniversaries. We communicate with our siblings as we negotiate our parents' needs—especially as they age. We gather together at their home.

When both parents die, there is a generational shift. It is a natural tendency to shift to the generations of family that we created. Our children and grandchildren now center on us—the eldest generation. When my mother—our last parent—died, my siblings and I recognized the normal shift in relationships. We lost a centering focus of our relationship—we no longer gather at our parental home for shared holidays or other occasions. We did two things to maintain our family's sense of identity and unity. We decided to have an annual family reunion on a Saturday close to our mom's birthday. Our children also decided to have occasional cousins' nights out every few months. Such efforts can hold at bay a sense of loss of our larger extended family being an inevitable casualty of parental death.

Inheritance and Legal Matters

The death of your second parent is likely the time when wills become probated and estates divided. A number of years ago, I decided to do some research on that issue. We often hear horror stories of inevitable conflicts that frequently follow painful ruptures of once close relationships. Instead my research indicated that the only real predictor of conflict was not the size of the estate, or the absence of a will, but rather the prior history of the family. Families who had close relationships and had demonstrated, in their past, the ability to resolve conflicts, divided estates with little difficulty. Those with a history of conflict found one more reason to fight.[6]

Two case anecdotes from the study illustrate this well. In the first, two brothers had fought their entire lives. Their mother died leaving an estate of around $10,000. At issue was $2,000 their mom had given to one of the brothers prior to her death. Was this a gift or a loan to her son? The difference was minuscule. Both brothers were financially stable. If it was a loan, one brother would receive $6,000, the other $4,000. If it was a gift, they inherit $5,000. They spent a collective total of $7,000 fighting it in court, yet each considered it money well spent.

The second case was very different. In this case the father died last—leaving assets of well over two million dollars to be divided among his seven children. He left no will. This was a family with a history of close ties and adept problem solving. At the request of the eldest child, all seven adult children gathered together in the family home. The eldest had posted newsprint throughout the dining room—noting their Dad's traditional gifts—$25,000 when each child or grandchild married, $50,000 when each child purchased their first home, and $10,000 each year for each grandchild's college expenses. The eldest son's newsprint indicated who had received these bequests and who was still "owed." He then suggested that these gifts be distributed and the remainder divided equally. As the eldest, he and his children had already received most of these funds. He asked for comments. Consensus quickly was reached supporting his thoughts, with two amendments—a certain amount of money should be set aside for the joint vacation their dad had always proposed, as well as a thousand dollars that should be reserved so they could all enjoy a dinner out that night.

The conclusion of my study was simple. Spend less time settling the estate; more time settling family.

Beyond the estate, is there an issue of dividing personal property? Who gets the piano or Dad's car or watch? We again found that well-functioning families developed procedures that caused little conflict. In some cases siblings took turns choosing, or kept a running tally of possible value to retain a sense of equity. In other cases, a trusted family friend or relative was asked to act as a mediator.

In the study, we asked one more question. Did family members feel a sense of guilt in financially benefiting from a parent's death? Most did not experience such guilt. They looked at any bequest as an expression of parental concern, a legacy, and the parent's final gift.

Complicated Relationships—Complicated Grief

Our relationships with our parents, however positive, certainly become more complicated as they age. Dr. Margaret Blenkner, a leading gerontologist (one who studies aging), coined the term *filial maturity* to describe the emerging relationship between adult children and their aging parents.[7] As parents age, we realize that they are not the awesome or awful powerful figures we once imagined them to be. We see them more as individuals with real needs, and we recognize that we may take increased responsibility for their care. Often this follows some form of crisis that drives that awareness home.

The moment I reached that state of filial maturity, I was a graduate student—home for a Christmas vacation. I admired my dad. He always seemed to have it together. He was a newspaper man, the circulation manager. Neighbors often asked him for assistance. Using the clout of his relationship with editors and reporters, he could often solve consumer issues or assist with other concerns. We lived in a two-family home with my sister and her family occupying the second floor. When my mom woke, she would go upstairs to assist my sister in getting her three daughters ready for school. One day we heard a great thump. When I came to investigate, I found my mother prone and unconscious at the bottom of the stairs. She quickly regained consciousness. My sister and I called for an ambulance but my dad was beside himself—panicked and anxious. I literally pushed him onto a chair and tried to calm him. That fall was not serious. We discovered that my mother had low blood sugar and simply had to eat a bit before tackling the stairs. I realized that my dad was not the strong, powerful figure that I always thought him to be. And I knew if anything ever happened to my mom, he would need a great deal of support.

Filial maturity captures the subtle changes that normally occur as parents age. We sometimes use the term *role reversal*. Yet that really does not capture the complex reality. Parents never become our children, even as we care for them. Dimensions of power and control still surface. There is a complexity and ambiguity even in the best relationships. For parents, it is difficult to be dependent on children, even as parents take pride and comfort in their child being there for them. As adult children we, too, may be ambivalent—proud to be responsible yet wishing we did not have the added tasks.

So even in the best situations, relationships with aging parents can be fraught with mixed feelings that can complicate your grief. Your grief will naturally be more complicated if your relationship with your parent was complicated. If the parent was abusive or absent, or if your relationship with that parent was difficult and conflictive, you may really struggle with your grief. It often helps to confront that ambivalence—perhaps in counseling. You may need to explore what you liked about the parent as well as what you did not like—what you miss or do not miss.

Sometimes it is the death of a parent, rather than your life together, that creates complications for your grief. Death—for example, by suicide—can cause numerous complications. You may feel guilty that you failed the parent. You may experience a sense of stigma and isolation, wondering if others are judging you—or your family—because of the manner of death. Homicides also generate complications. You resent the unwanted media attention or police investigation. The trial and sentence (or lack thereof) reopens your wounds.

While the loss of a parent may be your first entry into grief, many people find the strength to cope with this initial loss. In fact, as you reflect later on this loss, it may remind you of your strengths and your limitations as you adapt to later losses. And it reminds you of a central truth. Your parents left their mark on you—left you legacies, and perhaps liabilities—not only in their lives but also in their deaths.

CHAPTER 8

The Loss of a Sibling in Adult Life

"Everyone always asks me how his wife and kids are doing. No one ever asks how I am doing. I knew him longest—for forty-nine years, literally from the moment he was born," Camilla said. Her brother, Tony, died at forty-nine years of age from a sudden heart attack. The unexpected death devastated the family. Tony left three children, the oldest fourteen. His wife, Ann-Marie, was struggling financially as well as emotionally to raise the children alone. Camilla tried to be there for them, helping Ann-Marie and her nephews in every way she could.

Yet Camilla resented that her own sense of loss was ignored. Tony was her kid brother, born when Camilla was five years old. Soon after he was born, their mother developed multiple sclerosis. Camilla became, even at her young age, a second mother to Tony. She never resented it. She used to joke that other girls had dolls that talked, walked, or wet, but she had the real thing. The others had Baby Alive (a hot toy at the time), but she had a live baby.

Camilla and Tony were very close throughout their lives. In fact, she was even the "best man" at Tony's wedding. Camilla married and divorced within a few years, without having kids. That was fine with her. She was focused on her career as a teacher and often wondered if, after a day working with second graders, she would even have any patience left for her own kids if she had them. Her nephews were surrogate grandchildren and she enjoyed the freedom to do things with them when she wanted. She was close to her sister-in-law, Ann-Marie, and always welcome in their home before and since Tony died.

It's been two years since Tony died, but Camilla is ambivalent about Ann-Marie's growing relationship with another man, Bill. Camilla likes Bill, a young widower whom Ann-Marie met in a support group. The kids like him as well. Yet Camilla worries that Bill will somehow displace Tony—especially with her nephew Phil, who was only four when Tony died.

Mostly though, Camilla feels that no one acknowledges her ongoing grief or concerns. She feels very much alone.

The Sibling Bond

Had Camilla been fourteen years old and Tony nine, everyone would have acknowledged her loss. School guidance counselors would likely be monitoring her grades. Her counselor might recommend a therapist or suggest a grief group. She might attend a summer grief camp where she could share her story with others her age. As an adult, however, Camilla grieves pretty much alone, even after forty-nine years of a complex and multilayered relationship: Tony was to Camilla brother and child, peer and protector.

You likely will know your siblings longer and more intimately than anyone else in your lives. They will probably be there after your parents die. You know them before you meet your spouses or have children. Growing up with them, you learned (and likely exploited) all their flaws. In crises, you leaned on their strengths.

The sibling relationship is unique—more equal than the often complicated dynamics that exist between generations. You are kin but without all the hierarchy. Camilla illustrates that: while she was often in a caregiving role to her younger brother, they were also peers. They giggled together and shared secrets. Though they were close, there were times they fought. Camilla has a small scar just over her right ankle—attesting to a time when her brother, then eight years old, plowed his snow sled into her, frustrated that Camilla kept throwing snow on him when he would not give her a turn on the sled.

Siblings are part of our own identity. We develop, in part, by our place in the family—eldest, youngest, or in the middle. The sexes of siblings, the years between us—whether two or ten—affects how we develop. To Tony, being Camilla's kid brother had its perks. The older kids who had a crush on his sister often let him join their games. He often joked about how their treatment not only gave him special status among his friends but bestowed a confidence that served him well as an adult.

You share distinctive perceptions and memories with siblings, like the smell of a vacation cabin or grandma's cinnamon toast or the time the car broke down in the middle of a blizzard. You even test your memories with your siblings—inquiring whether events occurred as you recall them. When a sibling dies there may be no one to share or validate those moments. Often these memories affirm the bond you share.

I can ease my older sister's stress at any moment by asking her if she had a "BM" today, as an aunt would do when caring for us one summer while our mother and father coped with a medical crisis. For my adolescent sister, it was always an extraordinarily embarrassing moment. She feared that our aunt would dose us with a nasty tonic if we answered no. My question always brings us to a time in our life when we felt close but also alone. It reinforces our sense of solidarity. Many siblings share such stories.

Complications of Losing a Sibling

Disenfranchised Grief

When a sibling dies when you are an adult, few acknowledge your loss. You are lower on what sociologists Patricia Robson and Tony Walter call "the hierarchy of grief."[1] If your sibling is married or partnered, that individual and any children have first claim to support. If your parents are alive, their grief is also recognized.

Your grief, however, is disenfranchised. You are expected to put aside any grief and offer support to the surviving spouse, your nephews and nieces, and your parents. You are unlikely to get sympathy cards.

This disenfranchisement may be especially profound if the sibling was a half- or stepsibling. Here the perception that the individual wasn't "really" your brother or sister can further diminish support. Yet the fact may be—however the relationship might be described—the individual was a brother or sister, companion, and friend to you.

You simply need to enfranchise yourself. In losing a sibling, you experience many secondary losses beyond the loss of perhaps your longest-lasting relationship. Now there is no one to share those special memories or to check your perceptions. The loss of a sibling, too, may change the feel of holidays or family events. It may be another reminder that your family is diminishing, reminding you of your own mortality. You have a right—and need—to recognize your own grief. And you may need to do things that allow you to express that grief. Camilla, for example, created her own simple ritual. Every year on Tony's birthday she lights a candle in the church where they were both baptized. She then has a quiet, solitary dinner at a little pizzeria—a special place from their childhood.

If you need support, the Compassionate Friends can offer sibling support groups for adults. GriefNet provides an Internet support group.

Sibling Relationships

Certainly one of the factors that will affect your grief reactions is the relationship you have with your sibling. Dr. Helen Rosen[2] describes two different dimensions of sibling relationships. One dimension is a social dimension—how much siblings interact with one another. This would range from *close*—meaning very frequent interaction—to *distant,* where siblings rarely have contact. The other dimension is more of an emotional one. Here relationships range from very *warm* ties between siblings, characterized by shared intimate relationships, to ties described as *hostile*—estranged or highly conflicted.

Camilla and Tony's relationship could be described as warm and close. They were strongly bonded, and they interacted frequently. They deeply loved each other and enjoyed each other's company. Tony's family was Camilla's family.

A close and hostile relationship would be one where siblings interact frequently but are often in conflict. That was the relationship of Landon and Latham. Only two years separated them, but they were often referred to as "battling brothers." The common physical confrontations of their youth became more verbal as they aged, but their conflicts never ceased. Every family event or discussion was tense as other family members tried to keep peace between the two.

Candace and Tanya's relationship was hostile and distant. Ever since an argument in young adulthood, they mostly avoided each other. Though they each try to be civil to each other at rare family gatherings, there is tension there as well.

Siblings can be warm and distant as well. Prior to his sister Diane's death Dennis had a good relationship with her, but life had taken them in very different directions. Diane was married to a consulate officer posted in Asia. Dennis is a widower raising two young children—juggling work with parenting. He thinks of his sister often and misses their visits and phone calls.

When you lose someone who is physically distant but very important to you, your strong attachment might very well be disenfranchised by others who note how little you actually saw each other.

If you have an extremely close and warm relationship like Tony and Camilla, you will have lost one of your closest and strongest attachments. If your relation is very hostile—whether close or distant—your grief may be complicated by the deep ambivalence and regrets that you feel at the time of the death. In such cases, you may be troubled by unfinished business—things you are sorry you said or did not say, or did or did not do prior to your sibling's death. You may have regrets, too, in a close but distant relationship—perhaps feeling you could have made greater efforts in bridging that distance.

When a Twin Dies[3]

In middle age, the death of a twin is a unique form of sibling loss. Narida came to me for counseling after the death of her sister—her identical twin. While she spoke about the loss of her long, intense, and very special relationship with her beloved twin, she said something that still sticks in my mind. *When I looked into the casket—it was like looking in a mirror.* She still has nightmares.

There are many different ways that twins can relate to each other. Some twins can relate almost as a single unit. When they were growing up, they may have dressed identically, were in the same classes, and even shared friends. They may finish each other's sentences. Their relationships can be close and warm—intensely so. Narida even spoke of the mystical connections they shared. *Sometimes I felt I could even feel her pain. The moment she died in the hospital, I actually suddenly woke—later I found it was right at the time she died.* In such relationships, the grief can be intense. Narida felt that she lost part of herself, and believed that the closeness and the intensity of the bond she shared with her sister could never be replaced.

Others may have a more interdependent relationship. While not as profoundly close, such twins grow up counting on each other. Their twin is the closest friend and a companion in many activities. These twins count on each other for advice and assistance. Each one's strengths compensates for any weakness of the other.

Other twins may define themselves by their differences. *He's the athlete, while I am the student*. Here it is the difference that defines. *She is the well-behaved one, while I am the rebel.* These twins may experience some ambivalence about being a twin, as well as ambivalence in the relationship with their twin. This ambivalence can also exist when twins have a highly competitive relationship, seeking to constantly surpass the other in any shared attribute or activity. Their grief can be complicated by that ambivalence, as well as by guilt over the nature of the relationship.

Some twins downplay the fact of twinship, the relationship no more or less special than any sibling relationship. As one twin, Nick, shared, *Frankie and I really don't stress the fact that we are twins. We are simply brothers who share the same birthday.*

The death of a twin can create unique issues in grief. You may feel you can never replace that unique bond and intangible, secondary losses as well. Even though Narida and her twin were both married and lived a few miles from each other, they would regularly share their wardrobes. Nick would miss the shared birthday celebrations—a tradition from childhood that they continued even after they began their own families.

The death of a twin also can reaffirm our own sense of mortality. Identical twins share the same genes, so anxiety about your own health and mortality can rise significantly when your twin dies. Narida's sister's death from cervical cancer made her much more conscious of her own health. She now regularly schedules semiannual medical examinations and regular cancer screenings.

While the grief of losing a twin can be intense, it may also be tempered by the deep appreciation you have for the relationship. Both Nick and Narida could acknowledge the value of their twin. Still, twins who did have strong attachments besides their twin generally do better than those who did not.[4] And while groups such as the Compassionate Friends offer sibling groups that might be of benefit, there is a specialized support group—Twinless Twins (twinlesstwins.org)—for a twin surviving such a unique loss.

The Invisible Hand: The Death of a Sibling We Never Knew

Eddy's brother died two years before he was born. Though he never knew his brother, he lived under his shadow. He was always being compared to his brother, and his parents were far more protective because of his brother's death. Eddy even wondered if he were a replacement or therapy child—a child who might never have been born if not for his brother's death, and whose purpose was to distract his parents from their grief.

You can be affected by the death of a sibling you never even knew—perhaps one who died before you were born, or while you were still in your infancy, or even a neonatal loss that your parents experienced when you were a child. Such deaths can affect you in many ways. First, you may grow up in families characterized by a constant sorrow—a perpetually depressed mood. For Eddy, the holidays seemed joyless. *We would go through the motions—gifts, stockings, and dinner—but there seemed to be no excitement. It was more: Let's get this over with as soon as we can. I am not sure that my parents ever enjoyed a holiday once Kevin died.*

Having faced the loss of one child, parents may also have increased anxiety about any surviving children. Because Eddy's brother had died in a freak accident at a water park, Eddy never went to an amusement park until he was an adolescent. As a young boy, he was never allowed to go to a pool or an amusement park whether on a school trip or with friends or even relatives. He was not permitted to go out for any sports, such as football, that his parents thought dangerous. He was usually under the watchful eye of a parent. As an adult, Eddy feels that his upbringing hampered his sense of self-confidence.

You may be compared to an idealized version of the deceased child. To Eddy that was an issue as well. *The priest comforted my mother by telling her Kevin was now part of the communion of saints. It was hard to grow up constantly compared to St. Kevin—who never really lived long enough to struggle with school or deal with the stuff of adolescence.* You may wish you knew this person who looms—though absent—so large in your life. Here, too, your grief can be disenfranchised by others—or yourself. Such losses can and do affect you, and you may need to mourn them.[5]

Coping with the Death of a Sibling as an Adult

Acknowledging Your Loss

Perhaps the very first task in dealing with the loss of a brother or sister is simply acknowledging that this is your loss. That may seem unnecessary—yet with all the attention focused on others such as partners, children, even your parents—it can be important so that you really understand the impact of this loss on yourself. You may have lost the longest relationship in your life.

Your family structures, relationships, and traditions may also change. You may have lost a close confidant—perhaps the only one who could verify facts of your childhood and memory. If your parents are still living, you may find your role in their lives is now changed. You may have to take on tasks once done by your sibling. You may find your parents are less available to you and your own children as they cope with their own grief. They may become more worried and anxious about you and other surviving children—even though you are now an adult—constantly questioning your health, lifestyle choices, or activities.

Your relationships with in-laws, nieces, and nephews may be different. You may have to adapt to new people in the lives of your brother's or sister's children. Here it may be important to respect the fact that their needs are different from yours. As Ann-Marie began to develop a serious relationship with Bill, Camilla recognized her own ambivalence and acknowledged Ann-Marie's right to form a new relationship, and the need of her nephews for a strong male influence in their lives. Camilla also wondered how she would fit in with this now changed family. Would she still be a welcome guest? Would she retain her relationship with her nephews? Eventually, Ann-Marie and Camilla were able to sit down and share their perspectives. Ann-Marie assured Camilla that her growing love for

Bill did not mean that Tony was loved any less, never wanting her children to forget their dad, and emphasized the important role that Aunt Camilla needed to have in the family. With Tony's parents deceased, only Aunt Camilla could share the stories of Tony's childhood with his children. Reassured, Camilla was once again proud to play a prominent role in Ann-Marie and Bill's wedding—this time as Ann-Marie's matron of honor.

Dealing with the Emotions of Grief

As with any loss, dealing with the death of a brother or sister can arouse strong and conflicting emotions. If your relationship on the whole was warm, you'll likely feel deep sadness, loneliness, and perhaps even anger at being abandoned by a lifelong companion. In more distant or hostile relationships, grief may be haunted by guilt—and perhaps anger that your brother or sister died leaving you with this burden. You may find yourself dealing with emotional residue from your childhood that surfaces yet again, such as jealousy or resentment. Jasmine always felt her brother, Trevor, was the favored child. Though the two were close and Jasmine really loved and admired her older brother, there were times that she had to admit to feelings of jealousy and resentment. Whatever he did seemed to eclipse whatever she accomplished. Her high school graduation, for example, paled next to his college graduation—only a week apart. Her wedding seemed overshadowed by Trevor's car accident. She ruefully noted he even died just as her first grandchild was being born. As Jasmine grieved Trevor's death, once again those same, familiar feelings of jealousy, anger, guilt, and resentment popped up.

Grief can be intense also when siblings die from self-destructive causes such as drug abuse, suicide, or other such actions. Here grief can be colored by feelings of shame, guilt, and anger. You may be angry at your sibling for the ways he or she lived as well as for the cause of the death. You may be ashamed of the circumstances or story and reluctant to share it with others, limiting your reservoir of support. You may even have a fear that the seed of destruction in your sibling's life will manifest itself in another brother or sister, in your or their children, or even in yourself.

You will want to name and confront whatever emotions you experience when you lose a brother or sister. Once you name them, you can find ways to examine and resolve these feelings. Jasmine needed to explore her ambivalence toward her older brother and to confront all the times he seemed to "steal her show," as she described it. Once she did so in counseling, she was able to find ways to process that ambivalence—in her case, writing a letter to her deceased brother.

Creating Rituals

Since the grief of siblings can be disenfranchised, and any role in the rituals surrounding the death can be minimal, you may wish to consider creating your own ritual. Dennis did this when his sister died. They had a close but distant relationship, since Diane and her husband were posted in Asia with the consular service. After Diane died from an infection, her funeral was in Washington, but Dennis held a memorial service in their hometown so their friends could attend and mourn his sister, too.

In addition to rituals around the time of death, such as memorial services or anniversary services, you may need to create your own personal rituals. These can be simple yet powerful; we will discuss them in chapter 12. Once Jasmine had written her letter, she decided to read it to Trevor by his gravestone. In the presence of her husband and an old friend, alternately crying and laughing, she read her letter to Trevor—reminding him that he was a good brother who had the incredibly annoying habit of upstaging, by design or happenstance, every major event in her life. She wondered how he would do it now that he had died—yet was confident he would find a way.

Remembering Your Brother or Sister

Your lifelong bond with your brother or sister—for better or worse—continues after death. They never cease being part of your life. The question is not whether you will remember them, but how and when you will choose to recall them. Family holidays, for example, offer an opportunity to name the elephant in the room and to acknowledge that someone who was so much a part of your life and other lives is now missing. It can be as simple as a toast that allows the name to be spoken, stories to be shared, and the cloud of silence to be lifted.

Camilla is putting together photo albums of Tony, encompassing his growth from a newborn baby till his death. She originally had plans to make three—one for each of his children. At Ann-Marie's suggestion she is now making five—including one for Ann-Marie and one for herself.

Our families form the strongest bonds in our lives, and when those bonds are severed, our grief can be profound. Brothers and sisters, whether full, step, or half, play a unique role in your life. Depending on your place in the family order, they may have always been there. They may have been friend and companion, babysitter or playmate, or even teaser and tormenter—sometimes all in the same day. You shared a home, a parent or parents, memories, and experiences. You have been part of one another's lives. You need to mourn their deaths.

PART 3

The Unacknowledged Losses of Life: Disenfranchised Grief

As devastating as the loss of a spouse (or of a child, parent, or sibling, at least in childhood) is, these losses are at least typically recognized and supported by others. Disenfranchised losses are not openly acknowledged, socially sanctioned, or publicly shared. They create a paradox. We experience loss, but we come to believe we do not have the right to grieve that loss. The very nature of these losses can complicate grief, but the usual sources of support are lacking. Persons with disenfranchised grief frequently suffer in silence, not knowing the true cause of their reactions, having no context in which to understand them, and receiving little support or recognition. It is critical to recognize your grief, even if it is disenfranchised, for only by acknowledging your own grief can you better cope with life's losses and even grow from them.

Even years after a bitter divorce, Jill still grieves the death of her ex-husband, who just died. Married for nearly fifteen years before they separated, Jill is surprised not only by her own grief but also by her children's responses. She resents her young son's profound sense of grief, since the boy's dad often canceled plans and visitations. She is equally concerned by her adolescent daughter's seeming indifference to the death. Friends seem unsupportive—questioning why she would grieve "such a creep." To Jill, despite their negative history, he was the one love of her life and the father of her children.

Often losses like Jill's are unrecognized and unsupported by other members of society, sometimes even by those experiencing them. While the concept of disenfranchised grief has been part of the professional literature for the past twenty years, it has rarely moved beyond specialists in the field.

In chapter 8, we noted that Camilla's grief over losing her brother was disenfranchised. If she had been twelve years old, more people would have understood her grief in losing a brother. But because she is an adult, her brother's wife and children get more attention. Few fully recognize the impact of the grief resulting from the loss of an adult sibling.

The loss of a job and source of identity can also create profound, disenfranchised grief. Not only is it hard for family and friends—in addition to the unemployed person—to recognize job loss as a source of real grief, but the pain experienced over this loss can be difficult to understand as a manifestation of grief.

Since I first introduced the concept of disenfranchised grief in 1989,[1] I have been amazed by its resonance. Often I receive letters from people who credit me for "naming" their grief. One, for example, was from a mother whose happy-go-lucky son lost a leg in a car crash after a night of drinking and driving. The son recovered from this crash and became a new person. Newly motivated to become a physical therapist, he worked hard in school and his grades rose from barely getting by to dean's list honors. He became active in SADD (Students Against Drunk Driving), speaking to local high school students with great conviction and credibility. Yet even as his mother acknowledged her pride, she also confessed her grief that the son she once knew never emerged from that collision.

During a speaking tour of Australia, I was scheduled for an interview with a major radio station in Sydney with the local shock jock. My hosts warned me that he would ridicule my ideas and me. Instead, we had an intense conversation about his most recent loss—the suicide of an ex-girlfriend. He stated on air that the idea of disenfranchised grief was the only one that spoke sense to him.

In the next three chapters, I explore various types of disenfranchised grief, from the deaths of individuals whom you may not know to losses other than death that generate grief reactions. It's important to remember that sometimes we disenfranchise whole categories of grievers—whether because of their age, characteristics, or the ways they grieve. All of these chapters retain one basic goal—to enfranchise the disenfranchised—including perhaps you.

CHAPTER 9

Broken Bonds: When Relationships Are Not Recognized

Earlier we met Steve, who is grieving the death of the love of his life. For the past three years he has had a clandestine love affair with a coworker, Henry, who had yet to emerge from the closet when he suddenly passed away. Steve wonders if the secrecy of the relationship, and the stress of Henry's hidden sexuality, contributed to Henry's heart attack.

No one knows about the relationship—an explicit promise when the affair began. Steve readily agreed. Steve, too, is partially closeted—out only to a few siblings, close friends, and some members of the local gay community. The state where they reside had not legalized same-sex marriage. Moreover the company where they work discouraged romantic relationships between employees, whether gay or straight. Steve attended the funeral with some coworkers who could not wait to leave the wake for a local bar. Steve bears his deep sense of loss alone.

Steve is experiencing chronic disabling grief. For him, levels of distress remain high. The idea that he may feel better is remote, and it seems almost disloyal to Henry's memory. He finds it difficult to work since the workplace is so full of memories.

Steve's grief is disenfranchised. While Steve has experienced a deeply felt loss, his own discomfort with his sexuality, as well as his promise to Henry to keep their relationship secret, inhibits his ability to seek or receive support from others. Though he had a prominent role in Henry's life, his role in the funeral rituals and memorials was minimal.

The Nature of Disenfranchised Grief

Every society has grieving rules. These are norms or expectations of how we are expected to grieve and how long we can grieve, and also whom and what we can grieve. As long as we stay within these rules, we can expect social support. Basically, we can grieve the deaths of family members. With disenfranchised grief, you may be deprived of the social recognition, comfort, and support that a ritual such as a funeral or memorial service can offer. In these cases, there are no sympathy cards to console you. Even though you grieve a loss, you have no perceived right to mourn that loss.

Often, social rules about grief are explicitly stated in regulations and laws that define who has control of the deceased's body or funeral rituals and in company policies on bereavement leave. The funeral becomes the vehicle by which grief is acknowledged and sanctioned, and where support is extended. The primacy of a family at the funeral reaffirms that these survivors have experienced a loss, and that their subsequent grief needs sanction, acknowledgment, and support. The rite of the funeral publicly testifies to the right to grieve.

We may be granted days off for bereavement leave for the deaths of family members—spouses, children, parents, or siblings. Yet we are given no days off for other deaths—such as the death of a best friend, an ex-spouse, or an animal companion. Nor are we allowed time off for bereavement leave for other losses that might cause us grief, such as a painful divorce or any other significant transition in our life.

We live in intimate networks that include both kin and non-kin. We form attachments to fellow humans, animals, and even to places and things. We experience a wide range of losses—deaths, separations, divorces, and other changes or transitions. When these attachments are severed by death or any other separation, we feel their loss deeply. Yet only kin have legal standing. And in the ways we grieve, we may experience, express, and adapt to loss in ways inconsistent with the expectations of others. Other people may disenfranchise our grief—failing to acknowledge or even understand our loss and grief, or to offer support.

It is not only society that abides by these rules. Grief therapist Jeffrey Kauffman[1] suggests that we ourselves can internalize or accept and believe these grieving rules. So we can disenfranchise ourselves—believing the grief we are experiencing is inappropriate, repressing our grief or converting it to feelings of guilt or shame. Steve is an example of just such a situation. Not at peace with his own sexual orientation or open in his relationship with Henry, he can share his grief only with a few trusted friends and family.

Societies value equality and rationality—meaning any policies should apply equitably to all. The grieving rules reflect that. Extending grieving roles to non-death situations or to non-kin would create organizational burdens. Workplaces might be forced to define "levels of friendship" or "types of loss." They might be required to broaden the concept of bereavement leave, at considerable cost. Acknowledging the death of kin alone makes organizational sense. It recognizes the grief of kin when a family member dies, at least symbolically. By limiting the acknowledgment of loss to family members it avoids confusion and potential abuse, affirming a single standard. These policies then serve to reflect and project societal recognition and support, again reaffirming and sanctioning familial relationship.

In a diverse society, even losses that are disenfranchised by society as a whole may be acknowledged within a smaller subculture. For example, the death of a gay lover may not be fully recognized by family or coworkers, but the grieving lover may be recognized and supported within the gay community. In Hispanic and other cultures the role of a godparent is acknowledged as important, and the loss of a godchild or godparent is acknowledged as a source of grief. What is disenfranchised in one culture may be supported in another.

Contexts of Disenfranchised Grief— Unrecognized Relationships

One of the most significant forms of disenfranchised grief occurs when our relationship with the person who died is not recognized or supported by others. Friends and family may validate intense and intimate relationships that exist outside of the marriage bond. Partners, lovers, or live-ins, gay or straight, and individuals in extramarital relationships, share attachments that may not be acknowledged or even condoned by the larger society. In the case of a partner's death—especially if the relationship is cloaked in secrecy—our ability to publicly grieve and play a role in important rituals like funerals, or even have access to bereavement leave, can be severely limited, which can stunt our ability to process our grief reactions.

Even now that same-sex marriage is legal in the United States, and levels of acceptance remain high, support and acknowledgment of grief may be limited. A same-sex couple I knew had been together for over thirty years and married as soon as it was legal in New York. One partner died in the past month. I searched locally and unsuccessfully for an appropriate sympathy card that explicitly acknowledged their relationship, but finally found one online. Later when I visited the surviving spouse, she noted the sensitivity of all their friends—and ruefully joked that she had received multiple copies of what she deemed to be the only two cards available.

We also retain strong bonds with friends, perhaps since childhood, but our own grief is often subordinated to that of their family.

We may work with a person for decades, daily sharing lunch or coffee, but after his or her death, receive little acknowledgment of that unique bond. If the death occurred after retirement, we might not read or hear about it until any rituals are long over.

Some women who choose to have an abortion experience grief. Others do not. A number of factors are associated with the risk of an intense grief reaction, including having multiple abortions; having a first abortion; ambivalence about abortion; feeling constrained by age, circumstances, or finances; or seeing the pregnancy as a failed solution to a problem (e.g., *He will marry me if I have his child*).[2] Personal characteristics also play a part. For example, a woman from a faith community that opposes abortion can have an agonizing faith struggle, although not inevitably. The decision to abort may also generate grief in fathers and prospective grandparents.

If you or someone you know is experiencing such a loss, validate rather than discount these feelings of grief. It may help to explore with a counselor or trusted confidant the pregnancy and the decision to abort. You may want to review the process of abortion—exploring what was helpful and what was not. Examine any unresolved spiritual issues or participate in a ritual. Drs. Dennis Klass and Amy Heath[3] note the Japanese have a shrine for aborted fetuses that allows a healing ritual for mothers to reconcile with their unborn. You may need to create your own ritual.

Another important, close relationship that is seldom publicly acknowledged is that between counselors/therapists and their clients, which can be intense. As a counselor, I have often found out, sometimes inadvertently, of a present or past client's death. The ethics of confidentiality keeps me from acknowledging the relationship or attending any rituals. While I have arranged for a colleague to contact my patients should I die suddenly (documented in an envelope to remain sealed until my death), I expect my clients would face the same quandaries. Even if they are informed of the death prior to any rituals, should they attend? How will they describe their relationship? Is there anyone who knows they are in counseling with whom they can share their sense of loss?

We may grieve relationships that existed in the past and mourn the death of an ex-boyfriend, ex-girlfriend, or ex-spouse. Carmen had been married nearly twenty-five years to Antonio, and they were planning a silver-anniversary cruise. When she found him in bed with a neighbor they went through an acrimonious divorce, but when he died two years later after an illness, she still grieved his passing. Few of her friends understood her grief. Some friends even ventured that his death was a sweet revenge. Before his illness, Carmen and Antonio had avoided each other. Any contact was through attorneys. When he was ill, Carmen decided to visit, but it was awkward visiting him at the hospital. She found little support as she struggled with her ambivalence and grief in the aftermath of that death. Carmen had to take vacation days to attend the funeral. Her workplace bereavement policies offered leave for present spouses but not ex-spouses.

We mourn the losses of celebrities and other public figures we never knew, as witnessed by the throngs who grieved the deaths of Michael Jackson, Nelson Mandela, Princess Diana, and Elvis Presley. In an increasingly connected online world, we can become attached to everyday people we have never even met physically. It is not unusual to develop strong ties with persons we interact with primarily—even exclusively—online in chat rooms or in multiplayer or online games. Chris was a young adult dying of muscular dystrophy. Now bed-bound, he loved to participate in the multiplayer, online game World of Warcraft, in which players take on avatars, join different tribes, and vicariously engage in war and conquest. The more time one invests in the game, the more power generally accrues to the avatar. Chris chose the role of a wizard he named Toxik. Since Chris had little he could do but play, his avatar Toxik became more powerful even as Chris continued to weaken physically. At his death, he instructed a brother to inform the players in this game. After his brother did so, the varied tribes called a truce to have a funeral for Toxik. This online event was remarkable: various players remarked on the person Chris and his avatar Toxik. The comments of one character, a dwarf, captured this spirit. "Toxik," he noted, "was my sworn enemy—but Chris was always a good friend, always willing to help you with technical issues in the game."[4]

The loss of an animal companion, a pet, can be a source of great grief. Sometimes that loss can be especially complicated when we feel compelled to end the animal's suffering with euthanasia. Here we may experience guilt and regret as a component of our grief.

In many cases, the loss of an animal may be a child's first experience of loss. Children generally are very resilient, but some might be more at risk for grief that can be disenfranchised.[5] For an older woman, a widow, like Eleanor, her dog plays many roles in her life—companion, protector, even fitness coach. As Eleanor shops for her dog's food or walks him, she frequently finds herself in conversation with other dog owners. Her dog motivates her, giving her a reason to rise every morning. A pet may even have a prior connection to an earlier loss. For Eleanor her dog connects her to her husband Eric, who gave her the dog one Christmas. She realizes that the eventual pain of losing him may not be acknowledged, and may even be ridiculed, by others.

For some people, an animal is somewhat of a surrogate child. A colleague and his wife, who chose to be childless, send family picture Christmas cards each year that include the couple and their dogs—all arrayed for the holiday.

When an animal dies of a condition similar to one that currently affects the owner or someone else in the family, we mourn more than the animal's death. Dogs, cats, and other animals die of heart disease, cancer, kidney failure, strokes, and immune deficiencies just as we do. Then it becomes a reminder of the seriousness of illness and the possibility of death.

The Complexity of Disenfranchised Grief

Though each type of grief can create particular difficulties and different reactions, disenfranchised grief carries its own special problems.

The very nature of disenfranchised grief creates additional problems for grievers, who have few sources of support.

Disenfranchised grief tends to intensify grief reactions. We may even feel ashamed by our grief. When her dog did die, for example, Eleanor felt embarrassed about her feelings. She wondered if her very natural tears were a sign of senility. Who, she wondered, would be that upset about a dog? The answer, of course, is anyone attached to the animal.

Ambivalent relationships and concurrent crises complicate grief. Steve, for example, deeply loved Henry, but resented the hidden nature of their relationship. Even after his death, Steve felt guilty at any thought that he could affirm that love, and he was angry when his coworkers joked about their suspicions of Henry's sexuality.

Death can lead to complex legal and practical problems. Bella lived with Ali for four years. When Ali died in an accident, Bella had no legal standing to sue, nor was she listed on a lease. She even had to struggle with Ali's parents over possession of joint property.

With disenfranchised losses, you may be excluded from an active role in caring for the dying. Rituals for a death may not be available or helpful, and you may be excluded from attending them and may have no role in planning them. You have no recognized role in which you can assert the right to mourn and thus receive such support. In such cases, your grief may follow more complicated pathways, becoming chronic or escalating. In some cases, you may be able to work such things through with your family—perhaps around the kitchen table, or maybe in therapy. This was not possible for Steve. His parents had no interest in dialogue or counseling. Steve was able to find support among siblings, friends, and his new church. Sometimes the reality is that you have to accept support wherever it is offered—realizing that some people, even those close to you, may not be able to offer the support you need. The same situations may apply beyond your family in the larger community where people do not recognize your relationship or your loss.

As you struggle with your grief, try to analyze the causes of *empathetic failure*. This means seek out why you are experiencing a sense of disenfranchisement.[6] What is keeping you from receiving the empathy you need after experiencing your loss? There may be many reasons. The first reason may be that you are not reaching out for support. The very secrecy of the relationship, or feelings of shame about your grief, may inhibit you from asking for support. Certainly this was a factor in both Eleanor and Steve's grief.

Sometimes the shame may have a spiritual component. Some faiths condemn homosexuality, homosexual behaviors, and sexual relationships outside of marriage. In these cases, faith complicates mourning. Here it may be helpful to explore your conflicts with counselors, including pastoral counselors, in order to find some resolution of any spiritual struggle. Steve's exploration led him to find a church that was open and accepting of his sexuality.

Empathetic failure also can result when your intimate network of family or friends, or larger community, are not supportive. They withhold support as a punishment for the attachment. Steve's parents were not supportive or sympathetic to his loss. Their own religious and personal views opposed homosexuality.

In some cases, others may simply not understand the attachment. Eleanor often lovingly complained of her dog—the extra work and additional expense. She often used the dog as an excuse to go home early or to limit her stays. None of it meant that she loved her dog any less, but when her dog died, many simply assumed that Eleanor would feel a sense of relief.

Sometimes you have to have the courage to share with others what you are feeling and to ask for the support you need. This may mean that you educate your community about the meaning of your loss. Sometimes you can be your own best advocate. Just a few decades ago, perinatal loss—miscarriages, stillbirths, etc.—were often hidden and disenfranchised. It was the advocacy of women who went public with their stories that made society aware of the grief they experienced. They enfranchised themselves and others through their advocacy.

You need not struggle through with your grief alone. Counseling is especially helpful when you are not getting support from family or friends due to distance, apathy, or disapproval.[7] With the situations underlying disenfranchised grief, you may not find appropriate support groups outside of larger metropolitan areas, but you may find that there are online support networks that can offer much—validation of your loss; support; suggestions for coping with your grief; and, most important, the hope that you can cope, even grow, as you deal with your grief.

However, you can create your own ways to commemorate the dead. Think for example, how the AIDS Memorial Quilt assisted those in any relationship—friend, partner, or lover—who were empowered to find their own voice in a memorial square. You may also choose to have a memorial service, perhaps even in your own home, inviting close and supportive friends to share your loss, grief, and memories.

We have many relationships in our life outside our families. We become close to friends, coworkers, mentors, teachers, coaches, and counselors—to name just a few. We may have intimate relationships outside the bonds of marriage. We become attached to public figures such as presidents or political and religious leaders, movie stars and sports figures, or other celebrities whom we never meet but still carefully follow. We love animals that come into our lives—our pets and animal companions.

One of our great human characteristics is that we have a wonderful capacity to love—a capacity that is not limited to kin. We can love across species and space. And whenever we experience a loss of anyone or anything we love—whatever the relationship—we grieve.

CHAPTER 10

Does Anyone Understand? Unacknowledged Loss

> Greta cries every Christmas. Over a hundred years ago, her great-grandfather carved a set of Christmas ornaments that crossed the Atlantic with the family as they migrated from Germany. As each child, then grandchildren, and even great-grandchildren married, they would receive an ornament—a tangible reminder of their roots. Under Greta's guardianship, the ornaments were washed away in the 1997 Red River Flood in North Dakota. To Greta, she has lost a legacy, a gift to generations past and present.

Grief is not always about death, but it always is about attachment and separation. Any loss can engender it. Often, people endure pervasive and intense distress without having faced the death of a loved one at all. Life events such as divorce, infertility, disability, or job loss are devastating and cause us to mourn and experience emotions similar to those who have experienced the death of a loved one. Yet with many of the significant losses we experience, we might not even recognize our own grief. Further, in these cases of unrecognized or disenfranchised losses, our grief is again often not validated or recognized by others.

This chapter strives to name and validate these losses, reminding you that you are not alone in your grief. The losses here are not meant to be an exhaustive list, but illustrative of the types you may grieve. You can grieve the loss of anything, anywhere, or anyone to whom you become attached. No list could name them all.

Illness, Disability, Change, and Loss

The Loss of a Person We Once Knew

Sometimes the people you love change in significant ways. They are still in your lives—but not the way you remember or once knew them. Illness often changes people, especially mental illness or dementia. Here you experience what might be called a sense of *psychosocial* loss, grieving the loss of the person you once knew.

In dementia, a person still is with us, but is not like the person we previously knew. The ties that bind us to one another, the shared memories, even the personality are no longer accessible. Physically the person looks the same but may seem, especially as the disease advances, only a shell of his past self. He may no longer engage in the same activities or seem to recognize or acknowledge us. Sometimes the changes can be startling. The mother of one of my clients grew up in the segregated South. Yet her daughter was proud that her mom had been active in the civil rights movement, even though her mom lost friends and alienated family. Her mother would proudly tell the story of how as an adolescent girl she shamed her all-white church into integrating services. Yet as her mom lapsed in dementia, she began using racial epithets. Her mother's language not only shocked her daughter but called into question her mom's true beliefs. Was she really the progressive person she believed her mother to be?

Other illnesses can create a similar sense of loss. A traumatic brain injury generally affects all levels of mental function. Communication abilities, memory, personality, and the capability to process information may all be affected. In some cases, individuals may make a near full recovery, but in other cases progress can be slow and uncertain. We may grieve people as they sink into mental illness, alcoholism, or drug use. The son of a friend prided himself on his neatness and appearance. He often showered and changed his clothes several times a day after playing a sport or after an accidental spill. His parents used to joke that if the boy ever went missing, it would be difficult to remember what he was wearing as he changed so often. In adolescence, the boy developed a drug dependency and the most obvious of many changes was his loss of personal hygiene. He now often slept in the same clothes days on end, rarely bathing.

While you grieve the loss of people as they used to be, you may lose other friends and family who also find it difficult to cope with these changes and avoid these people, too. These, too, are losses.

Positive changes can also engender grief when a person becomes different from the individual we knew and loved. For Tristan, it was the religious conversion of his brother. He was initially delighted that his brother found some faith even if it was more intense than his own beliefs. But Tristan soon found it difficult to relate to his born-again brother, who no longer wanted to share a beer and was always witnessing to Tristan and his family. They now see each other only on holidays.

Similarly, Abigail was proud that her husband joined Alcoholics Anonymous after a long struggle with addiction that nearly ruined their marriage. Yet she misses the "people, places, and things"—especially the pub-based dart club that was a shared activity and a place where they socialized with many other couples—that her husband now avoids in order to remain sober. They celebrate New Year's Eve at an alcohol-free party sponsored by his local AA chapter in a church basement, rather than in the expensive clubs they once frequented. Abby is proud of her husband and supportive of his efforts at sobriety, even as she grieves aspects of her former life.

Anticipatory Grief and Illness

Apart from mourning the loss of personalities and shared activities, we experience losses as we ourselves and the person we love surrender our health and vigor, functional abilities, significant activities, or treasured roles. We now feel very different from a prior self.

Anticipatory grief is a term that referred to the grief felt about someone with a life-limiting illness; friends, family, and caregivers felt it in anticipation of an eventual death. We now understand *anticipatory grief* or what Dr. Rando, a prominent grief therapist and author, prefers—*anticipatory mourning*—as a reaction to all the losses experienced in an illness.[1]

These losses are significant. They can include increased physical disability, and the inability to do even mundane activities. Mental acuity can diminish, with the loss of concentration. The sufferer may have to give up roles once treasured, perhaps retiring from a job or giving up recreational pursuits. For one colleague, among the first symptoms of multiple sclerosis was a balance disorder. Her first loss was to give up skiing, a family activity that had spanned three generations.

The loss of health—even the prediction of loss—contained in a diagnosis can be a source of grief. We lose our assumptive world. All our plans, thoughts, sense of the future, or even our sense of safety and security are now challenged. The future we know is not as we once imagined it. For Craig, his wife's diagnosis of pancreatic cancer dashed their retirement dreams of travel and possibly relocating to Tuscany. As any illness progresses, we continue to experience additional losses and grieve each one.

Disability and Chronic Sorrow

Disability—including developmental disabilities—can lead to disenfranchised grief. In many cases, expressions of grief are seen negatively by others. We admire persons who take disability in stride. We expect parents to love a child whatever the disability. To express grief often runs counter to these social values.

However, some people do feel *chronic sorrow*,[2] and live with a constant sense of grief. For some people who live with a disability—or with someone who has a disability—grief is a constant companion. Often, this sense of sorrow surges at different moments. A mother of a child with intellectual disabilities (once called mental retardation) loves that child deeply, yet she also grieves the opportunities and experiences that her child will likely miss because of that disability. Her grief spikes at certain times; for example, when she has just received an invitation to a friend's daughter's wedding. The invitation reminds her that her daughter will never marry or have her own children. Yet she also feels bad that she is grieving, and feels she should love and accept her child as she is.

Parents of children with developmental disabilities may also be disenfranchised if their child predeceases them. Many parents have shared with me that others often expected them to feel a sense that the death of a child or adult with a disability was "a blessing in disguise." Now they would no longer have to worry about their child or plan for after they, as caretakers, aged or died. The grief that the parents experienced, and the strong loving relationships they had forged, were often discounted.

To deal with chronic sorrow, you may need to find confidants, counselors, and support groups that can assist you as you grieve. Above all, you need to have your grief acknowledged. You may need to deal with the complicated and ambivalent feelings you have as you struggle with disability—your own or that of others. And you may learn from the struggles of other ways in which you can best cope with your grief.

Relational Losses

Grief and Divorce

When I did my first research on disenfranchised grief, I focused on ex-spouses who often compared their grief at the time of their ex-spouse's death with the grief they experienced at the time of the divorce. At that time, professionals spoke of the "psychological sequelae" or secondary injuries or aftereffects associated with divorce. Those experiencing it called it "grief."

Divorces engender grief. Like death, divorce shatters your assumptive world. You rarely go into marriage assuming that you will divorce. And as with death, divorce creates all forms of secondary losses. As one divorcee said, "You divide the money, the children, the house, the furniture—even the friends." Among secondary losses associated with divorce may be financial security. All parties are likely to experience changes in their standard of living—some may be drastic. You may feel humiliated by the circumstances of the separation and stigmatized by the divorce. Self-esteem may suffer. You may find the idea of any intimate relationship distant. You need to name all these secondary losses and review strategies to cope with the inevitable changes that will occur.

Other factors complicate grief. You may be highly ambivalent about the divorce—perhaps desiring to exit a bad relationship while anxious and fearful of an uncertain future. Other emotions like guilt or anger frequently run high. And as with any loss, you need safe places in which to express these complex emotions, and safe persons with whom to explore them. Friends and family may be reluctant to offer support, or they may share anger and resentment toward the ex-partner and not understand why you would experience any grief reactions other than a deep sense of relief that the onerous bond is now broken. Depending on your faith and faith community, you may have spiritual struggles over the legitimacy of our divorce. Divorce is one of the few life transitions that many adults experience that is devoid of any form of ritual.[3] In fact, it may be useful to develop a ritual that marks that transition.

In addition, you now have to create a new relationship with your ex-spouse. A divorce ends a marriage but rarely a relationship—especially if there are children. There will inevitably be times when ex-spouses are in each other's company.

Divorce is not only hard on the couple; it hits children particularly hard. In fact, some new research shows that, for many children, the loss of a father or mother through divorce, especially if the noncustodial parent takes little role in the child's life, can be more problematic than the death of a parent.[4] Unlike death, the constant conflict at home that often leads to divorce can center on children, exacerbating the child's sense of guilt. Moreover, children receive mixed messages at the time of a divorce. *You should love him. He is your dad—miserable son of a bitch that he is.* Many family-friendly movies like *The Parent Trap* offer the seductive message that a capable child can heal the breach. But children usually cannot and should not be expected to assume adult roles.

Even in-laws feel grief as a significant relationship is severed. One client told me that after her ex-spouse's death, she was finally invited back into her in-laws' cousin's club—repairing once significant relationships severed, albeit temporarily, by the divorce.

Loss of a Relationship

You do not have to be married to lose a significant relationship. A study of young adults indicated that slightly over a quarter of the large sample indicated that a romantic breakup was their most serious loss to date and eclipsed others.[5] Young adults are particularly vulnerable. They may have just left home—for college, career, or military service—leaving support systems behind. They are seeking social approval and trying to demonstrate both mastery and competence—all challenged by a loss. Yet challenges remain even as young adults pass into maturity.

The disenfranchisement of grief is often significant here—particularly for adolescents or young adults. Your grief may be minimized as you are urged to get over it and find someone new. Adolescents and young adults may even be told that they will experience such losses often as they grow—a statement as comforting as reminding a child who lost his first beloved grandparent that he will eventually grieve the surviving three!

The grief is quite real. Dr. Louis LaGrand, in his study of young adults, found intense manifestations of grief including crying, insomnia, and even digestive difficulties.[6] What you need when you experience such a loss is basic to any grief reaction—the normalization of your feelings, education about the grief you are actually experiencing, assistance in finding and fashioning support, and assistance in regaining a sense of self-esteem that may have been challenged.

Breakups can include feelings such as abandonment and alienation. The other has left or been left, but we may have no idea what happened to that individual. We may not even have a good sense of the reasons underlying the alienation. Dorika has not seen her son Lajos for two years. As an adolescent, he had serious issues with drugs and resultant conflicts with his parents. He ran away from a rehabilitation program, and for a while his whereabouts were unknown. He has now returned to their city and Dorika and her husband know where he lives, but Lajos refuses any contact. They assume he is still using drugs but, in fact, know little of his present life. Dorika longs for a day she can reconcile with a clean and sober son—one whom she once knew and loved. She constantly reads death notices looking to see if his name appears, and wonders if she would even know if he died.

Other times adults disappear and children go missing. Military personnel can be missing in action, and people are lost without a trace after an event such as a natural disaster or terrorist attack. These types of losses are sometimes called *ambiguous losses.*[7] In such cases, it is difficult to achieve any meaning. We have a story with no real ending. We veer, as Dorika does, between hope and hopelessness. Here even the term *grief* may seem a betrayal—a premature capitulation to a loss that we still deny. We feel we are giving up for lost what yet might be found.

Sometimes grief is complicated even when we know that a person has likely died, but there is no body and we do not really have a sense of how that person's story ended. In March 2014, a Malaysia Airlines flight disappeared. Survivors still struggle with grief—complicated by the fact that the fate of the flight has never been established.

Adoption

There are three groups that experience grief in an adoption—relinquishing mothers (and sometimes fathers), adoptees, and adopting parents.[8] Relinquishing mothers obviously grieve giving up a child they have carried through pregnancy. Relinquishing mothers in past generations were often forced into giving children up for adoption, which made them feel guilty, ashamed, and angry. Mothers wonder where their child is and how well he or she is doing. Some may fantasize about an eventual reunion, while others dread the return of the child to a now changed life.

Once the adoptee learns that he or she has been adopted, a sense of grief often follows. Adoptees sometimes struggle with intimacy, if they had early attachment difficulties. Identity is often an issue as adoptees struggle, especially in adolescence and early adulthood, with fears and fantasies of their birth parents; feelings of being different; guilt over searching for information about birth parents that may be interpreted as a lack of appreciation for the parents who raised them; and guilt, shame, and anger over a sense of abandonment. After all, to be chosen by someone else means to have been unwanted by another. Yet despite these inherent conflicts in adoption, adoptees are, in fact, overall no less successful or satisfied than children raised by their biological parents.[9]

Adoptive parents have their own issues with grief. Their losses vary but can include infertility, the loss of a biological child, and even the loss of the experience of pregnancy. As the adoption process unfolds, they may fear that the process will not be finalized—that something will occur that will terminate the adoption. Later there can be conflicted feelings as their child struggles with identity and seeks contact with the relinquishing mother. The meaning of each of these losses and conflicts will be different for each adoptive parent.

Experts recommend open and ongoing communication between adoptees and adoptive parents to allow information, thoughts, and feelings to be acknowledged and processed.[10] This is unlikely to be a "one-time tell-all" but rather an ongoing process. Rituals—for example, acknowledging the finalization of the adoption—create a forum for such exchanges as well as opportunities to symbolically recognize the event.

Foster Care

Grief is endemic in foster care. A foster child loses not only parents but the world he or she once knew. Everything is different now—different school, different teachers, different family, different friends, and different rules. The foster child may even experience a loss of "inappropriate independence." Here the child can no longer do the things he or she once was able to do in an unstructured, chaotic household. He or she may now have to go to school, observe a regular bedtime, and give up meals of Twinkies and Coke. While these are inappropriate freedoms for a young child, their loss is still keenly felt.

In all these losses some foster children experience a sense of secondary gain that will increase a sense of ambivalence about any eventual return. After a conference where I had addressed foster parents, when we sat down for a luncheon, an eight-year-old boy approached me to show me his Game Boy. He told me he received it on his past birthday—a gift from his foster parents. He was especially excited as this was the first time he had ever received a birthday gift. For seven years, he and his birthdays had been neglected by a drug-dependent mother. Consider the complex feelings this boy is now likely to have toward his birth mother.

The foster parents I trained were wonderful people, making sacrifices daily for their children. Many of them legitimately look at themselves as rescuers. Yet the children's grief and loss complicate the relationship.

Foster parents also experience loss. As foster parents, you are given two paradoxical messages: *Love the child as if he or she were your own,* and *Remember this is temporary care so do not get too attached!* It is not unusual for foster parents to experience multiple losses as children are moved in and out of their homes.

Of course, relinquishing parents have losses as well. They have lost their children and feel stigmatized. They lost control to a bureaucracy and court system seen as unsympathetic to their plight.

Incarceration

When someone you love is incarcerated this, too, is a disenfranchised loss and carries with it shame. I once had a seven-year-old client who was grieving the loss of his stepdad, now in prison. I was the only person, aside from family, with whom he could share his grief. To everyone else his father was "working in Alaska." While this family could keep a secret, in other cases families must deal directly with the stigma that someone in the family is now in prison.

Any grief is complicated. You feel fear and anxiety for the persons because prisons are dangerous. You have fears over the ways the person will change in prison. You may have to deal with concurrent crises and contend with the loss of income, legal costs, and possibly fines that threaten our financial present and future. Even visiting can be both expensive and humiliating as you undergo long, bureaucratic lines, and searches of property and person.

Even the time of release may create feelings of grief. The incarcerated family member will have changed in one way or another—perhaps now drug-free and better or perhaps colder, angrier, and more distant. Whatever the change, we now have to adjust to their changes—as they have to adjust to the ways that we've changed in the interim.

Loss of Identity

Some losses affect your very identity—they challenge how you view yourself, as well as how you present yourself to the world. The loss of employment or the losses of a spouse or child change your sense of identity, but here the focus is on three that directly confront your identity.

A loss of functionality tests your sense of self. Your identity is challenged when you lose the ability to do things that were once important to you. Victor, for example, was always fascinated by cars. He attended a high school that actually included automotive training. Later he matriculated to a technical school, receiving an associate's degree in automotive engineering. He became a mechanic with a racing crew. It was all he ever wanted to do and he loves everything about it—the racing, demonstrating the technical skill it requires, the travel, even the camaraderie and banter. Now, diagnosed with a degenerative muscle disease, he knows he will soon no longer be able to continue. Financially he is secure, but this loss is more than the loss of a job. It is the loss of all he ever wanted to be.

A loss of reputation also challenges your sense of identity. You want others to see you as you believe you should be seen. Yet sometimes charges, rumors, or innuendoes haunt you and mar your sense of self. Even as you deal with this on legal or interpersonal levels, you still grieve a loss of your reputation—your public self.

Infertility is a loss to both women and men that strikes on many levels, including identity. From early in childhood, you think about the family you would like to have. As you marry, your plans, hopes, and dreams seem more tangible. But infertility may then strike at these dreams, as well as their links with sexuality. As Darcy Harris, a therapist who has treated infertile couples, notes, there is a troubling paradox in seeking treatment for infertility.[11] On one hand, you understand that the treatments—expensive, invasive, and psychologically and physically stressful—can be unsuccessful. You cope with fears that you may never parent your own biological children. Yet the very nature of treatment intensifies commitment to the role of parenting. Counseling is helpful, allowing you to name and explore your grief, and receive support as you cope with the inherent losses of infertility. It allows you to examine the underlying meaning of the loss. Do you mourn the inability to reproduce, or rather the desire to parent? If it is the latter, you can explore options such as adoption or foster care.

Transitional Losses

Every transition in life—no matter how positive—has an undercurrent of loss. At graduation, you celebrated your achievement and looked forward to the next phase of life. Yet you also recognized you're leaving behind friends, teachers or professors, and places and activities. There are also implications arising from the birth of a child. You may have anticipated the event for years and be overjoyed in the birth of new life. But you also know life will be different now; over the next couple of decades, your own freedom will be limited—and for a shorter period, so will your sleep.

Every change brings an element of loss. Nevertheless, in many life changes the gains are far more potent than the losses. Yet even in the most positive transitions, elements of loss can be experienced.

Developmental Losses

As you age, you inevitably experience changes. You give up activities as you take on new responsibilities and engage in different endeavors. Waiting for the school bus with my grandchildren recently on the second day of school, I heard a young neighbor complain to his mother that he went to kindergarten *yesterday*! His mom patiently explained he would now go five days a week—unlike his two-day-a-week preschool. The boy looked at her with disappointment, tears in his eyes. *This changes everything!* he complained.

It does. Everything changes as you continue through the life cycle. Some changes you take in stride, but others affect you deeply. The thrill of passing your driving test and earning your license held so much meaning, a mark both of accomplishment and maturity that promised new freedom and adventure. Now imagine the pain and grief when, through age or disability, you are forced to surrender that license and all it has meant.

Other developmental changes contain different meanings.

Loss of Employment

Unemployment and infertility are two of the most unrecognized losses in adulthood. When you meet strangers at a party or some other place, the first two questions you often ask to establish connection are: *What do you do? Do you have children?*

One of the most profound losses, as an adult, is the loss of employment. When you lose a job, you not only lose income, the most tangible loss, you may have other tangible losses as well. Health may suffer. No longer covered by employment health insurance, you may find it difficult to continue medications, physician visits, or other medical procedures. You also lose relationships you developed at work. Losing employment may lead to other losses such as relocation. You lose your assumptive world. You may have believed that if you worked hard, you would be rewarded. Your sense of a just world is threatened, as is your sense of self-esteem. We often define ourselves by what we do, so when you are not earning an income, you may see yourself as less worthy. In addition, no matter what the reason for dismissal, it is difficult not to see it as a personal affront. So along with whatever efforts you take to find a new position or retrain, you need to acknowledge your loss and confront your grief.

Other Transitional Losses

Every transition involves loss, including physical transitions such as relocation or migration. In relocating to another neighborhood, city, region, or nation, you will experience a series of losses of life as it previously or "once" was. Depending on both the distance and cultural difference, these losses may be minor or substantial. Spiritual transitions, such as changes or abandonment of faith, also involve elements of loss of what you believed about the world. Other such losses may include the loss of familiar forms of worship, and relationships with persons with whom you formally worshipped. Psychological transitions such as coming out include changed relationships, expectations of life, and—at least initially—challenges to self-esteem. Acknowledging and validating loss is a critical component of the coming-out process.[12]

Material Loss

The reality is that we get attached to *things*. Your home and possessions have meaning to you. To Greta, the loss of family Christmas ornaments was the most devastating aspect of a flood because it destroyed family history and marred a legacy.

In some cases, material losses can be multiple and catastrophic. A burglary of your home not only robs you of possessions and cash, but also of a sense of safety. In a fire, irreplaceable heirlooms, meaningful possessions, and photographs documenting your life and those of your family can be lost. Naturally, any loss of possessions will depend on the meaning you bestow upon them. To someone else, in another context, the loss of ornaments may simply be a reason to update belongings, but when you lose a possession that has meaning, you will grieve its loss.

Grief is not so much about death as it is about loss. A deceased colleague of mine, Richard Kalish, stated it simply and clearly. *Anything that you have, you can lose; anything you are attached to, you can be separated from; anything you love can be taken away from you. Yet, if you really have nothing to lose, you have nothing.*[13]

CHAPTER 11

Acknowledging the Disenfranchised

Randy, an older man with intellectual disabilities, lived, for most of his life, with his widowed father. Randy and his dad were always close. Randy grew up at a time when educational services for individuals with intellectual disabilities were limited outside of large state institutions. Randy's dad was a baseball scout and when Randy was a boy would often take him on scouting trips. Randy loved the trips and the time alone with his loving dad. They would constantly sing, "Take me out to the ball game." When Randy was sixteen years old, he found a job in a local warehouse. His coworkers were patient and understanding. When his father became weaker and more infirm, Randy moved to a group home. People there were kind. Most Sundays, Dad would come and spend some time with his son—usually eating lunch out. The visits stopped when his dad's condition worsened and he entered hospice care. Randy's sisters told him on their occasional visits that Dad was ill and would visit when he was better.

After his dad died, Randy's family did not want him to

to reflect on the drawing or scene they created. The Dougy Center (dougy.org) and the National Alliance for Grieving Children (nationalallianceforgrievingchildren.org) offer information and resources available for children, such as grief groups or even camp programs for children who are grieving. A range of books is available for children of different ages dealing with losses. These, too, can validate a child's grief, offer advice on coping, and affirm hope that the pain will not last forever.

It takes courage to grieve. For children, it takes courage to recognize and cope with uncomfortable feelings. For adults, it takes courage to trust children to do so. Yet there is little alternative. As adults, we need to recognize the full scope of children's attachments and help them grieve as best they can.

Older Adults

Just as we try to protect the very young, we frequently attempt to protect the very old. A number of years ago, Marge, a neighbor and good friend of my mother and my aunt Marie, died after a long stay in a nursing home. My sister called me with the news. Our mother had already died, but my aunt, nearing ninety years of age, was still alive—frail but mentally very sharp. "I'm not going to tell Aunt Marie," my sister stated. "It would just upset her." I demurred and reminded her that Aunt Marie had a right to know that a friend—even one she had not seen for a number of years—had died, to decide if she wished to attend the funeral. I reminded my sister that my aunt had survived the loss of her husband, one of her sons, her parents, and all her siblings. I was sure she could handle Marge's death. My sister agreed, with one proviso—I had to accompany her as we told my aunt.

Immediately when we arrived together, my aunt suspected something was wrong. As we sat down, my sister acknowledged that we had some bad news to share. I saw my aunt steel herself for the inevitable blow. "We just heard that Marge died," we announced. Within a moment, my aunt seemed visibly relieved. "I thought she died years ago," Aunt Marie shared. "I never heard anything after she was admitted to the Leeland" (the name of the long-term care facility). My aunt then added that many people seemed to think older people could not handle bad news—reminding us of all she coped with during her life.

My aunt decided to send flowers and attend the wake. As we drove her home, she noted how few of her friends had survived. She made us promise to tell any remaining friends when she died, noting that while it was sad to attend Marge's funeral, she was pleased to have the opportunity to say good-bye to her good friend.

We try to protect people who are, by definition, survivors. Older individuals do not need secrecy but support. They who have coped with a lifetime of loss are not strangers to grief. Often, our best intentions to protect simply generate and prolong pain. For instance, Elaine, also in her nineties and residing in an assisted living facility, was quite frail. Her son decided to keep the fact that his sister, who lived on the opposite coast and rarely visited, had died, reasoning that Elaine rarely saw her daughter, so it would be merciful to spare her that grief. But, Elaine missed the constant—often humorous—cards her daughter would send and the occasional phone call. Elaine wondered if she had offended her daughter, which caused her unnecessary pain.

But what should we do when older people with dementia lose someone they loved? This question has no clear answer because we know so little about how someone with dementia experiences and understands loss. But the loss of cognition should not be compared with the absence of emotion. Grief in dementia may be evident in changes of behaviors, as well as unusual or increased manifestations of agitation or restlessness.

Some persons with dementia may not be able to be aware of loss. They may have a vague sense that something is not right, or that some significant individual, perhaps one they cannot identify, is missing. Persons with dementia may confuse the present loss with earlier losses. For example, a bereaved spouse with dementia may believe that a parent rather than a spouse has died.

In other situations, persons with dementia may be unable to retain the information that an individual has died. They may ask repeatedly what happened to that person and even mourn the loss only later to reiterate the same question. In such cases, it is natural for you to be frustrated. It is difficult to understand that such behaviors are normal in the disease and not indications of inadequate explanations. As one daughter caring for her mother with dementia noted, *Each time she asks about Dad, I feel like I have been stabbed with a knife. I know she must miss him, but why can't she remember? Why does she always have to ask? Can't she understand that he died?*

Naturally, expressions of grief by individuals with Alzheimer's disease or other dementias are affected by factors including the extent of the disease, loss of awareness, immediacy of the lost relationship, and ability to communicate their reactions to the loss. These factors are likely to change as the disease progresses. At some point, the person with dementia will not retain any memory of the person who died.

It is critical to be sensitive to that loss. Are there any patterns to their reactions? Do reactions or questions come at a particular time of day? Do they seem prompted by any particular events, persons, or other cues? Sometimes it helps to experiment with different ways of handling their questions. For example, might it be helpful to return to a picture or memory each time the person with dementia questions the loss or expresses a sense of grief? In other cases, it may help to remove any mementos or pictures that seem to generate grief in the person with dementia.

In this difficult time, it is critical for you as the caregiver to remember the importance of self-care. You can only take care of others as well and as long as you take care of yourself. Finally, you must acknowledge your own grief—for the person who died, for the losses you experience as you watch someone you love decline with dementia, and even for the changes you experience as you give up activities you enjoy in order to take on new responsibilities.

Persons with Intellectual Disabilities

Like Randy, persons with intellectual disabilities experience loss and grief that can be expressed in many ways—physically, emotionally, cognitively, spiritually, and behaviorally. Crying, silence, withdrawal, sleep disturbances, physical complaints, and resistance to change are not uncommon.

Depending on the level of disability, however, persons with intellectual disabilities may have a difficult time understanding death. They may struggle with the notion that death is permanent, constantly asking when the person who died will return or when they can speak with that individual again. Sometimes their emotional expressions are distorted. Whenever Randy became agitated or nervous, he would giggle and he told me the story of his father's death with a nervous titter. Some persons with intellectual disabilities may have a "positive bias," a sunny disposition that masks their deep sense of loss. Others may have severe conceptual or speech limitations that make it difficult for others to understand their needs.

Yet whether or not someone can be understood is a poor measure of whether they themselves can understand. All but perhaps the most severely disabled feel and understand the loss of someone they know and love.

It helps to validate that loss and not disenfranchise it. Some caregivers are overprotective and try to spare persons with disabilities the pain of grief. Caregivers may be fearful of their own abilities to cope with grief and pain that are difficult for us to understand, and so avoid dealing with it. People with intellectual disabilities have the same needs as we all do when grieving; they need to be supported by others. They need to have their concerns addressed and their questions patiently answered. They should have opportunities to participate in funeral rituals in a way that is comfortable. This may mean that a private time be set aside so that they can attend a special viewing with their closest family and friends. It may mean that they attend the funeral rituals with the special support of someone they trust.

Randy's group home counselor was his advocate. He stressed

to the family Randy's need to grieve. He accompanied him to the funeral. Since Randy's disability sometimes led him to misinterpret social cues, the counselor practiced with Randy the ways to interact at a funeral. Randy was fine. As individuals offered condolences, he would firmly take their hand and quietly thank them for their support. Like all of us, persons with intellectual disabilities, individuals like Randy, need choices—and the respect that choice denotes.

All grief is ultimately individual and unique. Our grief is a combination of the highly individual relationship we shared with the person who died, as well as the distinctive ways that we each cope with loss. We all form attachments and experience loss, whatever our score on a test of intellectual abilities and functioning.

Disenfranchising Deaths

Death, we are often told, is the great leveler. Yet that, too, is a myth. The ways we die influence not only the grief we experience but the support we have. Think, for example, about the brave men and women who die in the service of others, in war or in the line of duty. We build monuments to their memory and publicly mourn their deaths as we celebrate their heroism.

Yet we mourn other deaths very secretly or in private funerals. We are reluctant to share about the death with anyone but trusted family or friends.

Stigmatizing Deaths

There are deaths that are stigmatizing due to suicide, homicide, or AIDS. In suicide, families may feel judged, or subject to the assumption that such events can occur only in families beset by problems. That reinforces our sense of security. It will never happen to us. The result is that if we are survivors of a suicide death, we may be very cautious in sharing our story and grief.

Many homicides create similar reactions. Lurid details underlying the circumstances of the killing may be presented in the media and in court proceedings. It is a common reaction in many homicides to attempt to discredit the victim—blaming them for being in the wrong place at the wrong time. We offer sympathy to victims considered "above reproach,"[2] but not to other victims whom we view in a different light.

Grief in many homicides is complicated by the terrible truth that we have a much greater chance of being killed by someone we know, maybe even love, than by a total stranger. We may grieve for the victim even as we sort out complicated feelings toward the perpetrator. Jeremy killed his own abusive father while trying to protect his mother. His mother's grief is profound—grieving not only the loss of a husband, however ambivalent their relationship had been, but also her fourteen-year-old son's loss of innocence.

AIDS is a stigmatizing disease because it is often associated with substance abuse or homosexuality. It also generates great fear. Christine's twin sons both died of the disease. She is frequently asked the question, "How did they get it?" She has learned to deflect what she considers inappropriate probing by saying, "The usual ways."

In other deaths, habits or behaviors such as smoking, alcoholism, or substance abuse are viewed as contributing to the illness. Tell someone the deceased died of lung cancer, and the inevitable question is, "Did they smoke?" This kind of judgmental comment disenfranchises grief.

If you are grieving such stigmatizing deaths, you may find comfort in specialized support groups or networks, such as Parents of Murdered Children (pomc.org), a group that offers support to all family members and friends, or Survivors of Suicide (survivorsofsuicide.com). The value of specialized groups is that they consist of people who own and know the stigma you are experiencing.

Traumatic Deaths

Traumatic deaths, such as car crashes, also can be disenfranchising. Legal constraints may inhibit you from seeking the support you need or even openly acknowledging your grief. These types of deaths usually entail criminal investigations and at least civil suits, if not criminal charges. In an adversarial legal system, any expression of sympathy can be misconstrued as an admission of guilt.

Derrick, a new teenage driver, crashed his car, killing a friend. He so much wants to reach out to his friend's parents but his lawyer will not permit that, fearful that anything he says may interfere with impending criminal and civil cases. His lawyer suggested that Derrick write a letter that the attorney could vet and give to the parents when he felt it appropriate. It is a poor substitute for Derrick, who so much misses the contact with his late friend's family.

Grieving Differently

We also can disenfranchise people who grieve differently—who experience, express, or cope with their grief in ways that seem unusual to us. In an earlier chapter we discussed the continuum of grieving styles. On one end of this continuum are intuitive grievers who feel the emotions of grief intensely and openly express their grief, crying or shouting or talking about their loss with others. Instrumental or "head" grievers experience grief physically or cognitively. *When I heard she died I just wanted to run. I thought about him all the time.* Instrumental grievers express their grief by talking and doing. We may disenfranchise individuals, including ourselves, who are not grieving according to how we believe someone should express grief. We feel powerless, even embarrassed, when we are with a man who is openly weeping. Similarly, we are confused when a woman grieves in a more instrumental or nonemotional style.

Time also plays a role. In the immediate aftermath of grief we understand emotional responses. We may even be suspicious of those who seem unwilling to display emotion. *Why aren't they crying?* Yet later, after a period of time, we may question those who still seem to express emotion. *Why are they still crying?*

You have to understand and enfranchise your own ways or styles of grieving, and find ways to express and adapt to your loss that work for you. A while ago, I met an older man jogging vigorously one morning. His wife had died recently. As we talked about his loss, he told me that running every morning helped. *I used to be a boxer,* he said. *I remember my coach always told me, "Lead with your strongest hand."* That is a lesson each of us can remember as we grieve.

Culture plays a role here as well. In some cultures more emotional displays are accepted—even expected, while in others such raw emotion is discouraged or censured. When I was a young adult, my Hispanic grandmother died. At the funeral, my family, well assimilated into American culture but of mixed Hispanic and Hungarian heritage, was embarrassed by the emotional behavior of her surviving friends who wailed loudly at the casket. One relative even recommended that, whenever they approached the casket, we should post a sign visible to those behind us stating "not our family." I wonder about how they might have viewed our absence of wailing. "Poor Josephine," they may have thought, "her family was so cold; no one wailed."

Each culture has its own expectations on how you are supposed to mourn. In some cultures, widows are expected to wear black for a time sometimes as long as a year, sometimes a lifetime. Generational differences in how you are expected to grieve change over time. The quiet stoicism of men in the past is no longer as strongly expected now in many segments of our society. However, one thing remains: When you violate these cultural or generational norms, you find that your support is limited—your grief disenfranchised.

Just as there is no one way to grieve a family member's death, there is no single type of loss that can "justify" your grief. You should not have your grief suppressed by rules on how or when you are allowed to experience it. Loss certainly does not abide by any rules. Whatever and however you grieve a loss, you need not do it alone. If family and friends seem not to understand or support you, you may have to find that support elsewhere—with counselors or in specialized support groups. In all of these conditions and circumstances, the goal remains the same—to enfranchise the disenfranchised griever.

PART 4

Helping Yourself—and Others

This section focuses on ways you can help yourself and others adapt to loss. Although there is no one prescription for handling grief, knowing your own coping patterns and understanding others' ways of coping can allow you to cope with loss and to grow from it.

Our ancestors knew well the power of rituals. There are ways you can enhance funeral and other memorial rituals and create your own therapeutic rituals. However, no matter how powerful such rituals are, they mark only the beginning of your journey with grief. You can incorporate the power of rituals at other times in your journey as you cope with particular issues in your bereavement. The power of ritual need not only be used once.

We will also explore the tasks you need to fulfill as you journey with grief. It is reassuring to know that you are not alone on this journey. One of the most promising aspects of end-of-life care is that there are resources that can assist you, whatever your path—self-help books, counselors, and support groups, as well as your own friends and families.

Some losses are more complicated than others. And some pathways, particularly the chronic and escalating grief patterns, are prone to more complicated reactions. We will discuss when self-help is not enough and where you can find the help you need as you struggle with loss.

Finally, change—however painful—offers opportunities to grow. Some people do grow in grief—emerging with new insights, enhanced skills, and even a deeper spirituality. I hope to empower you not only to cope with loss, but to grow from grief. This can be a very special legacy to those you loved and now mourn—a terrible blessing touching you even in the midst of your loss and pain.

CHAPTER 12

Making Rituals Meaningful[1]

Dr. Catherine Sanders was a pioneer in the study of grief. But she was more than that. She was a wife and mother, a neighbor who sang in the church choir. At her funeral, three speakers—her daughter, a colleague, and a fellow member of the choir—each spoke of the Catherine Sanders they knew.

Her daughter recalled Catherine was a military wife living on Coast Guard bases. As a military family, they moved a great deal. Yet as they moved from home to home, Catherine would make sure that the common rooms—bathrooms, living rooms, dining rooms, and kitchens—were always the same color, in an attempt to maintain some sense of stability in her children's lives.

Her neighbor, a crusty New Englander, told how her reserve melted before Catherine's easy, warm, Southern charm. Catherine had transplanted herself after retirement from the mountains of North Carolina to be on the shores of Lake Champlain in Vermont to be nearer her daughter and grandchild. "I suppose," Catherine would joke, "I am doing this retirement all wrong. Who moves north?"

A colleague shared Catherine's scholarly achievements and contributions to the field, and the kindness that she showed in mentoring younger colleagues. Once shy, Catherine had found herself among the fellowship and banter of colleagues who had become close friends.

Each person—whatever their role in Catherine's life—left that day hearing about the Catherine they knew and loved. Yet each learned something new—something else to admire—about her.

Some funerals are special in that way. They offer a portrait of an individual that allows us to mourn the death even as we celebrate a life. Funerals help us cope with loss, but even beyond the funeral, we can use rituals to make transitions as we journey with grief.

That should not be surprising. From our earliest ancestors, humans have found solace in ritual. Even before writing, there was ritual. Prehistoric and nomadic humans would return to the same places, every year, to carry out rituals and lovingly bury their dead.[2] Rituals are *liminal*—they exist in the sacred space between the conscious and unconscious, affecting us in deeply emotional ways.[3] They are one of our most ancient and effective methods for handling loss.

Making Funerals More Meaningful

Research has clearly demonstrated funerals' and memorial services' therapeutic value.[4] Funerals first confirm the reality of the death. Whether a body is present or not, it is difficult to sustain denial of death at such rituals. Rites assist in the expression of grief while simultaneously offering a structure that contains grief. In these places and times we can cry, laugh at funny memories, and openly express our grief in other ways. Funerals stimulate our memories and allow us to share stories. In a disorganized time, funerals allow us to "do something." As your friends and family gather to comfort, a funeral reminds you that you have support. Even in your loss, you are not alone. This affirms that while you face a loss, you are part of an intimate network—a community of family and friends that continues. Funerals and memorial services offer possible meanings for the loss, reminding us how our beliefs—whatever they might be—speak to us in our loss. We create meaning in our bereavement and share it within our group.

Funeral rituals can become even more meaningful when they offer opportunities for mourners to participate at their own levels of comfort. I mentioned earlier a young adolescent girl who had died in a bicycle accident. Her parents incorporated her friends in all sorts of ways in her memorial service—in a choir, a middle school glee club, as ushers, pallbearers, and readers. Their participation reaffirmed how special their daughter was to her peers and allowed them to be more than passive spectators. By giving them central roles, her parents and the ritual acknowledged their place in their friend's life. My family was equally intentional when my dad died. Each of his children and surviving friends offered brief eulogies. The grandchildren served as pallbearers. His pastor officiated. Every action and tribute highlighted the unique ways my dad had touched lives.

The most effective funeral rituals are personal, highlighting the life and unique contributions of the person who died. Eulogies, video and photograph presentations, and other personal narratives about the deceased can help do this. Most people, like Sanders, live in a variety of worlds, and mourners can need to speak to the multiple identities of an individual. My students know me one way, my colleagues have a different perspective, and my family sees still another side. Participatory and personal funerals are inclusive, making everyone feel that they are truly part of the ritual.

You have to remember that funerals should not be used as opportunities to resolve personal issues if you have a highly ambivalent relationship with the person who died. Colleen had such a relationship with her mom. For thirty years her mother, Eileen, had been a weekend alcoholic, functioning well in her work as a nurse but bingeing on weekends. After she retired, she drank constantly, which led to her early death. In her eulogy, Colleen openly and angrily addressed her issues with her mother, which shocked both Eileen's coworkers as well as many of the patients who had come to pay their respects. Some things are better left for close confidants; a therapist; or even a small, private ritual.

To have a meaningful funeral, you may need to *translate* these rituals so everyone understands their importance or symbolism. In an increasingly diverse society—spiritually and culturally—we cannot assume that all attendees will recognize the significance of the stories, music, or other parts of the service. When Deborah's husband died of ALS, the service ended with the song "Singin' in the Rain." Gil was an engineer by vocation, but a bluegrass musician by avocation who played with a local band. One of the band's inside jokes was that one of their regular gigs was an open-air concert hosted by a large outdoor flea market. Since both the market and the open-air concert were "weather permitting," the band would open with a bluegrass rendition of "We'll Sing in the Sunshine." After being diagnosed with ALS, Gil told his wife, "We learned to sing in the sunshine, now we will have to learn to sing in the rain." Sharing that story with those attending the funeral ensured that the meaning of the song did not get lost.

Funerals, Memorial Rituals, and the Disenfranchised Griever

Funerals and memorial rituals can be problematic for disenfranchised grievers. In many types of disenfranchised losses, there are no rituals. For example, while divorce is a common enough life event in many sections of the world, few mark it with ritual. In many cases of job loss, not only is there no opportunity for any form of ritual, but there might not even be an opportunity to take proper leave. It is not unusual for persons who are terminated to be notified at the end of the workday, or after being informed to be then escorted out of the building.

In other cases, you may exclude people unintentionally—perhaps to protect them from what we believe will be a difficult event. For example, you may not offer young children or individuals with intellectual disabilities opportunities to decide if and how they would wish to participate in rituals. At other times, distance and information may impede participation. Many of us have close friends—from childhood, college, professional life—all over the United States and the world. It is likely that many will not hear of friends' deaths in time to decide whether it would be feasible to attend a funeral.

The exclusion of attendees at a funeral can be symbolic rather than physical when a family wants to focus on their own grief. The role of a friend or similarly close relationship may simply be ignored, unrecognized, or unacknowledged. Even if they attend the funeral and are expected to be there out of respect for the deceased and in support of the family, their own role in the life of the deceased may be overlooked. In middle age, Lucy had that experience when her closest friend died. *Hannah was my best friend—ever since high school. We went to college together. Even though we were both married and lived in different cities, we would talk at least once a week. Our families would vacation together every year. And early each December, we would meet in New York City for a long weekend of Christmas shopping. When she died, of course I went to the funeral. The family was glad to see me. But they had a large bulletin board full of photographs. Not one included Hannah and me or even our families together. I almost wanted to shout, "I was part of her life, too."*

In some situations, the exclusion is deliberate, meant to show disapproval of a lifestyle, relationship, or individual. You may not want an ex-spouse or a lover to be at the funeral. Whether the exclusion is intentional or not, funeral directors, celebrants, clergy, and others involved in planning rituals can have a critical role in assisting families in reviewing their decisions. Sometimes we simply need encouragement and information to widen the circle and incorporate individuals such as children, persons with developmental disabilities, or others in the rituals.

When exclusion is deliberate, ritual leaders such as funeral directors and clergy can ask about the implications of a decision and offer options. One funeral director described a case where an adult son directed him to "make sure his father's mistress doesn't show." "I told him I am not sure how I could do that. We could, I explained, have a closed funeral where he would supply a list of acceptable guests and only those listed names would be admitted. Or I could ask every woman who came in if they were the deceased's mistress. The son saw the difficulty of his request. I suggested an option—I would call the woman and invite her to come for a private viewing. He discussed the option with his family and they approved. He later thanked me for helping the family avoid an uncomfortable time."

Creating Alternative Rituals

Public Rituals

As important as funeral and other memorial rituals are, they also have limitations. They may exclude—intentionally or not—certain grievers. Distance or role may preclude participation, or the ritual does not meet the diverse spiritual or cultural needs of different mourners. Here creating alternative ritual opportunities has value.

Over the years, I have become very close to a small group of colleagues who meet once a year at a conference of our professional association. Each Saturday of the conference, once a year, we have a long, enjoyable evening together. Over time we decided to join together for a fall reunion—about midway through our conference year, at the homes of different members. We are getting older and we are aware that should something happen to one of us, it may be a while before everyone knows. A few members have already died. In these cases, not everyone could attend the funeral. We developed our own ritual—a tontine. When a member of the group dies, we monogram a series of glasses with that person's name. At our Saturday night dinners, we bring out the glasses, toast, and reminisce about our deceased friends. The last person alive will keep the collection. I find it both reassuring and comforting to know that I will be so remembered. After all, we have been together so long.

You also can create rituals to acknowledge your own special relationships—perhaps with coworkers or clients. For example, an agency that placed HIV-positive children in foster care developed a ritual to use whenever a child died. Often, the social worker and nurse team worked closely with the child and any biological family, as well as the foster family. While the team attended the funeral, their role was supportive as they assisted other mourners such as foster and biological family. In this agency-based ritual, they had an avenue to express their own grief and to be supported by their colleagues. Similarly, many hospices or hospitals may allow or encourage small staff rituals that acknowledge the loss of a particular patient.

Alternative rituals, such as those at a workplace, can allow other mourners an opportunity to acknowledge their unique relationship and their own personal sense of loss. Alternative rituals can also be used to acknowledge a distinct aspect of a person's identity. Many service clubs or fraternal organizations such as the Elks have their own ritual, perhaps performed at a visitation or as part of a funeral that acknowledges that the deceased was part of that organization.

Alternative rituals offer a way to acknowledge a special relationship or a unique identity, and they also can be useful in addressing issues of diversity. We belong to different cultures and have different beliefs. My aunt Nina was a real freethinker and agnostic. Most of the family is Christian. When Aunt Nina died, she instructed her daughter, Wendy, to have a big party in her honor—no funeral, no service. Nina's family came, but it was clear that they were far from pleased. Her daughter wanted to respect her mom's wishes but also recognized the needs of her extended family. She invited them to have a religious funeral distinct from the memorial celebration.

Alternative rituals can address not only different religious or spiritual needs, but also cultural needs as well. One Greek American client shared his story when his sister died. *My family is very emotional. Part of our culture is that we weep at a funeral. It is a mark of respect. I knew my brother-in-law's family would be appalled. We were very controlled at the funeral, out of consideration for them. But later we returned to the grave site and grieved in our own way.*

Funeral rituals mark the *beginning* of your journey with grief. Many faith traditions have varied rituals that mark other points in our journey. For example, Jews have a ritual called *yahrzeit* that marks the first anniversary of the death. Jews may also mark the anniversary of the death with an unveiling or dedication of the memorial stone. Catholics may celebrate anniversary masses. In addition, many Christians use All Saints' Day, November 1; or All Souls' Day, November 2, to commemorate those who died. Many faith traditions join together for December's winter solstice or Longest Night services that remember the special issues that we might face as bereaved individuals in the midst of Christmas or Hanukkah celebrations.

The point is that you can create your own rituals whenever you feel you need them—on holidays, or perhaps the anniversary of the death, or other milestones in our life. These rituals can be as simple as a private visit to the cemetery or as elaborate and public as you wish. One bereaved family of a slain state trooper sponsors an annual event each year in his memory to raise funds for a charity. Hundreds of friends, family, and state and local police attend this all-day affair.

We can incorporate the deceased in other rituals, perhaps offering a holiday toast in their memory. My son was very close to his grandmother. One of his disappointments is that she did not live long enough to attend his wedding. We began that wedding by lighting a candle to commemorate all those whom we loved and in order to symbolize their spiritual presence in our hearts and memories.

Stops on a Journey: Therapeutic Rituals

As I began counseling clients, I became interested in using ritual within the therapeutic process. Ritual is powerful, so I invited clients to create their own rituals as they needed them during their journeys with grief. No matter how someone grieved, a ritual was valuable. Rituals resonated with the instrumental or head grievers' need to engage in action, as well as the intuitive or emotional grievers' desire to express their feelings. In addition, these rituals bridged participants' spiritual/humanistic beliefs and their cultures. Some designed rituals that they did alone, while others included family or friends. These rituals spoke to different needs at varied points in their journey.

Rituals of Continuity

Continuity rituals acknowledge the continuing bond we have with the person we have lost. Examples are lighting a candle on a holiday or birthday to acknowledge and remember someone we loved, laying wreaths at memorials to fallen soldiers on Memorial or Veterans Days, and laying flowers on graves on holidays such as Mother's Day or Father's Day. The display of the AIDS Memorial Quilt or the Donor Quilts (for families to honor their deceased organ donor members) allow a wide range of individuals touched by the loss—family, friends, lovers—to symbolically state that these individuals memorialized still remain part of the fabric of life.

Rituals of continuity can be useful even when the loss is not a death. One foster parent, for example, gives a departing foster child a memory book of pictures acknowledging the child's stay. The parent also acknowledges her own loss with a collage of photos that includes all the foster children who had been part of her family and her life.

Rituals of Transition

Rituals of transition mark a change or movement since the loss experience. In one of the most powerful rituals of transition I ever witnessed, a middle-age woman, Lela, shared that her husband died following a long chronic illness. Prior to the illness, her husband had been healthy and strong. As Lela said, her husband did not do sick "well." Caregiving was stressful for both. Years later, Lela still found it difficult to remove her wedding ring, but was now ready to begin to date again. She could not date with a wedding ring on her finger, yet could not seem to remove it without having an emotional crisis.

As we discussed this quandary, she realized that the ring had great meaning for her. During the difficult time of the illness, they would often argue. But every night, they would go to bed together, clasp their hands so that their rings touched and repeat their wedding vows "in sickness and in health." This gave them the strength to face another day. It became clear that since the ring was placed in a ritual of great significance, it would have to be removed in a ritual. We planned a ritual with the priest at the church where she was wed. One Sunday afternoon, after mass, with her family present, the priest called Lela to the altar. He repeated the vows, now in the past tense. *Have you been faithful in good times and bad, in sickness and in health?* Lela could affirm, in the presence of her witnesses, that she had. *May I have the ring now,* the priest intoned. She later reported it came off "as if it were magic." We had already determined what to do with the ring. At the time of her husband's death, he was so emaciated by disease that the ring fit very loosely on his finger. After he died, Lela removed it and kept it. The priest later took both rings, and had them interlocked and welded to the frame of her wedding photograph—symbolizing that this vow was now completed.

Rituals of Reconciliation

Rituals of reconciliation allow an individual to offer or accept forgiveness, or to finish unfinished business. I once counseled a young girl, Rosa, who was dealing with the death of her mother, an IV drug user, from AIDS. Throughout the daughter's life, she had been placed in a kinship foster home each time her mother relapsed into drug use. Naturally, Rosa had a high degree of ambivalence toward her mother. I asked Rosa where her mother was now. Rosa replied her mother was a ghost. She explained her spirituality by saying that when good people died, they went to heaven and received angels' wings. Bad people went to hell, burning up to be skeletons. In between, people became ghosts. As Rosa explored and resolved her ambivalence, she announced one day that her mother could now go to heaven, Rosa having reached a point where she was able to forgive her mother for her addiction and neglect. We created a ritual where her mother received angels' wings, and through that, her daughter's forgiveness in the ritual itself. On a picture of her mother, Rosa pasted angels' wings she had made out of a doily. Then she asked that we burn the photograph (with the wings) so that her mother could fly to heaven. I thought it interesting that the mother still had to burn, even in a somewhat purging fire.

Rituals of Affirmation

Rituals of affirmation allow us to say thank-you for the legacies we have received from the deceased or lost person or lessons learned in the experience. Tyrone had felt deeply his dad's concern as Tyrone had struggled with alcoholism. Unfortunately, by the time Tyrone became alcohol free, his father had lapsed into early-onset dementia and soon died. Now each year for twenty years, Tyrone marks another year of sobriety by visiting his dad's grave—thanking his father for his patience and support, and reassuring his dad that he's kept his promise to him to become—and remain—sober. As part of the ritual he pours out a can of beer at the grave site—repeating his father's admonition to him to "just pour his beer down some drain."

Kyle also benefited from a ritual of affirmation. Kyle's dad died when Kyle was only four years old. His father's last act was to ask his friend, Kyle's godfather, to take special care of him. His godfather became a surrogate father to Kyle. As Kyle reached adolescence, he created a ritual to thank his father for putting such a supportive adult in his life. At a family ceremony, Kyle's godfather gave him the watch that his father had entrusted to his care, while Kyle thanked his dad for all the gifts he had given him—especially his mom and godfather's continuing love and support.

Creating Rituals

In creating therapeutic rituals, you need to remember a few things. First, rituals always emerge from your own story. Your rituals will be as individual as you are. Your story will suggest what type of ritual may be needed at that particular time.

Second, effective rituals have visible elements that also have symbolic significance. To Lela, the ring symbolized her commitment to her husband in sickness and health. For Rosa, the wings represented her forgiveness for her mom. Tyrone's pouring out beer was both a sign that he had respected his dad's wish and a pledge of sobriety.

You also can decide if you wish anyone to witness your ritual. Some rituals are inherently private, but others, such as Lela's, need witnesses to have therapeutic benefit.

You also need to plan rituals. Your planning affects the nature of the ritual you wish to have. As Lela and I planned her ceremony, I asked what would happen to the ring once she removed it. If she had held onto it, it might very well have ended up back on her finger. The decision to allow the priest to arrange to have it linked with her husband's and welded to their wedding photograph not only precluded that possibility, but provided a satisfying symbolic sense of the completion of a vow.

You may have to address practical considerations as you plan. Lela had asked friends and family to travel some distance to attend her planned ritual. Her ceremony would begin after the twelve noon mass—an anniversary mass for her late husband. We figured it would end sometime after one o'clock, but the church was an hour away from Lela's home. Would she just thank everyone and dismiss them? Lela decided she needed to rent the church's fellowship hall and cater a light lunch.

Finally, in addition to planning such a ritual, you need to find some way to process what you experienced. *How did you feel in the ritual? What were your thoughts during the ritual? What felt right? Was there any aspect that did not seem to work well? Is there anything you still need to do?* There are many ways you can do so—with a counselor, a friend, or even as you reflect in a journal.

As you design a ritual, you want to design it in such a way that it does not intrude upon or complicate the grief of other mourners. I was counseling a widow whose beloved husband had died. In the course of the time we spent together, it became clear that her husband had had a long and sustained, but totally unsuspected, affair with someone who was continually doing rituals at her husband's grave site. Whatever your relationship to the deceased, you have a right, a need to grieve—but that does not need to be exercised in a way that tramples on the rights or memories of other mourners.

Grief is not just an experience you have at a certain point in time. It is a lifelong journey. So it is fitting that, at various times in your life, you remember and mark your loss and your love. Ritual provides a way to do just that. It is a powerful therapeutic tool—validating grief and allowing opportunities for catharsis. Rituals offer support and meaning, even in the midst of loss. They allow you, in a uniquely individual way, to remember, to mourn, and to continue—perhaps even grow as you journey with grief.

CHAPTER 13

When Self-Help Is Not Enough

Darlene was not handling the death of her husband, Franco, well. She has been crying constantly for almost a year since his death from a massive stroke at age fifty-five. Since her husband's death, she sees little improvement in her ability to cope. Sometimes she even thinks that she has no reason to live without Franco. She misses him terribly. The smallest reminder—a song, a photograph—can trigger grief. Just two days before she had left dinner with friends when one ordered shrimp scampi—the same dish Franco always ordered. Given her highly emotionally charged behavior, Darlene has found herself more isolated.

She also is having problems at work. Her company was very sympathetic and supportive at first, and gave her two weeks bereavement leave with full pay. But they are becoming impatient with both her performance and her attendance. Her constant lateness and many absences have placed her job on the line. She finds it difficult to get up in the morning and only gets to sleep after a few stiff drinks.

> Even her relationships with her family have suffered. She complains of loneliness, yet frequently dismisses invitations to visit with her children and their families with the comment "You don't really want a sad widow around." Finally her daughter dragged her to a grief therapist. Darlene credits that intervention with not only saving her job but possibly also her life.

Self-help is sometimes not enough. For many, loss leads to other issues and problems: depression, anxiety, alcoholism, or substance abuse. It may make us physically ill or self-destructive. Significant loss increases our chance of illness and may actually kill us. It affects our mental health as well. Estimates now indicate that, following a significant loss in their lives, somewhere between 10 to 20 percent of grievers have more complicated reactions that will need mental health assistance. In fact, in the revision of the *Diagnostic and Statistical Manual of Mental Disorders* (*DSM-5*)—the guidebook of the American Psychiatric Association—complications to grief are noted in a variety of different conditions including depression, anxiety, and adjustment disorders. Moreover the *DSM-5* suggests that a new diagnosis—persistent complex bereavement-related disorder—merits further study for possible inclusion in a subsequent revision. The manifestations of this newly proposed disorder include a sense of meaninglessness in life, extreme bitterness and anger about the loss, and a feeling that a significant part of the self has died, creating an emotional numbness. Clearly, not all of us can handle grief on our own.

Complications of Grief

Grief and Physical Health

Chapter 2 has an extensive discussion of the ways that grief can affect your health. However, it is well to review that discussion here. There clearly is a great deal of research that indicates that physical symptoms and disease can be real complications of grief—especially for older persons when a spouse dies.[1] Grief is stressful, and stress negatively influences our health. Then most people die from chronic conditions that are affected by poor diet, use of alcohol or tobacco, and lack of exercise that are shared in a relationship. Finally, when a spouse dies, the surviving spouse may change his or her lifestyle and neglect health.

The take-home piece is that when you are grieving, you should carefully monitor your health and health practices. It is critically important at a time when you are under stress to maintain your patterns of exercise, to eat and sleep well, and to take any medications as prescribed. You should be careful of engaging in bad health practices such as self-medicating, abusing alcohol, or engaging in other self-destructive behaviors.

Grief and Mental Health Issues

Typical grief differs from mental illnesses. We know that typical grief is a normal reaction to loss—the price we pay for love—a syndrome with a range of reactions that include physical, emotional, behavioral, social, spiritual, and cognitive responses. The *DSM-5* addresses grief in a number of ways.[2] Typical reactions to grief (called uncomplicated bereavement) are listed under a broad category of "other conditions that may be a focus of clinical attention." This means that while typical grief is not an illness, individuals can benefit by discussing their reactions with a mental health professional. In fact, it suggests that counseling may be helpful for other losses mentioned in this section, including separation, divorce, or loss of employment. You often are the best judge of whether you think you need counseling. The encouragement of family and friends that you should seek counseling would suggest consultation even if only for the reassurance that your grief is not complicated.

The *DSM-5* lists a number of mental illnesses that can be triggered or complicated by a loss. One of the changes in the most recent edition of this document was to remove the "bereavement exclusion" from the diagnosis of a major depressive disorder. The exclusion meant that, except under rare circumstances, a diagnosis of depression should not be given to someone who had just experienced a loss. This was done to avoid confusing typical grief reactions with symptoms of depression and perhaps overmedicating individuals journeying with grief. However, in retrospect, it seems foolish to say when you can lose a leg or a job you can be diagnosed with depression, but not when you lose a spouse. In any case, the *DSM-5* tries to carefully differentiate the two—noting, among other things, that depression is a more persistent reaction, while grief is likely to be experienced as waves of loneliness and sadness. It also notes that while in grief you might experience guilt and regrets, in depression you are likely to experience a loss of self-esteem. In addition in grief, if you think about dying, it is likely because you wish to be with the person who died, while in depression you may entertain suicidal thoughts because you feel worthless or unable to cope with the pain of your depression.

If you think you are depressed and you experience, over a period of time (two weeks) a depressed mood—such as loss of interest or pleasure in activities once enjoyed; changes in appetite or sleep patterns; fatigue, apathy, or other such reactions that seem to impair your ability to function—you should seek assistance. You should be especially sensitive to such reactions if you have had a history of depression or you are aware that depressions run in your family. Normal treatment generally involves both grief counseling and the use of antidepressants.

A significant loss can trigger an anxiety disorder. The *DSM-5* makes the distinction that while grief involves yearning for the deceased, fear of separation from other attachment figures is the central factor in separation anxiety disorder. This means that the loss you experienced not only generates grief for the person who died, but makes you constantly anxious that you will lose others to whom you are attached. As with any mental disorder, this does not mean momentary feelings of anxiety, but rather sustained reactions that persist over time and impair your ability to function in key roles. For example, ever since her mother died, Aleah has become increasingly anxious that other family members will die. She constantly calls her husband, Caleb, at work, to check that he is well—so much so that a supervisor has noticed. Aleah herself hates to go to work—a job she once treasured—as she is fearful that something will happen to her children when she is at work. Finally, the *DSM-5* suggests that a condition called persistent complex bereavement-related disorder be considered for further study as a trauma, or stressor-related, disorder. This would mean that an individual has an extreme difficulty adjusting to the loss of another that severely impairs the ability to function in life.

Other Complicating Conditions

While many people are resilient or experience typical grief reactions, some pathways are more complicated. In *chronic grief*,[3] distress begins at a relatively high level and remains so. Over time, there is little improvement—at least without professional assistance—in the level of distress experienced. You may even recognize that your grief is complicated, acknowledging that somehow you have not been able to adjust satisfactorily to the loss and to reengage in life. Even years later, a small reminder or a fleeting memory can cause upset and generate tears. The strong surges of grief never seem to abate. In fact, after a few months, the lows you are experiencing in your journey with grief are just as intense, come as often, and last as long. You are "stuck" in your grief.

Grief groups may not be as helpful, at least in the beginning. You should seek professional evaluation. Here there are likely complications to your grief. Experiences such as a persistent, unending yearning for the person who died, an intense sorrow and emotional pain, a preoccupation with the deceased and the circumstance of the death, and a continuing emotional disruption of our lives that becomes disabling, are all symptoms of what has been proposed as persistent complex bereavement-related disorder.[4]

Gail fits this pattern. She is dealing with the death of her sixteen-year-old daughter for over two years now, and she recognizes that many friends are tiring of "being supportive." One cousin reminded her, somewhat harshly, that after a year she should "move on." To Gail, grief is a continuous companion. She constantly thinks about her daughter and finds herself crying often. She feels she "goes through the motions" each day at home, but even still much is left undone. She has taken a leave of absence from teaching and has no plans to return. The thought of seeing girls walking through the hallways frightens her. For Gail, even the idea that she may feel better is not only remote; it almost seems disloyal to her daughter's memory.

Chronic grievers such as Gail may need encouragement and support to seek professional assistance. Gail, for example, would benefit from a psychological assessment of the factors underlying her intense reaction to her loss. There are some new, very promising therapies such as complicated grief therapy that can assist grieving individuals like Gail.[5] This approach combines education about grief with a safe and structured retelling of the experience of the loss as well as attempts to find meaning within the relationship and loss. The therapy is sensitive to recognizing that grief involves dealing with the loss, reconstructing life, and creating new life goals after that loss.

Another complicated pathway is *escalating grief*. Here you may seem to do well at first, but as time continues the sense of loss and grief increases rather than abates. This may be a form of delayed grief.[6] There are a number of reasons for such a reaction. In some cases, you may not have much social support at the time. When Anne's adult son, Dan, suddenly died of a heart attack, all attention, including Anne's, was focused on Dan's wife and young children. Only later did Anne begin to focus on her own loss and her own grief.

Sometimes another loss or event might trigger this escalation. Father Jim was an Episcopalian clergyman whose dog had just died, and his grief was inconsolable. He was troubled by his reaction since in the past year he had buried both his mother and a beloved uncle and handled both losses well, presiding over the funeral and the burial rituals. He comforted other family members and successfully handled all the details, probating wills and handling estates with efficiency and wisdom. He was described as a tower of strength by those around him. "What kind of person," Jim asked, "could handle the death of these two wonderful human beings and somehow break down for a dog? What does it say of my relationships?" It became clear that Jim suppressed his grief over these earlier losses, submerging it in the multiple tasks he felt he needed to accomplish. The loss of his dog was fully his own. There was nothing to do but mourn. Now, he mourned all his losses.

If you are experiencing escalating grief, seek counseling to determine what factors may be intensifying your grief. Counseling may be especially helpful here since a lack of support may have led to this escalation, and support may be limited as considerable time has passed since the original experience of loss.

We continue to learn more about the complications of grief.[7] For example, grief can be *exaggerated* where one or more manifestations of grief, such as anger or guilt, are far out of proportion, or *masked* where another condition—perhaps substance abuse or alcoholism—conceals the underlying difficulty of grief.[8]

Most of us will experience typical grief when we experience a loss. However, for a variety of reasons, others of us may have more complicated reactions to a loss. Here is when self-help may not be enough. Here is when we need professional help.

There are reasons why grief can become complicated.[9] If you have a history of prior mental health issues such as depression or anxiety, a major loss can trigger a relapse. You also are more likely to have complicated grief reactions if you have had a history of early significant losses. When you have experienced these early losses in your life, your ability to bond or attach to others may be impaired. You seek the attachment to others, yet never quite trust it. You hold back—making your relationship somewhat ambivalent—thus complicating your grief.

The nature of the relationship also matters. If you have a highly dependent relationship with the person who died, your grief will be more complicated. In a highly dependent relationship, you feel helpless without the other person. You feel overwhelmed—you even wonder if you can survive without his or her support. If your attachment to the person is extreme, you may feel that you are diminished by the loss—a part of you is now missing.

If the deceased was highly dependent upon you, you may feel that you have failed that person. Even in a normally dependent relationship of a parent and a young child, it is not unusual for parents to feel they failed their child. This is one reason why the death of a child is, in and of itself, complicating.

Highly ambivalent relationships can be complicated. Here the mixed feelings—you love and hate the person simultaneously—torment your grief. Here you are likely to have unfinished business—things you said or did or things you failed to say or do.

Sometimes it is information you learn about the person after the death that complicates your grief. For example, parents grieved the death of an adolescent son who died of a drug overdose. Their son had been an honor student and star athlete, and at first they assumed that the overdose was some form of terrible accident or a result of peer pressure. Later, they found out that the son had been under police surveillance for a while as a suspected drug dealer in his high school. Their fears were confirmed when they found a hiding place in their son's room where he had over two thousand dollars and a stash of illegal drugs. In another incident, a wife learned that her husband, who traveled frequently on business, had a mistress and son in another area. In both these situations, the image of their loved one was dramatically challenged after the death. They realized there was a side of that person they had never known—casting doubt on all they believed and trusted about that person.

Grief also can be complicated by the nature of the death. Violent and traumatic deaths also challenge your assumptions. You may have to struggle with the issue of preventability—coping with what-ifs—if you are haunted by all the ways this loss might have been avoided. On the other hand, long, extended periods of illness when you are heavily involved in caregiving can increase ambivalence and complicated grief. Here you are overwhelmed by your responsibilities. It is natural and easy to feel that you just wish this would end—adding to guilt.

Finally, circumstances can complicate your loss. It is difficult to deal with one loss, but if you are coping with multiple losses in a short time, or struggling with other issues such as health, employment, or income, dealing with your loss is certainly more difficult. If your grief is disenfranchised you may find counseling useful, as other sources of support may not be available. And finally, grief is more difficult if, for one reason or another, you have to cope with it alone—that is, support is not available.

Seeking Support

When to Seek Support

The first reason to seek professional support is that you believe you might need or benefit from grief counseling or group support. Even if your grief is not complicated, such support can help in a number of ways. First, it can reassure you that your reactions to this new and difficult reality are what you might expect. It is often common, especially as you experience your first significant loss, to wonder if your reactions are unusual or problematic. Counseling can reassure you that these reactions are natural and normal responses to a situation that is anything but normal or natural. Second, you can explore the ways you are coping—acknowledging your strengths and learning to compensate for any weaknesses in coping. Here you can better deal with difficult situations. Finally, counseling offers tangible support, as well as the reassurance that you can get through your loss.

You also should consider grief support when your own support system is limited or unavailable. As you age, you may find that you outlived many of the people you once counted upon to help you get through a crisis. In other cases, for example, if you are away at college, deployed with the military, or working far from your home, you may have a support system that is either dispersed or distant. Here support groups or counselors can fill in the gap.

Clearly if you are harboring self-destructive thoughts, such as committing suicide or thinking of hurting others, you should seek immediate help. If your grief is disabling—that is, you cannot over time function in key roles because of depression, anxiety, or some other aspect of your grief—you need professional assistance. If you have a personal or family history of depression or anxiety, seeing someone may help you avoid triggering such reactions.

Other reactions may indicate that your grief, in fact, is more complicated than you may have realized. If you cannot speak of loss without intense grief, or a minor event triggers strong grief reactions, in these cases you are consumed by the loss—your loss and grief are the dominant themes in life. There seems to be no respite from your grief. Again, if grief, over time, is really interfering with the quality of your life, if you think you will never get over your loss, self-help may not be enough.

How and Where to Get Support

You want to find a mental health professional—a mental health counselor, therapist, psychiatrist, psychologist, social worker, or pastoral counselor—who has a current understanding of grief. The paradox is that grief counseling is often regarded as a core counseling skill, meaning that any counselor should be able to provide it, but many counselors have not kept current and are using older models, such as the theory that everyone has to experience certain stages such as denial, bargaining, anger, and depression before reaching a stage of acceptance. Seeing someone steeped in these older models would be like going to an oncologist using therapies and methods current in 1969! You want a therapist to recognize the individual ways that we grieve as well as the fact that we continue a bond with our loss.

There are good sources to ask for referrals. Hospices often have bereavement counselors on staff as well as local sources of referral. Funeral homes also may keep lists for referrals. Dr. Katherine Shear at the Center for Complicated Grief at Columbia University (complicatedgrief.org) has developed and pioneered a very promising complicated grief therapy, and can offer referrals to clinicians trained in that approach. Both the Association for Death Education and Counseling (adec.org) and the Hospice Foundation of America (hospicefoundation.org) also offer referrals.

Whatever the source of referral, you should always interview any counselor prior to engaging in a therapeutic relationship. There are a number of questions you might ask. Among them are: *Do you have any special training or certifications in grief counseling? Are you a member of the Association for Death Education and Counseling, or any other professional organization related to grief counseling? What are some of the theories and approaches that inform your counseling?* Here you want to be very cautious if they mention stage models. I would use therapists who offer answers like Margaret Stroebe and Henk Schut's dual process model, Therese Rando's Six R processes, or Worden's task model. Another question: *What approaches do you use for treating more complicated forms of grief?* Current approaches to treating complicated grief such as complicated grief therapy, or restorative retelling—among many other approaches—tend to use similar approaches that include cognitive therapies and education about the grief process. In addition, they often apply some form of imaging, where you imagine conversations with the deceased.

Grief is not an illness but a normal, albeit transitional, experience of life. Yet at times your grief can be complicated, and self-help is not enough. If you need to seek out professional support, be sure that you are being supported by someone who understands the very individual pathways of grief—your pathway.

CHAPTER 14

Growing In and Through Grief

In the summer of 1981, John Walsh was a partner in a hotel management company when his six-year-old son, Adam, went missing. The police had a somewhat nonchalant attitude, reassuring him that missing children often shortly return. Sixteen days later, Adam's severed head was found in a drainage canal over a hundred miles from home.

John deeply grieved the death of his son, and he memorialized Adam by founding the Adam Walsh Child Resource Center—a nonprofit organization that advocated for missing and exploited children. The Center helped pass new laws that created a national directory of sex offenders and facilitated interagency cooperation in locating missing children. Many stores now have instituted a "code Adam"—a store lockdown when a child is reported lost in the store.

John was later convinced that a serial killer, Ottis Toole, murdered his son based on Toole's later recanted confession and then a deathbed confession allegedly made to his niece. John hosted *America's Most Wanted*—a reality show that helped

> capture approximately a thousand fugitives. Walsh believed that if such a national program had existed earlier, Toole and his sometime accomplice, Henry Lee Lucas, might have been apprehended before Toole had kidnapped Adam.
>
> While none of this can bring Adam back, John Walsh had choices within his grief. He chose to make the Adams of the world—the other missing and exploited children—safer, as a legacy to his son's death and life.

Grief can have a mysterious math. Some are deeply diminished by a loss. Others grow despite—perhaps even because of—loss. Blooming widows are able to use the death of a spouse as a spur for growth. Some children shaken by parental loss seek achievement and power as a way to adapt to their sense of vulnerability.[1]

It may seem insensitive to speak about how we grow in grief—perhaps even cruel. After all, in the midst of your pain, it is tactless to attempt to say there may be a silver lining on that very dark cloud of your loss. In counseling, I usually do not even bring up the topic until a client first mentions how he or she has grown even in their grief—noting new sensitivities, skills, or insights. Then, and only then, do I feel confident to ask the question, *Have you noticed any growth in other areas?*

Yet the truth is that ultimately you have to decide whether you will grow up or down from your encounter with loss. Loss will change us. Our lives will now be different. That is an unalterable aspect of loss. You have no choice that your life will change. You do have choice about *how* it will change. You can learn from the stories of people who choose to "grow up" as they deal or have dealt with loss. These lessons remind you that you can do more than simply cope with loss—you can learn that grief, however painful, offers opportunities for growth.

Growing in Grief

Two University of North Carolina professors, Drs. Lawrence Calhoun and Richard Tedeschi, have extensively studied what they term *posttraumatic growth*.[2] They define posttraumatic growth as the positive changes that we experience as a result of our struggle with traumatic events, such as a significant loss. Such events are transitional lines or turning points in our life. We now look at our life as having parts—before and after our loss.

Drs. Calhoun and Tedeschi are deeply sensitive to the suffering these events entail. Yet they note that in many spiritual traditions, perhaps all, there is recognition of a central human truth—that the remarkable nature of human beings is that sometimes in suffering we are opened to looking at reality in new ways, that sometimes suffering engenders growth. Dr. Joanne Jozefowski calls the ability to create positive meaning from negative experiences "spiritual alchemy."[3] Growth can occur in a number of areas.

Changes in Lifestyle

Sometimes the death of another becomes a wakeup call. These deaths can sharpen our own awareness of mortality. You may decide to examine your own life and make changes to enhance your own lifestyle practices and your health. When I was a lifeguard in the late sixties and early seventies, we prided ourselves on our deep tans. We were both unaware and probably uncaring about any health risks. Decades later, when one of my friends from that era developed and subsequently died from melanoma, we heeded his call to be preventive in having annual skin checks—something I have done now for over two decades.

For others, the death of someone you care about may change your lifestyle practices in many ways. You may diet, seek to eat healthier, exercise more, cease the use of tobacco, or limit alcohol. Death can be a stark reminder that the choices you make may very well determine not only how you live but how long.

Relating to Others

You can also grow in your relationships with others. Sometimes you are touched by the compassion and care of others. Denise, for example, became more caring, open, and giving after her divorce. She reflected on how much she needed and counted on the support that she received from her family in that difficult time. She had been so focused on her relationship with her husband, and her sense of betrayal when she learned of his affairs, that she rarely was there for her friends. Yet she was deeply touched that, despite that, they were there for her. She now pays it forward—anxious to be supportive to those around her. She describes herself as far more compassionate and open to receiving—and giving help.

For Thomas, the death of his dad was a life changer. They had good rapport, but after college, Thomas married and worked about three hundred miles from his dad. Busy with work, wife, and children, Thomas had little time for anything else. He and his dad spoke once a week—a scheduled Sunday call. He wanted to visit, but outside of alternating Christmas and Thanksgiving holiday visits with his in-laws, they almost never got together more than once a year. When Thomas received the shocking call that his dad had a massive heart attack, he rushed to the hospital—getting there minutes after his father had died.

For a long time, Thomas dealt with the guilt and unfinished business of his relationship. He wished he'd visited more often, talked more frequently, and told his dad how much he loved him. Now, after that struggle, he is far more open with his mother, wife, children, siblings, and friends. He continues the weekly call with his mother but frequently calls during the week as well. He hugs his children daily and shares his feelings often. No matter how sudden the loss of anyone else might be in the future, Thomas has resolved that there will no longer be any unfinished business.

Reaffirmation and Renewal of Personal Strengths and Skills

While a loss can make you aware of how dangerous and unpredictable the world can be, it also makes you aware of how tough and strong you really are. At the time of your loss, you wonder how—or even doubt if—you can survive. Yet you do. When you do, you become aware of your own hidden strengths. You discover that you are more powerful and more self-reliant than you ever imagined—that you can deal with tragedies you never thought you could survive. You now become more confident in your abilities to handle difficult life events. You have survived before; you can survive again.

In the absence of someone who played important roles in your life, you may have to master new skills. They may be domestic skills—cooking, cleaning, or handling family finances. Or you may now have to run businesses or take on tasks you never imagined.

Indira worried constantly what would happen to her if her husband, Viji, died. She had married right after college, moving directly from her father's house to her husband's. Viji handled all the finances. She barely knew where their bank accounts were. They had a good marriage for nearly twenty-five years and had two sons—one just starting college, the other in high school before Viji was diagnosed with pancreatic cancer.

The first year after Viji died was rough. Her parents came from India for the funeral and stayed for nearly seven months, helping her master the new skills she needed. As she learned these new skills, she found that she had a talent for managing finances. More than that, Indira recognized strengths she never dreamed she had. Reserved, almost subservient in her relationships, she now had to assume the leadership of the hotel her husband owned. She also had to manage her two boys—especially the younger son, who acted out a bit after his dad's death.

Like Indira, we can be surprised at our resilience and acquire new skills. You may even find that you are stronger and more adept than you imagined. You may gain a stronger sense of self, discover new talents, and assume new roles.

You may even find that your loss generated significant changes that in some way made the world better—creating new laws, or something more local such as a safety rail or traffic light where none had been before. However significant such changes are—in yourself or society—they do not bring the person back. Yet that is not the choice. The choice is how you deal with the loss you experienced. The choice is to grow up or grow down.

New Possibilities

A significant loss can lead, over time, to significant development. As you change and grow in response to the loss, you find more new interests and paths than you ever expected. For Indira, out of necessity, she had to take charge of her late husband's fledgling hotel business. At first she was overwhelmed by the responsibilities, but within a short time, she realized she enjoyed the work. In the beginning she thought the work provided a diversion from her grief, but soon she realized she actually enjoyed the challenges. In the years since her husband Viji's death, she now has come to own two hotels and manages two others.

Dr. Catherine Sanders began her quest to understand her own grief after the accidental death of her adolescent son. Gaining a doctorate in psychology, she was a successful author, researcher, and therapist—a pioneer in the study of grief. She even hosted one of the first psychology radio shows in the 1980s in Charlotte, North Carolina.

The point is that sometimes loss makes you look at yourself and your world in a new way. You can no longer live the life you formerly lived, however much you wish to do so. Yet sometimes, as you are forced by your loss to look at life in a new way, you find new opportunities and possibilities.

Appreciation of Life

Loss teaches that life is fragile and unsure. This can be terrifying, or it can remind you that each day is precious. You can now acknowledge that life is a gift. As part of that awareness, your priorities change. You have a greater sense of what is important and less patience with the trivia of life. You may decide you need to spend more time doing what you wish with the people you love—your family and friends.

In the course I teach on Counseling Individuals with Life-Threatening Illness, we watch a film called *Death*. This documentary captures, in a vivid and realistic way, the last days of a middle-age man, Albro, as he is dying of cancer. Albro speaks candidly about the regrets he has over his life. Often, he reminds us, there were things he wished to do—go to a movie or other simple pleasures. Instead, perpetually short of time, he would clean his apartment. He had planned that when he would retire—an event he would now never experience—he would have more time to do as he wished. Even watching the film annually fills my class and me with a renewed appreciation of life. I regain the strength not to always be caught in the endless activity of life but to take the time to do the things that I really enjoy—ski with family and friends, catch a movie, or watch my grandchildren play. The old joke is relevant here: Nobody ever lies on their deathbed thinking, *I wish I'd spent more time in the office.*

A Deepened Sense of Spirituality

A final growth that Calhoun and Tedeschi found in their research was spiritual change—a deepened sense of spirituality. Loss often challenges your spiritual beliefs. Some may find their faith so shaken that they never regain it. Others may find their community and rituals get them through the loss. You now have a new appreciation of your beliefs. They have sustained and supported you through the crisis. You know, far more than you previously did, how much your beliefs count and mean. But others find that out of this spiritual struggle, new insights and a stronger spirituality emerge. Like the biblical story of Jacob, it may be a very intense struggle—one where you feel you are wrestling with God.

After a loss, the world does not seem to follow such neat and fast rules. You may now accept that not all questions can be answered, and embark on deeper sense of spiritual quest.

Growth versus Resilience

Posttraumatic growth is a transformative response that arises out of our suffering through loss.[4] Resilient grievers' assumptions about the world are less likely to shatter when facing a loss. Some resilient grievers experienced growth through adversities earlier in life, so they are able to cope with current loss. If you are handling the current loss well, you need not worry that you are not experiencing some of the growth discussed in this chapter. You simply can take comfort in your resilience.

Empowering Growth

Reflecting on What Is Lost and What Is Left

The first step in transforming loss is to recognize what is lost and what is left.[5] By that, I mean first you really need to understand the scope of your losses—that is, how the loss affects your life, including all the secondary losses that accompany it, and how that loss deeply affects your sense of self. For Helen, for example, the death of her only child, Carey, as a young adult brought with it not only the loss of a child but many additional losses as well. Her close relationship with Joyce, Carey's girlfriend, would be changed as it would with all of Carey's friends who once frequented her home. She acknowledged that her dreams and wishes for grandparenthood would have to be abandoned. Even her identity as a mother seemed somewhat challenged. In counseling, we explored what it means to be a mother when your only child dies.

Yet we also had to explore what she had now, and to determine how she would remember her son—what memories to bring and what memories to leave behind. Helen realized she had continuing bonds she retained with her son. She had rich memories of Carey and could affirm that she would always be Carey's mom—that was part of her biography that could never be altered. And she could appreciate all the legacies Carey had left. We talked about how fossilized animals leave an imprint that continues to be visible long after their deaths. I asked Helen to recount Carey's imprint on all aspects of her life, including her mannerisms and gestures, the way she spoke, her work and leisure, her own ways of relating to others, her feeling about herself and others, her personality, and her values and beliefs. We then explored what imprints she wished to affirm and develop, as well as any she would like to relinquish and change. As we concluded these sessions, Helen reaffirmed the bond she would continue to maintain with her son.

EXERCISE ON LIFE IMPRINTS[6]

Think of taking a seashell and placing it in wet sand or clay. It would leave an imprint. The people in our lives also leave imprints. Some of these are legacies that strengthen us. Some might be liabilities that we need to overcome. Yet others leave their marks or imprints upon us. These remain even in our loss. Think of a person whose imprint you would like to trace.

What impact did the person have on . . .

- My mannerisms and gestures: _____
- My way of speaking and communicating: _____
- My hobbies and pastime activities: _____
- My basic personality: _____
- My values and beliefs: _____

What imprints do I wish to affirm and develop? _____

What imprints would I like to relinquish and change? _____

Recognizing and Using Your Strengths

Growing in grief is never easy, but it is a choice you can exercise. Perhaps it is the major choice that we are offered. Sanders thought so. In her research, she found that when we grieve we ultimately have to choose between death, maintaining our current state, or growth. But how do we grow?[7]

The first step is to take personal stock. The very fact that you have lived this long indicates that you do have strengths in reserve. Even if you have never faced a loss like the one you are experiencing now, you likely have experienced prior losses and crises in your life. Reflect on these. *What helped me get through these events? What strengths did I have that helped me through those times? Am I overlooking strengths that helped me in the past?* These strengths can be external strengths, such as the support that others can offer, or inner strengths, what you have inside yourself like your spirituality or ability to cope. Ask yourself, *How do my spiritual beliefs or my philosophy of life speak to me about this loss?*

Sometimes you have to reexamine these strengths. One client, when I asked that question, noted that her husband had really helped her deal with the deaths of her parents. Now, she reminded me, it was his death she was mourning. I asked her how her husband helped. She replied that he let her share her feelings, never judged them, and always reassured her that she would get through this. After all, he was there. I then reminded her that the strength her husband offered was both careful listening and a supportive, unconditional presence. I asked who could offer that type of support to her now. She was able to recognize that both her daughter and her sister could provide those same essential strengths.

You do not have to grieve alone. You can make connections with family and friends and with others as well. Varied organizations such as faith-based communities can provide both opportunities to find help as well as opportunities to help. Support groups can also be helpful. They allow contact with others who have experienced similar losses and trauma. As you hear others speak of their strengths, you will be reminded of your own. As you hear others discuss how they handled varied events and difficulties, you might recognize what you could do.

Experimenting with Your Grief

When I was in kindergarten, we cut open milk cartons, placed soil in the containers, and planted seeds for bean sprouts. I suppose the lesson was to see how plants grow—something city kids do not always experience. For me though, the real lesson was patience. Each day as I watered my plant on the windowsill, I anxiously searched for signs of growth. It took time.

Grief, too, takes time. Sometimes you want to get over it so rapidly that you lack the patience to let the process unfold. You expect to wake up one day and be "better." You need to give yourself time to grieve, but like watering a plant, you can sometimes test how far along you are in the process.

You can experiment. By this I mean that you can test yourself as to what you can do. Helen, for example, indicated that she wanted to make a scrapbook of Carey's life—one for her and one for Carey's girlfriend, Joyce. Yet she said it was just too painful, so she put it aside. I challenged Helen to experiment—to periodically assess if she was ready to begin the scrapbook today. There was to be no pressure. After all, it was only an experiment. She did try a number of times and found she could not continue. It was just too painful. One day, though, she proudly showed off the beginnings of her scrapbook. The day before, she had experimented and found she was now ready.

Choosing and Choosing to Grow

You also have smaller choices throughout grief. *Who will I spend the holidays with this year? How shall I mark the anniversary of the death?* Sometimes you drift into these decisions—taking the path of least resistance. In my counseling, I constantly pose that as a choice—emphasizing that you can empower yourself to make these decisions.

Once you have made them, you can assess how well they worked for you. In doing so it is important to focus on what went well and what did not. For example, the first Christmas after Carey's death, Helen decided to spend part of it with her sister's family and to have breakfast with Joyce. They shared stories and memories of Carey and cried and laughed together. It was very satisfying. Dinner with her sister's family was more mixed. Carey's death was the elephant in the room. No one quite knew whether to say something about it or not. Finally Helen broke the tension with a toast to her son. At that point, her family knew it was safe to speak about Carey. She had allowed a nephew to drive her to the party. She later realized that was a bit of a mistake. By the early evening Helen was beginning to tire, but her nephew and his family were still enjoying the time. They did not leave for a few hours—exhausting Helen.

As we analyzed the event later in counseling, Helen could congratulate herself on her good choices. Visits with Joyce and with her sister were safe places to spend the holidays. The toast to her son was a helpful gesture and important symbol to the family that it was not only appropriate but important to include Carey. She realized that, in the future, she would do well to bring her own car. She would do so at Easter. As she reviewed the day, Helen felt more confident in her own abilities—more at ease in making decisions. She could celebrate her response to the challenge of the holidays. After all, her instinctive first response was to attempt to forget the holidays. She knew she could make decisions that would allow comfortable connections even as she grieved. That would bode well for the future. Small choices empower bigger ones.

Keeping Perspective

Another part of growth is keeping your perspective in grief. Review how you are changing as you cope with loss—celebrating, like Helen, your small triumphs. I begin each support group for surviving spouses by asking, *How has your story changed since the last session?* Here the survivors focus on what they learned, new insights they received, or new skills that they have mastered.

Part of perspective is focusing on the future. When I work with individuals or support groups, as we approach the end of our time together, I always ask what they would say if I meet them a year from now. What would have changed in their lives? What are their goals? I find such questions allow them to focus more on what they still want out of life—even as they cope with loss.

In her later years, Sanders even began to develop the notion of a sixth phase of grief she called *fulfillment*—a point at which you could look back on your own life in a way that integrates the earlier loss into the fabric of your life.[8] In fact, she believed that in this phase your life journey only made sense given the experience of loss. While the loss was neither welcomed nor anticipated, you could no longer imagine what life would be like without that loss. This sense included a belief that you have done well, not only despite the loss, but in a very real way because of the loss. The underlying themes, played out in the life of Sanders and so many others who have journeyed with grief, is that however painful and inexplicable the loss was, we have grown in ways we never imagined. Not that we wished to pay the price of our loss, but since we were not given that choice, we did choose to grow. There is no greater legacy to your loss. I hope that will be your choice—and your legacy.

ACKNOWLEDGMENTS

First and foremost I have to thank my agent, Jennifer Gates from Zachary Shuster Harmsworth, for her vision for the book. Without her this book would not exist. I also need to acknowledge both Jennifer Gates and Jacob Moore's contributions to the proposal. I am most appreciative to Dr. Charles Corr, my mentor and friend, for his constant and consistent editorial comments, as well as to Richard Dickens and Tonie Papaleo for their suggestions.

It is fitting to acknowledge, in a special way, all those colleagues whose work is recognized in so many end notes. They are more than a footnote, as their ideas and contributions stimulated and nurtured my own thinking and this book. I thank colleagues like Thomas Attig, George Bonanno, Lawrence Calhoun, Charles Corr, Stephen Fleming, Earl Grollman, Terry Martin, Robert Neimeyer, Danai Papadatou, Colin Murray Parkes, Therese A. Rando, Henk Schut, Katherine Shear, Margaret Stroebe, Richard Tedeschi, and J. William Worden for all they have contributed over so many years.

My many colleagues in the Association for Death Education and Counseling and the International Work Group on Death, Dying, and Bereavement also provided constant support. Leslie Balmer, Robert Bendiksen, John Birrell, Dana Cable, Phil Carverhill, Chris Hall, Neil Heflin-Wells, Gail Martin, Lu Redmond, Sherry Schachter, and

Deiann Sobers, to name a few, provided, over many years, stimulation and camaraderie.

My own college has been so supportive for over thirty years. I will always appreciate the freedom and opportunity to develop professionally that I have had at the College of New Rochelle, and the stimulation offered by my graduate students. I would like to acknowledge the support of President Judith Huntington, Provost Dorothy Escribano, Vice President Colette Geary, Dean Marie Ribarich, and Associate Dean Wendi Vescio. Three who share interest in palliative care and grief, Claire Lavin, Dennis Ryan, and Lynda Shand, also have stimulated my thinking in this area, as well offering the support and collegiality so evident at the college. For many of those years, Vera Mezzacuella, our faculty secretary, has generously offered all types of assistance. Once, again, I thank her. Our division's administrative assistant, Diane Lewis, keeps everything else operating with cheery efficiency.

For over twenty years, I have had the privilege of being a consultant to the Hospice Foundation of America (HFA). This has helped me professionally in so many ways. Each year, preparation for a new teleconference and accompanying book continues to make me stretch my professional knowledge. In addition, I have enjoyed the professional stimulation and personal friendships of the so many wonderful people I have met there including the late Jack Gordon, Myra MacPherson, David Abrams, Lisa Veglahn, Norman Sherman, and the staff—past and present. I have to give special thanks and mention to my frequent collaborator and coeditor, and always friend—HFA's CEO, Amy Tucci.

I am fortunate to live in a community that really is one. For that I thank my neighbors Paul Kimball, Allen and Gail Greenstein, Jim Millar, Robert and Tracey Levy, Fred and Lisa Amori, Chris and Dorota Fields, and all my friends in my community. They keep me grounded.

Most important, I need to acknowledge all those in my personal life who are always a source of pride and joy. My son, Michael, and his wife, Angelina, my grandson Kenny, and granddaughter Lucy make it all seem so worthwhile. I treasure them always.

I appreciate the gift of godchildren as well—William James Rainbolt, Austin Rainbolt, Scott Carlson, Christine Romano, and Keith Whitehead. They and the other members of my intimate network of family and friends including Kathy Dillon; my sister, Dorothy, and my brother, Franky; and all of their families as well as Eric Schwarz; Larry Laterza; Ellie Andersen; Jim, Karen and Greg Cassa; Lynn Miller; Kim Rainbolt, Lisa, Cody and Ciara Carlson; Tom and Lorraine Carlson; Ken and Elaine Gilmore; Chris and Mary Anderson; Linda, Russell, and Ryan Tellier; Liz Galindo; Peter Levins; and Diane, Evan, and Jesse Brohan provide nurturing, encouragement, respite, friendship and, most important, laughter. The Internet has allowed contact with once long-lost friends. To that technology, I owe renewed ties to Ed Hodges, Alice Hum, Kathy Nacey, and Bruce and Lynne Prochnik—all of whom were important presences as I navigated childhood and adolescence, and now not only offer warm reminiscence but continued friendships.

Finally, I have to acknowledge the careful, instructive, and incredible editing, help, encouragement, and infinite patience of my editor, Leslie Meredith and the staff at Atria. And, of course, I need to acknowledge all those people who in their own struggle with grief taught me much about loss—and life.

APPENDIX: RESOURCES

Self-Help Book Distributors

- The Centering Corporation (centering.org)
- Compassion Books (compassionbooks.com)

Both are book services offering a wide range of resources for individuals who are grieving.

Sources of Information, Referral, and Support

- Alive Alone (alivealone.org): Offers information and support for parents who have lost an only child or all their children.
- Association for Death Education and Counseling (adec.org): A professional association for grief counselors and others in the field. Offers information including a current list of certified grief counselors.
- Camp Erin (moyerfoundation.org/programs/camperin.aspx): A network of children's bereavement camps supported by the Moyer Foundation.
- Center for Complicated Grief, Columbia University School

of Social Work (complicatedgrief.org): Offers referrals to therapists trained in complicated grief therapy.

- Dougy Center (dougy.org): Based in Oregon, this center offers support groups for grieving children. While locally based, it also can provide information on programs, based on their model, operating throughout the country.
- Gilda's Clubs: These clubs are independently offered in many sections of the country for individuals and families struggling with cancer. Check locally for the nearest club. Many offer services to individuals grieving a death from cancer.
- GriefNet (griefnet.org): This very rich Web site offers over fifty e-mail support groups, as well as access to a range of resources including books and music.
- Hospice Foundation of America (hospicefoundation.org): Offers grief information and programs for both counselors and the general public.
- National Alliance for Grieving Children (nationalallianceforgrievingchildren.org): Provides information and referral to counseling, camps, and support groups for children and adolescents throughout the country.
- Parents of Murdered Children (pomc.com): Offers information and referral to families victimized by homicide.
- Share (nationalshare.org): Offers support for pregnancy and infant loss.
- Survivors of Suicide (survivorsofsuicide.com): Offers information and referrals to families where an individual has died by suicide.
- The Compassionate Friends (compassionatefriends.org): A major support group for parents where a child of any age has died. It also provides services to siblings and grandparents. The Compassionate Friends offers information, resources, and connections to local and online support groups.
- Twinless Twins (twinlesstwins.org): Provides information and support for twins who have experienced the death of their twin.

Web Opportunities to Create Memorial Sites

- MuchLoved (muchloved.com/gateway/muchloved-charitable-trust.htm)
- Virtual Memorials (virtual-memorials.com)
- Legacy.com (memorialwebsites.legacy.com)

NOTES

Chapter 1: The Myths and Realities of Grief

1. Elisabeth Kübler-Ross, *On Death and Dying* (New York: Macmillan, 1969).
2. Kenneth J. Doka, ed., *Disenfranchised Grief: New Directions, Challenges, and Strategies for Practice* (Champaign, IL: Research Press, 2002).
3. Kübler-Ross, *On Death and Dying.*
4. See Kenneth J. Doka and Amy S. Tucci, eds., *Beyond Kübler-Ross: New Perspectives on Death, Dying, and Grief* (Washington, DC: Hospice Foundation of America, 2011).
5. See Doka and Tucci, *Beyond Kübler-Ross.*
6. Sigmund Freud, "Mourning and Melancholia" (1917), in *The Standard Edition of the Complete Psychological Works of Sigmund Freud*, James Stachey, ed., vol. 14 (London: Hogarth Press, 1957), 239–60.
7. While grief clinicians and researchers had started challenging this idea of detachment decades ago, the more recent publication of Dennis Klass, Phyllis R. Silverman, and Steven L. Nickman's book *Continuing Bonds: New Understandings of Grief* (Washington, DC: Taylor & Francis, 1996) made a persuasive case.
8. Nancy Berns, *Closure: The Rush to End Grief and What It Costs Us* (Philadelphia: Temple University Press, 2011).
9. Carol Staudacher, in her book *Men & Grief*, expresses this succinctly: There is only one way to grieve. That way is to go through the core of grief. Only by experiencing the necessary emotional effects of your loved one's death is it possible for you to eventually resolve the loss. See Carol Staudacher, *Men & Grief* (Oakland, CA: New Harbinger, 1991), 3.
10. Camille B. Wortman and Roxane Cohen Silver, "The Myths of Coping with Loss," *Journal of Consulting and Clinical Psychology* 57:3 (June 1989), 349–57.

11. Kenneth J. Doka and Terry L. Martin, *Grieving Beyond Gender: Understanding the Ways Men and Women Mourn* (New York: Routledge, 2010).
12. To George A. Bonanno, a well-respected Columbia University psychologist writing in *The Other Side of Sadness: What the New Science of Bereavement Tells Us about Life after Loss* (New York: Basic Books, 2000), loss is an inevitable aspect of the human condition. Since we have always coped with loss, we have developed a remarkable capacity for coping with loss well—even growing, not in spite of it, but because of it. To Bonanno, most people need to process grief only minimally, and few need, or even benefit, from professional assistance and intervention. Ruth Davis Konigsberg, a journalist, makes similar claims in her book, *The Truth about Grief: The Myth of Its Five Stages and the New Science of Loss* (New York: Simon & Schuster, 2011). This is not surprising since Konigsberg draws heavily from Bonanno's research. Konigsberg's book is more of a journalistic exposé. Her theme is that a "grief industry" has developed that perpetuates the mandates of grief counseling as well as the myth of stages.
13. We have always recognized that reality. The British psychiatrist Colin Murray Parkes is, in many ways, the father of contemporary grief studies. He began working with Dame Cicely Saunders, the founder of the modern hospice movement, in St. Christopher's Hospice outside of London. He wrote an important research article decades ago entitled "Grief Counseling: Who Needs It?" His conclusion rings true today. See Colin Murray Parkes, "Bereavement Counselling: Does It Work?" *British Medical Journal* 281:6232 (July 5, 1980), 3–6.
14. George A. Bonanno, Camille B. Wortman, and Randolph M. Nesse, "Prospective Patterns of Resilience and Maladjustment During Widowhood," *Psychology and Aging* 19:2 (June 19, 2004), 260–71.
15. Therese A. Rando, ed., *Clinical Dimensions of Anticipatory Mourning: Theory and Practice in Working with the Dying, Their Loved Ones, and Their Caregivers* (Champaign, IL: Research Press, 2000).

Chapter 2: The Experience of Grief

1. Colin Murray Parkes, Bernard Benjamin, and R. G. Fitzgerald, "Broken Heart: A Statistical Study of Increased Mortality among Widowers," *British Medical Journal* 1:5646 (March 22, 1969), 740–43.
2. J. Richard Williams, "Effects of Grief on a Survivor's Health," in *Living with Grief: Loss in Later Life*, Kenneth J. Doka, ed. (Washington, DC: Hospice Foundation of America, 2002), 191–206.
3. Jie Li, Margaret Stroebe, Cecilia L. W. Chan, and Amy Y. M. Chow, "Guilt in Bereavement: A Review and Conceptual Framework," *Death Studies* 38:3 (March 2014), 165–71.
4. The term is used by Jennifer Elison and Chris McGonigle in *Liberating Losses: When Death Brings Relief* (Cambridge, MA: Perseus, 2003). It also is evident in work on posttraumatic growth; see Lawrence G. Calhoun and Richard G.

Tedeschi, eds., *Handbook of Posttraumatic Growth: Research and Practice* (Mahwah, NJ: Lawrence Erlbaum Associates, 2006).

5. See Louis LaGrand, *After Death Communication: Final Farewells* (St. Paul, MN: Llewellyn Publications, 1997).
6. LaGrand, *After Death Communication.*
7. LaGrand, *After Death Communication.*
8. C. S. Lewis, *A Grief Observed* (New York: Bantam, 1963).

Chapter 3: Your Journey with Grief: Understanding the Process

1. Derald Wing Sue and David Sue, *Counseling the Culturally Diverse: Theory and Practice*, 6th ed. (Hoboken, NJ: John Wiley & Sons, 2013).
2. See Donald Woods Winnicott, "Transitional Objects and Transitional Phenomena," *International Journal of Psycho-Analysis* 34:2 (1953), 89–97.
3. Pauline Boss, *Ambiguous Loss: Learning to Live with Unresolved Grief* (Cambridge, MA: Harvard University Press, 1999).
4. Kenneth J. Doka, ed., *Disenfranchised Grief: New Directions, Challenges, and Strategies for Practice* (Champaign, IL: Research Press, 2002).
5. Froma Walsh and Monica McGoldrick, eds., *Living Beyond Loss: Death in the Family* (New York: Norton, 1991).
6. Isabel Fearon, Patrick McGrath, and Helen M. Achat, "'Booboos': The Study of Everyday Pain among Young Children," *Pain* 68:1 (November 1996), 55–62.
7. Sue and Sue, *Counseling the Culturally Diverse.*
8. Susan Nolen Hoeksema, "Ruminative Coping and Adjustment to Bereavement," in *Handbook of Bereavement Research: Consequences, Coping, and Care*, Margaret S. Stroebe, Robert O. Hansson, Wolfgang Stroebe, and Henk Schut, eds. (Washington, DC: American Psychological Association, 2001), 545–662.
9. Colin Murray Parkes, "Bereavement Counselling: Does It Work?" *British Medical Journal* 281:6232 (July 5, 1980), 3–6.
10. Margaret S. Stroebe and Henk Schut, "The Dual-Process Model of Coping with Bereavement: Rationale and Description," *Death Studies* 23:3 (April-May 1999), 197–224.
11. For an extended discussion see Therese A. Rando, *Treatment of Complicated Mourning* (Champaign, IL: Research Press, 1993).
12. Catherine M. Sanders, *Grief: The Mourning After: Dealing with Adult Bereavement* (New York: John Wiley & Sons, 1989).
13. In his seminal book *Grief Counseling and Grief Therapy*, Dr. J. William Worden offers a task model that exemplifies the value of our new understandings of grief. Worden identifies four major issues that need to be addressed as we grieve. I have added one more task to Worden's list. J. William Worden, *Grief Counseling and Grief Therapy: A Handbook for the Mental Health Practitioner*, 4th ed. (New York: Springer, 2009).
14. Charles A. Corr, "A Task-Based Approach to Coping with Dying," *Omega: Journal of Death and Dying* 24:2 (1991–92), 81–94.

15. Thomas Attig, *How We Grieve: Relearning the World*, rev. ed. (New York: Oxford University Press, 2011).
16. Attig, *How We Grieve.*
17. Sanders, *Grief.*

Chapter 4: Your Style of Grieving

1. Terry L. Martin and Kenneth J. Doka, *Men Don't Cry . . . Women Do: Transcending Gender Stereotypes of Grief* (Philadelphia: Brunner/Mazel, 1999); and Kenneth J. Doka and Terry L. Martin, *Grieving Beyond Gender: Understanding the Ways Men and Women Mourn* (New York: Routledge, 2010).
2. This test was developed by Dr. Terry Martin and is included in Doka and Martin, *Grieving Beyond Gender.*
3. Colin Murray Parkes, "Bereavement Counselling: Does It Work?" *British Medical Journal* 281:6232 (July 5, 1980), 3–6.
4. Birgit Wagner, Christine Knaevelsrud, and Andreas Maercker, "Internet-Based Cognitive-Behavioral Therapy for Complicated Grief: A Randomized Controlled Trial," *Death Studies* 30:5 (June 2006), 429–53.

Chapter 5: When Your Spouse Dies

1. Therese A. Rando, *Treatment of Complicated Mourning* (Champaign, IL: Research Press, 1993).
2. J. William Worden, *Children and Grief: When a Parent Dies* (New York: Guilford Press, 1996).
3. Worden, *Children and Grief.*
4. Muriel Spark, *Memento Mori* (New York: Macmillan, 1959).
5. J. Richard Williams, "Effects of Grief on a Survivor's Health," in *Living with Grief: Loss in Later Life*, Kenneth J. Doka, ed. (Washington, DC: Hospice Foundation of America, 2002), 191–206.
6. Linda J. Beckman and Betsy Bosak Houser, "The Consequences of Childlessness on the Social-Psychological Well-Being of Older Women," *Journal of Gerontology* 37:2 (March 1982), 243–50.
7. Vicky Whipple, *Lesbian Widows: Invisible Grief* (Binghamton, NY: Harrington Park Press, 2006). Whipple's book offers an account of the specific issues faced by lesbians negotiating widowhood. Kenneth J. Doka, ed., *Disenfranchised Grief: New Directions, Challenges, and Strategies for Practice* (Champaign, IL: Research Press, 2002) provides a larger discussion of disenfranchised grief including how it pertains to same-sex relationships.
8. Erin Linn, *I Know Just How You Feel: Avoiding the Cliches of Grief* (Cary, IL: Publishers Mark, 1986).
9. Worden, *Children and Grief.*

Chapter 6: When a Child Dies

1. Therese A. Rando. *Treatment of Complicated Mourning* (Champaign, IL: Research Press, 1993).

2. William Feigelman, John R. Jordan, John L. McIntosh, and Beverly Feigelman, *Devastating Losses: How Parents Cope with the Death of a Child to Suicide or Drugs* (New York: Springer, 2012).
3. Feigelman et al., *Devastating Losses.*
4. Reiko Schwab, "A Child's Death and Divorce: Dispelling the Myth," *Death Studies* 22:5 (June 1998), 445–68.
5. J. William Worden, *Children and Grief: When a Parent Dies* (New York: Guilford Press, 1996).
6. Jennifer L. Buckle and Stephen J. Fleming's book *Parenting After the Death of a Child: A Practitioner's Guide* (New York: Taylor & Francis, 2011) presents the results of a study on this topic, offering sage advice to parents struggling with this issue.
7. One of the earliest research pieces challenging the idea that we detach from the deceased was a study of bereaved parents published almost thirty years ago. It found that parents, even seven to nine years after the loss of their child, spoke of a continuing "empty space." Their strategies for coping with this empty space varied. Some tried to fill the emptiness by engaging in diverting activities. Other bereaved parents moved on by trying to get over it. Still others retained an ongoing connection to their deceased child. See S. G. McClowry, E. B. Davies, K. A. May, E. J. Kulenkamp, and I. M. Martinson, "The Empty Space Phenomenon: The Process of Grief in the Bereaved Family," *Death Studies* 11:5 (1987), 361–74.

Chapter 7: When a Parent Dies

1. Mark W. Speece and Sandor B. Brent, "The Development of Children's Understanding of Death," in *Handbook of Childhood Death and Bereavement*, Charles A. Corr and Donna M. Corr, eds. (New York: Springer, 1996), 29–50.
2. Kenneth J. Doka, "The Awareness of Mortality: Continuing Kastenbaum's Developmental Legacy," *Omega: Journal of Death and Dying* 70:1 (2014–15), 57–66.
3. Doka, "The Awareness of Mortality."
4. Marian Osterweis, Fredric Solomon, and Morris Green, *Bereavement: Reactions, Consequences, and Care* (Washington, DC: National Academy Press, 1984).
5. Both Hope Edelman in *Motherless Daughters: The Legacy of Loss* (Boston: Da Capo, 2006) and Allison Gilbert in *Parentless Parents: How the Loss of our Mothers and Fathers Impacts the Ways We Raise Our Children* (New York: Hyperion, 2011) specifically address this issue.
6. Kenneth J. Doka, "The Monkey's Paw: The Role of Inheritance and the Resolution of Grief," *Death Studies* 16:1 (January 1992), 45–58.
7. Margaret Blenkner, "Social Work and Family Relationships in Later Life with Some Thoughts on Filial Maturity," in *Social Structure and the Family: Generational Relations*, Ethel Shanas and Gordon F. Streib, eds. (Englewood Cliffs, NJ: Prentice-Hall, 1965), 46–59.

Chapter 8: The Loss of a Sibling in Adult Life

1. Patricia Robson and Tony Walter, "Hierarchies of Loss: A Critique of Disenfranchised Grief," *Omega: Journal of Death and Dying* 66:2 (2012–13), 97–119.
2. Helen Rosen, *Unspoken Grief: Coping with Childhood Sibling Loss* (Lexington, MA: Lexington Books, 1986).
3. Joan Woodward, *The Lone Twin: Understanding Twin Bereavement and Loss* (London: Free Association Books, 1998).
4. Woodward, *The Lone Twin.*
5. Diane Kempson and Vicki Murdock, "Memory Keepers: A Narrative Study on Siblings Never Known," *Death Studies* 34:8 (2010), 738–56.

PART 3: THE UNACKNOWLEDGED LOSSES OF LIFE: DISENFRANCHISED GRIEF

1. Kenneth J. Doka, ed., *Disenfranchised Grief: Recognizing Hidden Sorrow* (Lexington, MA: Lexington Books, 1989).

Chapter 9: Broken Bonds: When Relationships Are Not Recognized

1. Jeffrey Kauffman, "The Psychology of Disenfranchised Grief: Liberation, Shame, and Self-Disenfranchisement," in *Disenfranchised Grief: New Directions, Challenges, and Strategies for Practice*, Kenneth J. Doka, ed. (Champaign, IL: Research Press, 2002), 61–77.
2. See Larry G. Peppers and Ronald J. Knapp, *Motherhood & Mourning: Perinatal Death* (New York: Praeger, 1980); and Larry G. Peppers, "Grief and Elective Abortion: Implications for the Counselor," in *Disenfranchised Grief: Recognizing Hidden Sorrow*, Kenneth J. Doka, ed. (Lexington, MA: Lexington Books, 1989), 135–45.
3. Dennis Klass and Amy Olwen Heath, "Grief and Abortion: *Mizuko Kuyo*, the Japanese Ritual Resolution," *Omega: Journal of Death and Dying* 34:1 (1996–97), 1–14.
4. Lisa Hensley, "Death and Disenfranchised Grief in Virtual Communities: Challenges and Opportunities," paper presented at the 31st annual conference of the Association for Death Education and Counseling, Dallas, TX, April 18, 2009.
5. Cyrus S. Stewart, John C. Thrush, and George Paulus, "Disenfranchised Bereavement and Loss of a Companion Animal: Implications for Caring Communities," in *Disenfranchised Grief: Recognizing Hidden Sorrow*, Kenneth J. Doka, ed. (Lexington, MA: Lexington Books, 1989), 147–59.
6. Robert A. Neimeyer and John R. Jordan, "Disenfranchisement as Empathic Failure: Grief Therapy and the Co-Construction of Meaning," in *Disenfranchised Grief: New Directions, Challenges, and Strategies for Practice*, Kenneth J. Doka, ed. (Champaign, IL: Research Press, 2002), 95–118.
7. Colin Murray Parkes, "Bereavement Counselling: Does It Work?" *British Medical Journal* 281:6232 (July 5, 1980), 3–6.

Chapter 10: Does Anyone Understand? Unacknowledged Loss

1. Therese A. Rando, *Clinical Dimensions of Anticipatory Mourning: Theory and Practice in Working with the Dying, Their Loved Ones, and Their Caregivers* (Champaign, IL: Research Press, 2000).
2. Susan Roos, *Chronic Sorrow: A Living Loss* (New York: Brunner-Routledge, 2002).
3. Terry L. Martin, "Divorce and Grief," in *Disenfranchised Grief: Recognizing Hidden Sorrow*, Kenneth J. Doka, ed. (Lexington, MA: Lexington Books, 1989), 161–72.
4. Judith S. Wallerstein, "The Long-Term Effects of Divorce on Children: A Review," *Journal of the American Academy of Child & Adolescent Psychiatry* 30:3 (May 1991), 349–60.
5. Louis LaGrand, "Youth and the Disenfranchised Breakup," in *Disenfranchised Grief: Recognizing Hidden Sorrow*, Kenneth J. Doka, ed. (Lexington, MA: Lexington Books, 1989), 173–86.
6. LaGrand, "Youth and the Disenfranchised Breakup."
7. Pauline Boss, *Ambiguous Loss: Learning to Live with Unresolved Grief* (Cambridge, MA: Harvard University Press, 1999).
8. This part of the chapter draws from the work of Sherry R. Schachter and Jennifer A. Schachter, "Adoption: A Life Begun with Loss," in *Counting Our Losses: Reflecting on Change, Loss, and Transition in Everyday Life*, Darcy L. Harris, ed. (New York: Routledge, 2011), 75–92; and Rose Cooper, "Unrecognized Losses in Child Adoption," in *Disenfranchised Grief: New Directions, Challenges, and Strategies for Practice*, Kenneth J. Doka, ed. (Champaign, IL: Research Press, 2002), 265–74. It should be noted that within the adoption community, the appropriateness of terms like *birth mother, natural families*, etc. are often debated. Recognizing this, I have tried to use the most neutral terms, such as *relinquishing mother*, *adoptee*, and *adopting parents*.
9. Hamilton, L., Cheng, S., & Powell, B., "Adoptive Parents, Adaptive Parents: Evaluating the Importance of Biological Ties for Parental Investment," *American Sociological Review* 72 (2007), 95–116.
10. Schachter and Schachter, "Adoption: A Life Begun with Loss."
11. Darcy L. Harris, "Infertility and Reproductive Loss," in *Counting Our Losses: Reflecting on Change, Loss, and Transition in Everyday Life*, Darcy L. Harris, ed. (New York: Routledge, 2011), 171–82.
12. Derek Scott, "Coming Out: Intrapersonal Loss in the Acquisition of a Stigmatized Identity," in *Counting Our Losses: Reflecting on Change, Loss, and Transition in Everyday Life*, Darcy L. Harris, ed. (New York: Routledge, 2011), 183–92.
13. Richard Kalish, *Death, Grief, and Caring Relationships* (Pacific Grove, CA: Brooks/Cole, 1985), 181.

Chapter 11: Acknowledging the Disenfranchised

1. David A. Crenshaw, *Bereavement: Counseling the Grieving through the Lifecycle* (New York: Continuum, 1990).

2. Kenneth J. Doka, ed., *Disenfranchised Grief: New Directions, Challenges, and Strategies for Practice* (Champaign, IL: Research Press, 2002).

Chapter 12: Making Rituals Meaningful

1. Much of my professional work has revolved around the use of therapeutic ritual. Some of the material in this chapter draws from a previously published chapter, "The Role of Ritual in the Treatment of Disenfranchised Grief," in Kenneth J. Doka, ed., *Disenfranchised Grief: New Directions, Challenges, and Strategies for Practice* (Champaign, IL: Research Press, 2002), 136–54.
2. Lewis Mumford, *The City in History: Its Origins, Its Transformations, and Its Prospects* (New York: Harcourt, Brace & World, 1961).
3. Arnold van Gennep, *The Rites of Passage* (Chicago: University of Chicago Press, 1960).
4. See Kenneth J. Doka, "Expectation of Death, Participation in Funeral Arrangements, and Grief Adjustment," *Omega: Journal of Death and Dying* 15:2 (1984–85), 119–29; and Therese A. Rando, *Grief, Dying, and Death: Clinical Interventions for Caregivers* (Champaign, IL: Research Press, 1984). While dated, both offer a good summary of research on the value of funerals—at the time an important topic for research. In the subsequent thirty years, less research on the topic has been produced, but it still affirms the value of meaningful ritual.

Chapter 13: When Self-Help Is Not Enough

1. J. Richard Williams, "Effects of Grief on Survivor's Health," in *Living with Grief: Loss in Later Life*, Kenneth J. Doka, ed. (Washington, DC: Hospice Foundation of America, 2002), 191–206.
2. American Psychiatric Association, *Diagnostic and Statistical Manual of Mental Disorders*, 5th ed. (Washington, DC: American Psychiatric Association, 2013).
3. This is what Dr. George Bonanno and associates described as the chronic depressed pattern.
4. Persistent complex bereavement-related disorder is noted in the most recent version of the *Diagnostic and Statistical Manual of Mental Disorders* (*DSM-5*) as a condition for further study. This means that while there is not a consensus among psychiatrists to include it as a mental disorder, there is enough evidence to propose further evaluation. It is likely that it may be included in later editions of the *DSM*.
5. The Center for Complicated Grief can offer information on therapists trained in the approach. Their Web site is complicatedgrief.org and they can be reached by telephone at 212-851-2701.
6. Interestingly, based on his research, Bonanno claims not to have found delayed grief in his study (see George A. Bonanno, Camille B. Wortman, Darrin R. Lehman, Roger G. Tweed, et al., "Resilience to Loss and Chronic Grief: A Prospective Study from Preloss to 18-Months Postloss," *Journal of Personality and Social Psychology* 83:5 (November 2002), 1150–64). Worden disagrees and notes that Bonanno's time frame may be too brief to pick up significant

cases. Worden also acknowledges this type of grief reaction is relatively uncommon; see J. William Worden, *Grief Counseling and Therapy: A Handbook for the Mental Health Practitioner*, 4th ed. (New York: Springer, 2009). Yet Bonanno's pattern of escalating grief may not be all that dissimilar to what Worden and others such as Rando observed; see Therese A. Rando, *Treatment of Complicated Mourning* (Champaign, IL: Research Press, 1993). Moreover, the phenomenon of delayed grief has been suggested since 1937; see Helene Deutsch, "Absence of Grief," *Psychoanalytic Quarterly* 6 (1937), 12–22.

7. Therese A. Rando, Kenneth J. Doka, Stephen Fleming, Maria Helena Franco, Elizabeth A. Lobb, Colin Murray Parkes, and Rose Steele, "A Call to the Field: Complicated Grief in the DSM-5," *Omega: Journal of Death and Dying* 65:4 (2012), 251–55.
8. J. William Worden, *Grief Counseling and Grief Therapy: A Handbook for the Mental Health Practitioner*, 4th ed. (New York: Springer, 2009).
9. See Margaret Stroebe, Henk Schut, and Jan van den Bout, eds., *Complicated Grief: Scientific Foundations for Health Care Professionals* (New York: Routledge, 2013); Therese A. Rando, *Treatment of Complicated Mourning* (Champaign, IL: Research Press, 1993); and J. William Worden, *Grief Counseling and Grief Therapy*.

Chapter 14: Growing In and Through Grief

1. Marvin Eisenstadt, Andre Haynal, Pierre Rentchnick, and Pierre de Senarclens, *Parental Loss and Achievement* (Madison, CT: International Universities Press, 1989).
2. Lawrence Calhoun and Richard G. Tedeschi, eds., *Handbook of Posttraumatic Growth: Research and Practice* (Mahwah, NJ: Lawrence Erlbaum Associates, 2006).
3. Joanne T. Jozefowski, *The Phoenix Phenomenon: Rising from the Ashes of Grief* (London: Jason Aronson, 1999).
4. Calhoun and Tedeschi, eds., *Handbook of Posttraumatic Growth.*
5. John M. Schneider, *Finding My Way: Healing and Transformation through Loss and Grief* (Colfax, WI: Seasons Press, 1994).
6. Robert A. Neimeyer, "Narrative Strategies in Grief Therapy," *Journal of Constructivist Psychology* 12:1 (January 1999), 65–85.
7. Catherine M. Sanders, *Grief: The Mourning After: Dealing with Adult Bereavement* (New York: John Wiley & Sons, 1989).
8. Kenneth J. Doka, "Fulfillment as Sanders' Sixth Phase of Bereavement: The Unfinished Work of Catherine Sanders," *Omega: Journal of Death and Dying* 52:1 (July 2006), 141–49.

INDEX

ABOUT THE AUTHOR

Dr. Kenneth J. Doka is a professor of gerontology at the Graduate School of the College of New Rochelle, and a senior consultant to the Hospice Foundation of America. A prolific author, Dr. Doka has authored, coauthored, and edited over thirty books on aspects of grief counseling, including *Disenfranchised Grief: New Directions, Challenges, and Strategies for Practice*; *Grieving beyond Gender: Understanding the Ways Men and Women Mourn*; *Beyond Kübler-Ross: New Perspectives on Death, Dying, and Grief*; and *Counseling Individuals with Life-Threatening Illness*. In addition to these books, he has published over one hundred articles and book chapters. Dr. Doka is editor of both *Omega: Journal of Death and Dying* and *Journeys: A Newsletter to Help in Bereavement*.

Dr. Doka was elected president of the Association for Death Education and Counseling in 1993. In 1995, he was elected to the board of directors of the International Work Group on Dying, Death, and Bereavement, and served as chair from 1997 to 1999. The Association for Death Education and Counseling presented him with the awards for Outstanding Contributions in the Field of Death Education in 1998, and Significant Contributions to the Field of Thanatology in 2014. His alma mater, Concordia College, presented him with their first Distinguished Alumnus Award. He is a recipient of the Caring

Hands Award as well as the Dr. Robert Fulton CDEB Founder's Award. In 2006, Dr. Doka was grandfathered in as a mental health counselor under New York State's first licensure of counselors.

Dr. Doka has keynoted conferences throughout North America as well as Europe, Asia, Australia, and New Zealand. He participates in the annual Hospice Foundation of America Teleconference and has appeared on CNN and *Nightline*. In addition, he has served as a consultant to medical, nursing, funeral service, and hospice organizations, as well as to businesses and to educational and social service agencies. Dr. Doka is an ordained Lutheran minister.